The Biomedical Basis of
Gerontology

The Biomedical Basis of Gerontology

David A. Hall
BSc PhD DSc

Life Fellow of the University of Leeds
Lately Senior Lecturer in Biochemistry in
Relation to Medicine, Department of
Medicine, University of Leeds

WRIGHT · PSG
Bristol London Boston
1984

Published by
John Wright & Sons Ltd, 823–825 Bath Road, Bristol BS4 5NU, England
John Wright · PSG Inc., 545 Great Road, Littleton, Massachusetts 01460, USA

British Library Cataloguing in Publication Data
Hall, David A.
    The biomedical basis of gerontology.
    1. Gerontology
    I. Title
    612'.67   HQ1061

ISBN 0 7236 0697 8

Library of Congress Catalog Card Number: 83–50884

Typeset and printed in Great Britain by
John Wright & Sons (Printing) Ltd at The Stonebridge Press, Bristol BS4 5NU

Preface

The flow of publications in the field of ageing
has increased dramatically over the past decade. By their very nature, however,
and no doubt in part due to the relatively circumscribed interests of their authors,
some have been very restricted in their approach. Biologists have attempted to
cover the fundamentals of the ageing process, clinicians have approached geriatrics
from a patient-oriented standpoint, and sociologists have presented their personal
evaluations of the relationship between the elderly individual and society: each
with little appreciation of the problems under consideration by workers in other
disciplines. Even in textbooks which by their titles would appear to be aimed at
the integration of the clinical and the biological fields, such as the various editions
of Brocklehurst's *Textbook of Geriatric Medicine and Gerontology* (1973, 1978), the
two approaches are separated. Such a dichotomy has been virtually inevitable,
however, since the majority of authors or editors have developed their interests in
ageing as a side-line to the discipline in which they were originally trained, and
have had little opportunity for analysing their own ideas and beliefs against those
of workers in completely different fields.

This is not intended to belittle the value of these publications, many of which
provide bench mark studies in age research, but the separate development of
gerontological and geriatric approaches is not conducive to the presentation of an
integrated appraisal of all aspects of ageing.

I have always held the belief that the study of ageing should be multidisciplinary
in nature (Hall, 1972) and that wherever possible each individual research worker
should be involved in as many diverse aspects of the field of which he is capable.

Speaking of physical chemists, in the preface to his book *Physical Chemistry*, E A. Moelwyn-Hughes (1940) stated:

'The complete chemist blows his own apparatus and solves his own equations.'

How much more true should this diversity of approach be for workers in any biomedical discipline. Unfortunately, such a holistic approach has tended to be deprecated by workers in the main streams of each individual discipline. They have tended to suggest that a gerontologist whose research develops along such broad lines must of necessity be a 'jack of all trades . . .' and therefore by definition '. . . a master of none'.

Notwithstanding this implied criticism which has pursued me through my career in gerontology, my early research experiences ensured that it was along such catholic lines that my contribution to age research should develop, whatever my consequent standing amongst those of my colleagues who concentrated on a more specialized approach. The first research programme on which I was engaged, during World War II, was aimed at the preparation of a stable textile fibre for camouflage netting from the polysaccharide alginic acid, derived from seaweed. Although this was undeniably a product-oriented applied research project with little, if any, direct relationship to either biological or clinical gerontology, it introduced me, on the one hand, to the concepts of fibre science, and on the other, to the hypothesis that chelation may provide an important stabilizing factor for organometallic complexes: both of which were to prove of considerable value to me in my subsequent studies on the ageing of fibrous components of connective tissues. This was followed by investigations of amino acid metabolism and analysis which directly paved the way for my entry into age research, and for the expansion of my interests via enzymology in general to a study of age-related changes in general to a study of age-related changes in lipid metabolism and of autoxidation in particular. My appointment in 1948 to the (then) relatively unique post of biochemist in a clinical department influenced the way in which my research interests have subsequently developed along the watershed between biochemical and clinical gerontology. Coupled with this, the organization, over the past 10 years, of five short courses on the *Biological Basis of Ageing*, within the University of Leeds, but catering for an international cross-section of gerontologists, geriatricians, biochemists, zoologists and nurses, has reinforced my belief in the necessity to examine the inter-relationship between the biology of ageing and the care of the elderly. Out of this determination has grown the decision to write this book, combining both clinical and biological approaches; using findings from the latter field to answer questions posed by the former and evidence provided by clinicians to help discriminate between the various theories of ageing which have been developed as the result of experimental studies at the biological level.

Whether such a close integration is possible or not remains to be seen. The reader should bear in mind that what follows represents the views of one individual. I cannot believe that my argument will be entirely unbiased, nor can I hope that my approach will prove to be all-embracing. No doubt the discerning eader will be able to differentiate between those chapters which deal with areas in vhich I and my closest colleagues have been personally involved and others which have included so as to present some semblance of completeness. I have considered t necessary to present such material in which I have maintained a vicarious interest)ecause, hopefully, among those who read the following pages will be some who ire coming afresh to age research. Were I to omit mention of all those aspects of ;erontology in which I have not been personally involved, such readers would be)resented with a very lop-sided theme.

Although I accept all responsibility for the views expressed, I must acknowledge ny indebtedness to those who have, over the years, worked with me and have from ime to time given me the benefit of their views on ageing at all its levels of :omplexity. First and foremost I must record my thanks to Professor Sir Ronald funbridge who introduced me to the often tantalizing, always absorbing, study of ige and ageing. Others who have from time to time been responsible for much hought-provoking discussion are my late colleagues Professor Fritz Verzar, Drs M. K. Keech, W. A. Loeven and T. Davies, together with: Mr C. M. Airey, Drs A.). Blackett, P. Burdett, R. J. Cox, J. W. Czekalowski, J. W. Czerkawski, S. S. Elridi, J. E. Gardiner, G. N. Graham, H. D. Griffin, P. F. Lloyd, R. S. W. Middleton, W. R. Miller, F. B. Reed, R. Reed, Miss H. Saxl, Dr R. S. Slater, Mr S. F. Switala, Drs J. D. Teale, I. S. Tesal-Smith, J. E. Wilkinson, Professors G. C. Wood and V. Wright, and Miss A. R. Zajac.

My thanks are also due to my daughter-in-law, Mrs Kate Hall, who has so gallantly tackled the preparation of the manuscript.

David A. Hall

References

Brocklehurst J. C. (ed.) (1973, 1978) *Textbook of Geriatric Medicine and Gerontology*, 1st and 2nd ed. Edinburgh, Churchill Livingstone.
Hall D. A. (1972) What has gerontology to offer geriatrics? *Symposium of Geriatric Med.* **1**, 32.
Moelwyn-Hughes E. A. (1940) *Physical Chemistry*. Cambridge, Cambridge University Press.

Contents

1   *Introduction*

1.1   **Definitions of Ageing**

1.1.1   *The Semantics of Ageing*

We have little difficulty in defining an old house, an old car or an old work of art, such as one of Leonardo da Vinci's drawings. The house is classed as a listed building, and the car given veteran status, because they were built or manufactured a certain number of years ago. The drawing may represent an early design for a helicopter and hence could be classed as modern, but because its passage down the centuries has been adequately documented and authenticated, it is accepted as a fifteenth century work of art. Such classification is much more difficult with a living organism, but is is essential that full documentation is available if a correct assessment of age is to be attempted.

The first necessity is an acceptance of the semantic meanings of certain words which are commonly used in the description of the ageing process.

In addition to such words as *age* and *ageing*, which themselves may have a number of semantic implications, many of the nouns and adjectives used in this field require some degree of rigid definition before it is possible to correlate and compare the observations of one worker with those of another.

1.1.2   *Old and Young*

Perhaps the most over-used and under-defined works appearing in reports of many so-called age studies are 'old' and 'young'. Many workers, especially those employing experimental animals, have in the past merely indicated a comparison of two groups to which these very vague adjectives have been applied. Of recent years this practice has improved to the extent that an increasing number of workers now stipulate the actual age or the weight of their animals. Many inbred strains of a single species, however, differ markedly with respect to life-span and it is essential to define the strain employed, so that the actual age of the group of animals being examined can be expressed in terms of the mean and optimum life-spans of the strain. Even here, however, difficulties can arise since environmental factors can modify the survival characteristics of an individual strain considerably. Blackett (1979) has, for instance, observed that under his conditions of husbandry there is little difference in optimum life-span between the so-called long-lived hybrid strain of mice LAF (C_{57}BLXA) and the short-lived inbred strain C_3H/Hc. It is, therefore, essential that definitions of the terms 'young' and 'old' be accompanied by the fullest documentation of the normal survival characteristics of the strain, including where possible survival curves prepared from a parallel population to that being experimented upon.

1.1.3 *Growth and Maturation*

It has long been a debatable question as to whether ageing studies should include those changes which precede the degenerative changes of old age. Some workers have suggested that ageing commences at conception and therefore that growth, maturation and senescence represent a continuum without any major discontinuity. Others contend that the ageing process is a discrete phenomenon only apparent in advanced age and should be treated separately from the developmental phases. It does not appear to matter which viewpoint is adhered to, so long as the research worker defines what he is looking at. In fact, although the major portion of the evidence presented below will relate to the later stages of ageing, considerations of some developmental phenomena are included, either because they represent all the knowledge at present available in a particular field, or because the changes which take place at this stage in life provide a basis on which subsequent senescent changes are built.

1.1.4 *Senescence*

This is a general term for a decrease in the efficient functioning of an organism with increasing age. Although Comfort (1979) obviously implies that the concept should be restricted to the later years of life

> 'Senescence is a deteriorative process . . . associated with a decrease in viability and an increase in vulnerability . . . and shows itself as an increased probability of death with increasing chronological age'

senescent changes can occur at any stage in the life process. In fact the term may be applied to the sum total of any group of effects which detract from the normal life-style. A certain degree of degenerative change is associated, on a statistical basis, with all levels of advanced chronological age and hence the appearance of such change substantially earlier than is to be expected can be described as *premature senescence*.

In the foreword to *Endocrinology and Ageing* (1981), Michael Green states:

'Age is not a diagnosis, but ageing is inevitable.'

That he should consider it necessary to introduce a publication devoted to the minutiae of ageing phenomena with such an apparent truism is a sad indictment of those clinical colleagues who often attempt to ease the minds of their patients by assuring them that their aches and pains are 'just due to their age'. As we advance in years even the fittest of us will show signs of deterioration. This is inevitable. The degree to which our faculties and our capabilities fail, however, varies from individual to individual. How then may we define this deterioration which comes to us all to a greater or lesser degree as we grow older?

There have been numerous attempts to formulate such a definition in ways which will adequately describe the changes in structure and function apparent in increasing age.

For instance, Warthin (1929) defined ageing as an involutionary phase in the development of the organism. Whilst Medawar (1952), more specifically, stated that senescence was:

'that change of the bodily faculties and sensibilities and energies . . . which renders the individual progressively more likely to die from accidental causes of random incidence.'

Strehler (1959) referred to ageing as a decrease in adaptation and again in 1962 as:

'the changes which occur generally in the post-reproductive period and which result in a decreased survival capacity on the part of the individual organism.'

Maynard-Smith (1962) pointed out that although the phenomenon of ageing might originate within an organism, the changes were also apparent in the organism's inability to respond successfully to external factors:

'(Ageing processes are) those which render individuals more susceptible as they grow older to various factors, intrinsic or extrinsic, which may cause death.'

All these definitions are relatively imprecise in concept, being essentially couched in philosophical terms. Finch (1976) on the other hand has suggested that, in the post-reproductive period, ageing is directly due to the dysdifferentiation of previously differentiated cells.

Everitt and Burgess (1976) have attempted to relate the post-reproductive deterioration to the rate of previous development phases. For them ageing is:

'a progressive deterioration of the organism after maturity of size, form or function has been reached and which is universal, intrinsic, progressive, and deleterious with time.'

Other definitions have invoked: loss of information (Comfort) and a decline in the production of free energy (Calloway, 1964). This latter suggestion does, in fact, encompass all other definitions. The development of an organized structure and an integrated functional system requires a considerable input of energy; energy which is subsequently dissipated as degenerative changes occur.

According to the Second Law of Thermodynamics, all systems tend towards a condition of maximum entropy, in other words towards a high degree of disorganization or 'rundownness'. Hence the highly organized, highly differentiated system which characterizes the mature adult organism must of necessity become disorganized, dysdifferentiated and by definition senescent, as age progresses past maturity. Calow (1978) has commented on this concept which represents ageing as a tendency towards maximum entropy, which he claims may not be operative in living systems. His main aim, however, was to explain the whole life process—maturation and degeneration included—rather than the ageing process alone. To account for the full range of such phenomena, he invoked:

'cycles of generation and degeneration rather than unidirectionality.'

From these various definitions it may be possible to distil a composite statement which covers all the requirements. The following elements will need to be included:
1. Ageing may be apparent throughout life, but is more noticeable in the post-reproductive period
2. Ageing lowers the functional capacity of cells, organs and entire organisms
3. Ageing results in the degradation of structural elements within the body
4. Ageing lowers the effectiveness of the response of the organism to internal and external factors, and
5. Ageing increases the likelihood of the ultimate dysfunction—death.

Before accepting these definitions it is necessary to appreciate the basis on which they are derived.

Over the past two or three decades, many of the existing theories of ageing and definitions of ageing outlined above have proved to be inextricably interwoven, leading to considerable confusion and in certain instances detracting from the significance of the fundamental findings of gerontological research. Comfort has pointed out that numerous workers in this field have tended to assume the very points which they set out to prove, thereby reducing the credibility of a major part of their contribution to the theoretical basis of age research. Obviously definitions must be separated from theories before the latter can be interpreted, and it is first of all essential to define not ageing itself, but the physical constraints which surround its assessment.

1.2 The Time Scale

First the time scale against which all chronological changes are measured has to be defined. Leaving aside all consideration of multidimensional time and the possibility that an individual can move backwards in time, other than as a conceptual exercise, it is generally accepted that time moves inexorably from the past through the present to the future. Moreover, sidereal time is believed to travel forward at a constant pace. The interval of time between any pair of physical happenings in the past will be identical to that between similar happenings when they occur in the future. For instance, the time taken for a weighted pendulum to swing through a given angle will be the same in 1984 as it was in 1982. It has, however, been suggested (Lecompte du Nouy, 1936) that this may not be true if one considers the timing of *physiological* events. The repair of the same defective physiological system may for instance take four or five times as long at 80 as it does at 20 years of age. Comfort has, however, criticized this concept of a distinct *biological time* commenting that du Nouy and more recently Reichenbach and Mathers (1959) are guilty of what is essentially a non-sensical comparison of so-called physiological and physical times which are, in fact, two evaluations of a single reality. There is, however, considerable confusion concerning the measurement of the passage of physiological time. Merry and Phillips (1981) have quoted Shock (1977) as stating that:

> 'in mammals, ageing is essentially a continuous process after maturation and proceeds at an almost uniform rate throughout life.'

This may well be true of certain age-related physiological functions (Shock, 1957), but is not universally the case. Hall et al. (1981), for instance, have shown that the rapid reduction in skin-fold thickness which occurs at ages above 65 is not a direct continuation of an effect which has been steadily increasing throughout life. There is a marked discontinuity at this age, and Hall and his co-workers have suggested that the loss of collagen which affects this reduction in skin-fold thickness is under completely different control before and after this threshold age (*see* p. 91). Moreover, although physiological activities such as pulmonary function, glomerular filtration rate, liver function, etc. decrease progressively with increasing age (*Fig.* 1.1) the concentrations and/or activities of enzyme systems in various tissues may change with age either linearly or in a curvilinear fashion (Wilson, 1973) (*Fig.* 1.2). Sometimes indeed the age regression lines for enzymes pass through peaks and sometimes through troughs at points intermediate between maturity and death.

Even those systems which demonstrate a progressive fall with age may not always react in an identical fashion, different systems at enzymic, physiological or anatomical levels exhibiting different rates of decrease. What is more, the negative regression against age of all these factors may vary from individual to individual. The net result is a non-continuous relationship between function and age at the level of the whole organism. Many individuals age more rapidly than others, but in any single individual the ageing process may appear to occur more rapidly during one period of life than another, and at a greater rate in one organ than another. It is almost as if the ageing process were being monitored by reference to a measuring stick which expands and contracts not only relative to other measuring aids, but also to different extents along its own length (*Fig.* 1.3).

Ries (1974) has suggested that it should be possible to assess a person's

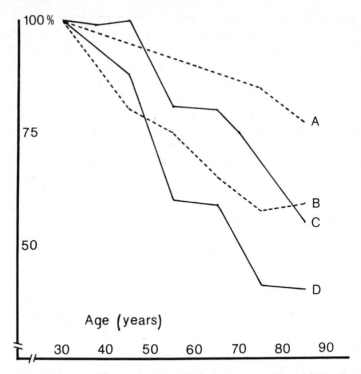

Fig. 1.1. Age-related changes of four typical physiological parameters (Shock N. W., 1959, Functional changes in aging. Program and Papers of Conference on Gerontology, Duke University. p. 123). A, condition velocity; B, vital capacity; C, glomerular filtration rate, and D, maximal breathing capacity. The figures for individual ages are expressed as percentages of the value for age 30, which is taken to represent the value for maturity.

biological age by the summation of the measurements of the 'age' of individual organs or physiological functions obtained by a comparison of absolute values with the age regression line for that particular factor. Not all possible measurements of age-related phenomena are, however, of equal importance. The greying and loss of hair, both essentially age-related effects, cannot be ascribed the same importance as can changes in blood pressure, liver function or renal clearance. Hence for any summation of age effects to be effective it is necessary to institute a weighting system. Unfortunately the degree of weighting required to equate measurements of hair loss and kidney function cannot as yet be assessed (if indeed it ever will) and if this failure is coupled with the realization that there is no way of knowing how many possibly important factors are as yet unmeasured or indeed immeasurable, it can be seen that a lot of thought is required before assessments of biological age which are representative of anything approaching a true record of an individual's physiological status, are available.

Hence, although it may be desirable for the concept of biological age to be retained as a working concept, its measurement is at present far from possible and it is necessary for gerontologists to retain the sidereal calendar as a measure of age.

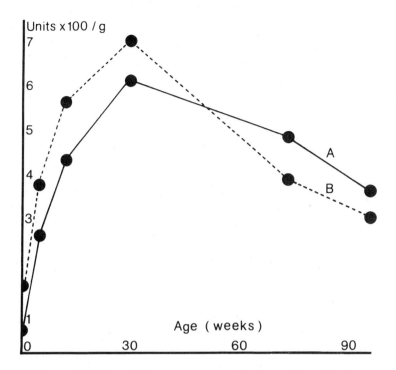

Fig. 1.2. Typical age-related changes in the enzyme content of rat tissues (adapted from Kanungo, 1980, *see* references for Chapter 5; Singh and Kanungo, 1968, *see* references for Chapter 2). The two curves relate to the amounts of lactic acid dehydrogenase present in (A) the skeletal muscles and (B) the heart tissue of rats aged 0–96 weeks. Similar development of enzymes during maturation followed by their subsequent disappearance has been observed for numerous enzymes, tissues and species (Wilson, 1972, 1973, *see* references for Chapter 5).

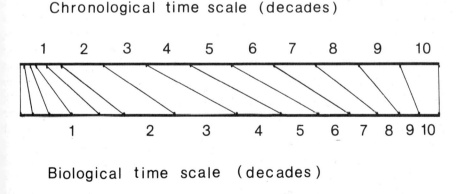

Fig. 1.3. Schematic comparison of chronological and biological time scales. Much more physiological activity can be packed into the first decades of 'biological time' than into those of later life, hence the length of that part of the biological measuring rod appears to be longer in the early period of life than a comparable portion of the chronological measuring rod. At the other extreme of life the opposite relationship applies.

Two patients, one with sparse grey hair, wrinkled skin, rheumatoid arthritis of the knees and defective hearing and another with a full head of hair which still retains its youthful colour, with smooth cheeks and still capable of taking long walks and appreciating Mozart, may both have the same date on their birth certificates. Within one year the appearance and functional capacity of the former may not have changed appreciably, whereas the latter may have suffered an unexpected cerebral thrombosis, precipitating many hitherto latent age-effects which will markedly change his life-style. Both these individuals will still be of the same chronological age, but their biological ages would appear to be reversed. The calendar and the clock are not ideal measuring aids for the study of biological ageing, but at present they are all that is available.

BOX 1.1

Shock (1981) has gathered together observations by 12 different groups of workers who, over the past 30 years, have attempted to correlate a variety of physiological factors with chronological age. Some workers report a very high correlation with age for certain functional parameters. For instance, Furukawa et al. (1975) record a value for τ of 0·880 for the accommodation of the eye and 0·83 for vibratory sensitivity of the finger, whereas for the same parameters other workers report correlation coefficients of less than two-thirds these values. With population size ranging from 38 to 1080, the significance of correlation coefficients above 0·50 varies considerably and the correlation may only be of significance in those instances in which the population size is greater than 400. The range of values varies markedly over the 12 sets of results, even for parameters measured in a similar fashion. For instance, the standard deviation (0·145) of the 9 reported correlation coefficients for systolic blood pressure with age is 31% of the mean value of 0·47. Measurements of the age correlation of diastolic blood pressure on the other hand show almost twice this degree of variation, the standard deviation (0·20) being 60% of the mean.

1.3 The Starting Point

To be effective, the measurement of any dimension whether it be a period of lapsed time or a distance in three-dimensional space requires a starting point and this is true of the measurement of the age of an individual. By common consent and the application of common sense, the initial point when measuring life-span is taken as the date of birth, but there are other milestones in life which could and have been employed for certain specific reasons. The other terminal, the date of death, would not appear to be of universal use since it is in the main unpredictable and any assessment based on measurements backwards in time from the point of death would have to be deferred until after this final act had occurred.

In human subjects two other intermediate milestones, puberty and (in the case of females) the menopause, may also be used for age measurements. Comfort has referred to the work of Tanner (1955) regarding the use of graphs to record the rate of change of stature over the age range 6–18 years. Each individual curve has a sharp peak followed by a dramatic fall, but the ages at which these peaks occur may range from 10 to 14 years. If the curves are plotted together any attempt to calculate a mean curve representative of a number of adolescents results in a broadening and flattening of the peak. If, however, the curves are plotted in terms of numbers of years before or after the age at which the rate of change of stature is greatest, i.e. before and after puberty, the peaks and the falling limbs of the curves are superimposed on one another and the mean curve has all the characteristics of each individual curve with a sharp peak and marked fall thereafter.

Although effective for certain measurements, the use of puberty as a universal milestone from which age measurements may be made, is rendered less than precise on account of the variations which, according to some workers, occur with changing cultural development.

Similarly, although the menopause may be an appropriate point from which to measure age in the female subject over 45 years old, the same variation with race and internal environment may occur.

Thus, just as the decision has been forced upon gerontologists to employ sidereal time as a measurement of age, so it would appear to be impossible to measure age in most instances from any other base line than that of the birth date of the individual. The extension of the length of the life-span by the addition of an essentially identical period of 40 weeks to account for fetal life does not appear to have much to offer, although it may ultimately be proved that premature birth or extended uterine retention may have a role to play in determining the future physiological life-style and life expectancy of the individual.

1.4 Cross-sectional v Longitudinal Studies

Another factor which has to be considered when studying age changes in groups of subjects, especially with a view to determining how various parameters change with age, is whether it is more appropriate to employ *cross-sectional* or *longitudinal* methods.

The method which has been employed with the greatest frequency is that involving cross-sectional assessment in which measurements of a particular parameter for a selected group of subjects of one specific age are compared with those of another age group. The difficulty here is that no account can be taken of the previous history of the older group. At the present time a group of 70-year-old subjects from 'developed' countries will have experienced the food shortages of World War I during their early youth, the depression of the 1930s in their young adulthood and the controlled dietary intake, but far closer psychological involvement, associated with World War II in middle age, whereas those under 35 and over 30 years of age, although they were reared during the years of post-war rationing, will have spent the rest of their lives in a relatively well-nourished state.

Inhabitants of third world countries may have suffered a similar degree of restriction in their fetal and perinatal diets to those who grew up in occupied territories during World War II, but their present social and economic status may be entirely different. For true comparison the history of each individual member of any group under study should be known. The easiest way to accomplish this is by means of a longitudinal study, where a cohort of comparable origin is followed throughout life, or for a major portion of it, and measurements taken at stated intervals over this period. This is the method employed in many animal studies where litter mates or at least animals of the same strain, born within days of one another, are followed for an appreciable portion of their life-span. In human studies, however, there are logistic difficulties. To follow an individual or a group of individuals merely from maturity to senescence entails the continuation of a single research project for at least 40–50 years. This is longer than the normal research worker's own span of activity. Hence it will be necessary for the research to be institution- rather than worker-oriented and for the methods of examination employed to be so far ahead of their time as to be acceptable to the next generation of research workers. It is highly unlikely that such a condition will be easily attained since the methodology of any worthwhile discipline develops pro-gressively and measurements made by one generation will hardly be acceptable to the next when they take over. In addition to this, there is the question of training. Any assessment which requires the co-operation of the subject who is being examined, such as the answering of a questionnaire or the performance of some mental or physical task, will of necessity provide biased results on the second or any subsequent occasions on which the subject is tested, since the task will become easier on repetition. Sometimes it is possible to make allowance for this, but not on every occasion. For instance, enhanced confusion which may reduce the effective-ness of a particular test which is repeated as a subject becomes progressively senescent, may affect any training effect, but if the aim of the test is to assess the fundamental confusion itself, results which are better than expected will be obtained due to the positive training element. Difficulties then arise in the analysis of such results since the positive effect of training will affect the negative effect of confusion to a variable and essentially indeterminable degree.

Therefore, although it would appear desirable to employ longitudinal methods wherever possible, so as to eliminate some of the cohort effects which can detract from the value of cross-sectional assessment, there are many pitfalls associated with undue reliance on the former approach. In fact, much can be gained by a combination of the two. Carrying out sequential cross-sectional studies using the same groups over relatively short periods of time permits the overall age-related changes which are associated with cross-sectional studies to be extended to increasing age. Obviously the larger the number of age groups and the greater the duration of the study the more chance there is for the longitudinal changes to link pairs of groups together to give a dynamic element to what would other-wise be a static cross-section throughout the age range (*Fig.* 1.4).

The best documented example of this type of investigation is the Framingham study (Study, 1968) but similar projects have been undertaken in Holland (van Zonnenfeld, 1954), in Leipzig (Ries, 1974) and in Basle (Gsell, 1968).

1.5 Animal or Human Experimentation?

As was pointed out in the previous section, an inordinate amount of time has to be spent on any meaningful longitudinal study of human ageing. This, above all else, would appear to point towards the importance of animal experimentation in age

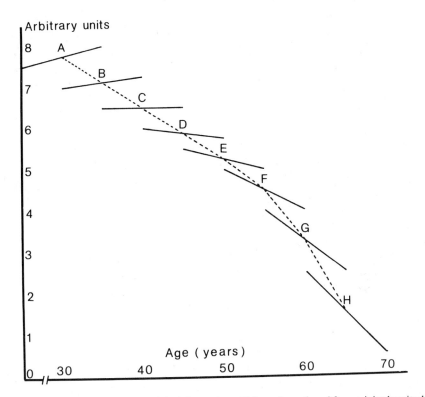

Fig. 1.4. A schematic representation of the information which can be gathered from a joint longitudinal and cross-sectional study of a typical ageing phenomenon. In this hypothetical instance, eight cohorts (A–H) aged 25, 30 . . . to 60 are each studied for a period of 10-years. The changes in the measurable parameter, indicated by the eight separate full lines, demonstrate the nature of longitudinal change taking place during each 10-year period, whereas the dotted line represents the cross-sectional change at the mid-point of the experimental period. Other cross-sectional comparisons can be obtained by joining the beginning or end of each longitudinal segment.

research. Most certainly, many profitable lines of age research have had their origins in animal experiments. Coupled with the relatively large numbers of animal studies which can be accomplished during a normal research lifetime the cost of experimentation with some animals is relatively low. Studies on variations in the life-span of the fruit fly, *Drosophila* sp., the house fly, *Musca domestica*, rotifers or paramecia can be accomplished in days rather than weeks or months. There are, however, two difficulties associated with the use of such small and short-lived animals. First, it is often impossible to carry out biochemical studies on individual tissues or even on individual animals, although the daily advent of increasing numbers of micro-analytical procedures is making this even more possible. Even where such methods are not available, statistical analysis can overcome some of the difficulties encountered with pooled analyses. The second obstacle is the improbability of the existence of any direct correlation between age-related changes in one phylum with those of another. Probably the main profit to be gained from insect studies is associated with their genetic variability, which permits various genetic correlations between morphology and age to be examined. These more primitive animals, the metabolic processes of which are relatively far removed from those of vertebrates, provide us, however, with information which can only with difficulty be extrapolated directly to the mammalian field.

Among small mammals, mice and rats have been employed for many ageing studies. Mice and rats have a life-span of from 1½ to 4 years, thus permitting a reasonable research project to be accomplished within the period of a normal research contract. One of the difficulties which has arisen from experimentation on such small animals, especially where cross-sectional studies have been involved, has been an inability to correlate the age of 'old' mice or rats with 'old' human subjects. How old, for instance, is the mouse which is comparable to a 70-year-old man? This can obviously be assessed more readily if mice of the same strain are followed from birth to death and groups culled for analysis at various ages. But the varying optimum life-span of different strains of mice makes it difficult to compare the relative ages of 15-month-old mice, or 2-year-old rats, with the ages of truly old human subjects. Too many workers have merely reported the age of their animals without relating this to the optimum life-span of the strain or, worse still, have merely referred to them as 'young' or 'old' without any reference to chronological age. One of the problems is that most of the mice and rats studied are laboratory bred, and although experiments with such stock gain from their genetic uniformity, it is difficult to compare their metabolic processes or their survival with those of their wild progenitors. A limited number of studies have been carried out on wild mice of local strains, isolated by geographical factors such as restriction to a single island but here again there are difficulties. First, since their dates of birth are unknown, their ages have had to be estimated on the basis of bone shape and size, or on the basis of external features such as tail taper (Hall, unpublished results) (*Box* 1.2), and secondly predation and climate may artificially restrict the age span of those animals which can be studied in the wild to 6–9 months, well below their potential optimum.

The use of larger animals, such as dogs, pigs and monkeys, etc. for age studies, presents two obstacles to the design of useful research programmes. First, they are longer lived and hence results take longer to amass. Secondly, their capital cost and caging and maintenance expenses are far greater than those for smaller animals. Against this must be assessed their greater metabolic similarity to human subjects and the fact that their greater size permits individual tissues and cell strains to be examined.

Although one may regard the main aim of gerontological research as being the elucidation of the problems of the ageing human subject, much can be gained from animal experimentation, especially when its results are considered alongside observations from the clinical field. Similarly, at the far extreme much can be gained from the study of ageing cell clones, for, although the metabolic processes in culture may be greatly simplified due to the removal of control mechanisms arising from other cell groups and tissues, it is this very simplification which permits stricter analysis.

BOX 1.2

The age of mice or rats collected in the wild can be measured by an assessment of tooth wear. This method, however, is only applicable to dead animals, and is then markedly time-consuming since all soft tissue must be removed before the weight of the teeth themselves can be obtained. A non-invasive, non-destructive method which is particularly useful in the case of the younger animals which constitute the normal populations which are subject to early death by exposure, disease and predation merely necessitates measurement of tail dimensions. The tail diameter is measured close to the root and the distance from this point to the tip. Assuming the tail to be essentially conical, its taper (Tan Θ) can be calculated from these dimensions.

$$\text{Tan}\,\Theta = \tfrac{d}{2e}$$

For dead animals the relative tapers of a series of tails can be calculated after excision from length and weight.

$$\text{Tan}\,\Theta = \frac{3W}{\pi e^3}$$

Tail taper appears to bear an exponential relationship to age as estimated from tooth wear.

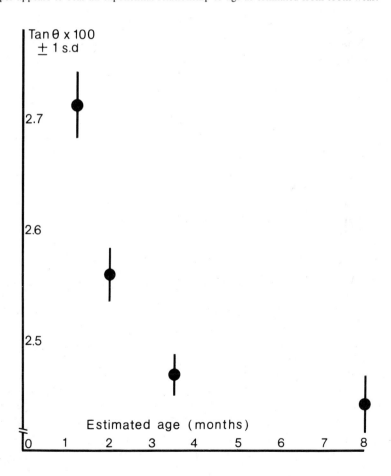

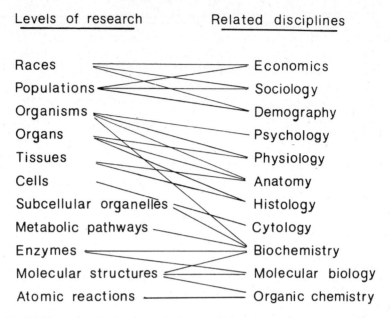

Fig. 1.5. The various levels of organization at which ageing studies can be carried out.

It is, therefore, apparent that ageing can and should be studied at a great variety of levels of organization (*Fig.* 1.5) using all appropriate animal and cell lines at each of these levels. From *Fig.* 1.5 it can be seen that the levels at which research can be carried out include a number lying above that of the intact organism. The relationships between the individual and society, between societies and between races and racial groups are essentially sociological and economic in character. The diagram, however, as well as showing separate levels of research, demonstrates the interaction of different levels of organization. Hence, although it would not be expected that age variations in, for instance, the glycolytic enzymes of the Krebs cycle would have any direct effect on the role played by a 70-year-old man in society, these enzymes in fact may by their effect on carbohydrate metabolism, and thus on the activity of the musculature of the individual, have physical and hence sociological significance even at the population level.

1.6 Criteria for the Recognition of Age Phenomena

Strehler (1977) describes four attributes which together determine whether a particular phenomenon can be described as meeting the criteria of being a factor in the ageing process.

The first of these is *universality*. He suggests that if any given phenomenon plays a part in the ageing process it should occur in all the older members of any one species. In this way, he eliminates a number of hereditary diseases which, although appearing preferentially in certain advanced age groups, are by no means present in all representatives of a species. He answers the vexed question as to whether this definition rules out such conditions as cancer, atherosclerosis and rheumatoid arthritis, by suggesting that it is not the pathological condition itself which has to be universally apparent, but the reduced resistance to pathological effects such as tumour growth, arterial degeneration or joint involvement, which therefore assumes the role of a true ageing phenomenon. Although a proportion of the aged population may never develop tumours because they are not subjected to one of the known tumour-inducing agents (such as carcinogens, viruses, radiation, etc.) while yet again others may not have the processes of joint degradation initiated by some endogenous or environmental factor, this does not detract from the suggestion that all members of the human species become more susceptible to these pathological changes as they grow older.

Strehler's second criterion for ageing phenomena is *intrinsicality*. By this he implies that for a change to be truly assessed as being due to ageing it must originate within the organism and not be imposed on it from outside. Thus the fundamental change in the artery wall represents the ageing factor which induces atherosclerosis and not any alteration in diet, even though this may itself be age-related. However, many elderly subjects develop food fads which determine whether their intake of saturated fats increases or not. Once the lipid is circulating in the blood, intrinsic changes in the vascular wall, which constrain it to remain in the arterial intima, determine the age changes in the vessel wall rather than the diet itself. Changes in the diet, if they are due to some psychological aberration on the part of the individual, may of course represent true ageing phenomenon, whereas changes in food intake which are imposed through economic stringencies would not. The question becomes more complicated, however, if changes in the subject's economic situation are dependent on intrinsic physiological factors which determine whether he is able to continue in gainful employment. These could be truly age-related. The whole concept of intrinsicality is rather like an onion with alternate layers of true ageing phenomena interspersed with interactive environmental factors. *Progressiveness,* the third of Strehler's factors, implies that ageing is a gradual rather than an acute occurrence. Studies of the epidemiology of cardiovascular disease are in the main restricted to the documentation of ischaemic incidents since these and not the development of the underlying atheromatous changes are the observable happenings. Similarly, changes in cerebral blood flow are usually not noticed until after the occurrence of a cerebral accident. These observable phenomena are *age-associated* in that they occur more frequently in subjects above a certain age, but they themselves cannot be regarded as *age-related.* Both, however, are the sequelae of changes which have been developing in the central or peripheral vascular system throughout the years. Such hidden occlusive changes represent the true ageing phenomena, the acute incidents are merely the markers which indicate that the progressive age change has reached a certain threshold of intensity at which an uncontrollable acute condition supervenes.

Cellular ageing (q.v.) does not result in complete dysfunction of any specific organ immediately one or two cells have died. In fact, the whole process of organ malfunction is progressive from the stage when the active forms of one or two enzyme systems are present in suboptimal concentrations, through the stage where sufficient intracellular enzymes are lost to result in death of that particular cell, to the situation in which a sufficient number of cells have died to preclude that organ from functioning properly. The proportion of cells which bring about such a dramatic change in the function of an organ varies from organ to organ, and may in fact be very few if cells with important function are lost, but once this critical stage is reached the stress thrown on the organism as a whole is usually sufficient to result in organismal death. At this stage, however, appreciable numbers of individual cells in all the organs of the body, including the one whose malfunction precipitated death, will still be viable even though they may be producing suboptimal amounts of their normal enzymes.

The fourth factor—*deleteriousness*—has been the one about which there has been the greatest degree of controversy since Strehler (1959) first proposed these criteria. It might be expected that since senescence has been described as a reduction in the viability of an organism, any change contending for assessment as a true ageing phenomenon would by definition be one which was deleterious to the functioning of the organism. From conception to death the organism passes through various phases. The fetal stage and that portion of life up to the attainment of maturity can be described as the *developmental phase*. This is followed by an adult phase during which many of the functions of the body are maintained at or near optimum capacity and this phase either imperceptibly or precipitately changes into an involutionary phase during which these changes, which are ultimately recognizable as *senile*, develop. It has been suggested that ageing commences at conception, but during the developmental and the first half of the adult phase the organs of the body are increasing their efficiency to an extent which completely dominates any degenerative process. If, however, we use as a definition of ageing, the broad statement: 'the response of the organism to the passage of time', the changes which result in increased efficiency during growth and development must be regarded as age related. Thus, for instance, it is known that the numbers of cross-linkage in connective tissue components—especially collagen— increase with increasing age (*see Table* 4.7) and Verzar (1963) suggested that such changes were due to ageing. This may be true in certain tissues, where the introduction of more cross-linkages is deleterious to the normal functioning of the organ of which collagen forms a part (eye, major cellular organs, etc.). In other tissues, however, an increase in cross-linking does not in itself detract from the properties of the tissue but may in fact increase its effectiveness (skin, tendon, etc.). In these tissues ageing does not occur until some degradative process assumes such proportions as to outweigh the stabilizing and strengthening effects of cross-link formation. The acceptance of the criterion of *deleteriousness* therefore implies acceptance of the more limited definition of ageing which Comfort proposed.

1.7 Conclusions

It may be deduced from the above that ageing is not the total response of an organism to elapsed time, but only to that portion of the overall life-span during which there is a reduction in the response to either endogenous or exogenous stresses. In other words, a reduction in the organism's ability to cope with stresses imposed on it by its internal or external milieu.

In measuring ageing use has to be made of measuring aids which are far from perfect.

References

Blackett A. D. (1979) *Study of the Effects of Antioxidants on the Ageing Process in Mice*. Ph.D. Thesis, University of Leeds.
Calloway N. O. (1964) A general theory of senescence. *J. Am. Geriatr. Soc.* **12**, 856.
Calow P. (1978) *Life and Cycles*. London, Chapman & Hall.
Comfort A. (1979) *The Biology of Senescence*, 3rd ed. Edinburgh, Churchill Livingstone.
Everitt A. V. and Burgess J. A. (ed.) (1976) *Hypothalamus, Pituitary and Aging*. Springfield, Ill., Thomas.
Finch C. E. (1976) The regulation of physiological changes during mammalian aging. *Q. Rev. Biol.* **51**, 49.
The Framingham Study (1968) An epidemiological investigation of cardiovascular disease. Sect. 19, Washington, DC, US Government Printing Office.
Furukawa T., Inoue M., Kajiya F. et al. (1975) The assessment of biological age by multiple regression analyses. *J. Gerontol.* **30**, 422.
Green M. (ed.) (1981). *Endocrinology and Ageing*. London, Saunders.
Gsell O. (1968) Die Basler Studie über longitudinale Alterns forschung. 1955–1965 (The Basel study of longitudinal age research, 1955–1965), in *Herz und Atmungsorgane im Alter. Deutscher Gesellschaft für Gerortologic.* **1**, 16.
Hall D. A., Blackett A. D., Zajac A. R. et al. (1981) Changes in skinfold thickness with increasing age. *Age Ageing*, **10**, 19.
Lecompte du Nouy P. (1936) *Biological Time*. London, Methuen.
Maynard-Smith J. (1962) The causes of ageing. *Proc. R. Soc. (Ser. B)* **157**, 115.
Medawar P. B. (1952) *An Unsolved Problem of Biology*. London, Lewis.
Merry B. and Phillips J. (1981) Basic gerontology. In: *Clinics in Endocrinology and Metabolism. Endocrinology and Ageing*. London, Saunders. p. 1.
Reichenbach M. and Mather R. A. (1959) The place of time and aging in the natural sciences in scientific philosophy. In: Birren J. E. (ed.) *A Handbook of Aging and the Individual*. Chicago, Chicago Press.
Ries W. (1974) Problems associated with biological age. *Exp. Gerontol.* **9**, 145.
Shock N. W. (1957) Some physiological aspects of aging in man. *Bull. NY Acad. Med.* **32**, 268.
Shock N. W. (1977) Systems integration. In: Finch C. E. and Hayflick L. (ed.) *Handbook of Biology and Aging*. London, van Nostrand Reinhold, p. 639.
Shock N. W. (1981) Indices of functional age. In: Danon D., Shock N. W. and Marois M. (ed.) *Aging: a Challenge to Science and Society*. Oxford, University Press, p. 270.
Strehler B. L. (1959) Origins and comparisons of the effects of time and high energy radiations on living systems. *Q. Rev. Biol.* **34**, 117.
Strehler B. L. (1977) *Time Cells and Aging*, 2nd ed. New York, Academic Press.
Tanner J. M. (1955) *Growth and Adolescence*. Oxford, Blackwell.
Verzar F. (1963) *Lectures on Experimental Gerontology*. Springfield, Ill., Thomas.
Warthin A. S. (1929) *Old Age, the Major Involution: The Physiology and Pathology of the Ageing Process*. New York, Hoebert.
Wilson P. D. (1973) Enzyme changes in ageing mammals. *Gerontologia* **19**, 79.
van Zonnenfeld R. (1954) *The Health of the Aged*. Assen, Royal Van Gorcum.

2

Theories of Ageing

2.1 Theories Related to Wear and Tear

Drawing an analogy with the chronological degradation of inanimate systems probably the most obvious group of theories of ageing ascribes the ageing process in the animal body to the wear and tear of bodily constituents. Many earlier workers, who studied ageing before the advent of more precise methods for its evaluation (Pearl, 1928; Warthin, 1929) subscribed to the suggestion of Weismann (1882) that senescence was an inherent property of all metazoa (although not of less highly organized forms of life). He suggested that the evolution of senescence has progressed hand in hand with the development of cellular differentiation and

'Death takes place because a worn-out tissue cannot forever renew itself.'

Certain tissues of the body at the end of their processes of differentiation do not develop further; their cell mass remains constant or declines, undergoing no further mitoses and this could well result in the wearing out of such tissue as is already present. The actual process of wear may well be initiated by factors outside the body; for instance, age-related joint damage may in part be due to excessive and unnatural use of the limb in question (*see* p. 111) or to the activation of a degenerative cycle by some earlier infection, as in the streptococcal induction of rheumatoid arthritis. The true age-related phenomenon would then be an increasing inability to make good the ravages of these external factors. Where external injury and the side effects of metabolism act in concert (Furth et al., 1954; Jones, 1956; Sacher, 1956) the effect is one of accumulated wear and tear. A specialized example of this is the often reported relationship between radiation and ageing. Alexander (1957) suggested that the observed shortening of life associated with exposure to ionizing radiations of more than a limited threshold level could be due to an acceleration of the rate of ageing. If this were so, 'natural' ageing might be correlated with the low levels of radiation always present in the environment. Although studies on the effects of radiation received a marked encouragement following the exposure of the inhabitants of Hiroshima, Nagasaki and the test atolls in the Pacific to irradiation from atom bombs, the suggestion that all-pervading radiation (albeit of cosmic origin) could be the cause of the normal ageing process, was made by Kunze as early as 1933. Using the very sensitive method of plotting survival curves for groups of mice of various strains (CBA, LAF, and C_3Hb) it has been demonstrated that the age for 50% survival can be reduced by $43 \pm 4\%$ after exposure to between 6·4 and 8·8 rad (Neary et al., 1957; Lorentz et al., 1954). It would appear that this degree of shortening of life-span is about the optimum obtainable, since roughly similar values are recorded irrespective of whether the dosage is administered daily or weekly. This was confirmed by Mole and Thomas (1961) who observed that the system which is susceptible to exposure appears to become saturated by radiation. The effect is apparently a function of the initial dose-time value rather of the overall exposure. Lindop and Rotblatt (1959, 1961a, b) however, who studied the effect of single doses of radiation on mice, showed that the reduction in life-span is not due to any one single cause but to the advancement in time of many of the normal causes of death. They pointed out that the development of each individual pathological condition was not speeded up or enhanced to a corresponding extent and hence irradiation per se cannot be regarded as having effects which are identical to those of ageing, although they do resemble them.

2.2 Cross-linkage Theory

Bjorksten first advanced the cross-linkage theory in 1941 and later expanded and modified it (Bjorksten, 1974). He suggested that macromolecules such as proteins and nucleic acids could become less metabolically active throughout life by the introduction of linkages joining them together. The theory has been supported by numerous studies, not the least important of which have been those based on Verzar's observations on collagen cross-linkages, although the direct relationship of these links with ageing is now doubted (Verzar, 1963, see p. 92).

Rudzinska (1952) observed the precipitation of a protein in the nucleus of the ageing ciliate *Tokophyra infusorium,* a finding which he ascribed to cross-link formation between pairs of protein molecules and not to dehydration as had been suggested earlier in studies of age changes in colloidal solutions (Růžicka, 1924; Marinesco, 1934). Verzar (1963) deduced, on the basis of changes in the physical properties of the proteins of tail tendons, that cross-links increased in number with increasing age. At that time such cross-linkages had not been identified but subsequent studies have demonstrated their existance (*see* Chapter 4) and they have now been characterized. Milch (1963) suggested that cross-linking agents might be derived as by-products of normal biochemical processes within the body, demonstrating that similar changes in the physical properties of collagen fibres to those occurring with increasing age could be induced by treatment with bi functional aldehydes such as glyoxal, malondialdehyde and succindialdehyde. O these, malondialdehyde is present as a degradation produce of lipid peroxidation and this observation links the cross-linkage theory with Harman's (1956) free radical theory.

2.3 Free Radical Theory

The free radical is a very unstable species of molecule, lacking as it does one of a symmetrical pair of electrons in an outer orbital which would otherwise balance the molecule by exerting an opposite direction of spin. In *in vivo* situations i attains full stability by the withdrawal of an electron from some other hitherto stable molecule. When such a molecule is a polyunsaturated fatty acid, lipid peroxyl ROO', lipid oxy RO' and hydroxyl OH' radicals are formed (Tappel 1968). Intermolecular linkages between the degradation products of such lipid oxidation products and either other lipids or proteins results in inactive polymers which at best are of little use to the cells in which they accumulate (Gedick and Fischer, 1959) and at worst can interfere with the cells' activity. Lipid protein complexes of this type have long been observed in cells throughout the body where they have been given the names age pigment or lipofuscin (Stubel, 1911) Hamperl (1934) showed that such complexes of lipid and protein were present in many types of cell and many workers have shown that the lipofuscin content of most tissues increases with increasing age (Deane and Fawcett, 1952; Sulkin, 1955 Blackett and Hall, 1981). There is, however, little direct evidence to associate the presence of these age pigments with cellular malfunction especially in the brain where accumulation might be expected to show a marked correlation with decreased mental capacity.

2.4 Waste Product Theory

In youth many macromolecules are produced in excess of the amounts required for the formation of new tissue. The excess production is balanced by enhanced catabolism resulting in the appearance of high concentrations of degradation products in the urine and faeces (*see* p. 88 for details of the appearance o hydroxyproline in urine following the degradation of collagen in the pre-pubertal human being). As cross-links increase in number the proportion of these macro molecules which can suffer complete degradation decreases and waste products are retained in the body. Many workers have suggested that the accumulation of such partially degraded metabolic products are a major cause of ageing.

2.5 Nucleic Acid Immobilization

In addition to proteins and lipids, probably the most important macromolecules in the body are the nucleic acids. There is evidence that they become linked firmly either to themselves or to protein with increasing age. Acharya (1972), studying pregnant rats, observed an increase in the frequency of DNA–protein–RNA complexes and in the molecular weight of the nucleic acid molecules themselves in both the brain and liver. Cutler (1976b) also reported an increase in the number of DNA–protein cross-linkages with age in rat liver and proved that the rate of accumulation was inversely proportional to optimum life-span in two other species of rodent—*Mus* and *Peromycus*. DNA can be extracted from young tissues but the percentage which is readily removable from liver decreases with increasing age (Amici et at., 1974). von Hahn and Fritz (1966) showed that the material extracted from aged organs has a higher melting temperature. Salser and Balis (1972) in contrast to Amici and his co-workers reported that the amount of protein-bound DNA remaining in liver after exhaustive extraction was independent of age whereas that in spleen and kidney increased and that in intestinal tissue decreased. In cultures of embryonic lung fibroblasts (Bradley et al., 1976) there was no evidence of increased insolubility as a function of *in vitro* passage number. This might indicate that this particular manifestation of ageing is dependent on the interaction of one cell species with another and cannot occur in monoclonal cultures.

The proteins with which nucleic acid is associated in nuclear DNA are members of a group of small basic proteins, the histones, and transcriptions of RNA necessitates the temporary separation of histone from the appropriate gene locus. Firm bonds between DNA and histone prevents the 'ballooning' of the chromatin strands which is associated with DNA/histone dissociation and hence with RNA transcription. Ageing cells contain DNA in a more firmly bound form and are less capable of producing their usual number of protein molecules and are hence less likely to function in a normal fashion.

2.6 The Rate of Living Theory

Reubner (1908) observed a direct relationship between the life-span of different species of animal and their metabolic rate. Both man and mouse expend about 2·9 kJ/g of tissue throughout their lives but the *rate* at which this is expended by the mouse is roughly 30 times greater than that for man. The mouse lives 2–3 years as opposed to the man 60–90.

Cutler (1975, 1976a, 1978, 1979) has related *maximum life-span potential* (MLP) and specific metabolic rate (SMR), which he combined as a product (MLP × SMR) to give a value, *maximum life-span potential calorie consumption* (MCC) which is a measure of life-capacity, to the *encephalisation quotient* (EQ) (Jerison, 1973) the degree of brain development over and above that required for normal bodily function. MLP is calculated from the equation:

$$\text{MLP} = 10\cdot839 \times (\text{brain wt})^{0\cdot636} \times (\text{body wt})^{-0\cdot225}$$

(Sacher, 1959). Sacher compared brain weight (in g) and body weight (in g) separately with maximum observed life-span and observed that although there was a relatively good correlation between either of these two parameters and life-span for a fair proportion of the animals studied, some, especially man, demonstrated a far longer life-span than might be predicted from either body or brain size. The incorporation of both parameters in one equation produced a much closer correlation (*Fig. 2.1*).

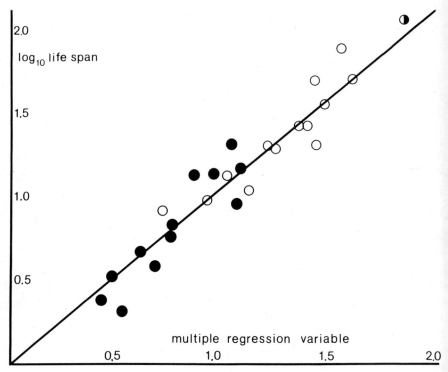

Fig. 2.1. The relationship between the logarithm of the life-span of man and animals of two different orders and the multiple regression variable—MLP (maximum life-span potential) $MLP = 10 \cdot 839 \times (\text{brain weight})^{0 \cdot 626} \times (\text{body weight})^{-0 \cdot 225}$. Closed circles: rodents; open circles: primates; halved circles: man. Derived from figures reported by Sacher (1959).

In Cutler's studies SMR was calculated from the equation:

$$SMR = 442 \cdot 74 \times (\text{body wt g})^{-0 \cdot 266}$$

(Brody, 1945) and the value for EQ from the equation:

$$EQ = 8 \cdot 33 \times (\text{brain wt g}) \times (\text{body wt g})^{-0 \cdot 666}$$

(Jerison, 1973). On the basis of these relationships Culter (1979) has been able to demonstrate that values for both MLP and MCC have increased during the evolutionary development of individual families of the animal kindom (*Fig. 2.2*). Those species which were destined to become extinct without phylogenic modification also demonstrated a very narrow distribution of values for MLP and MCC.

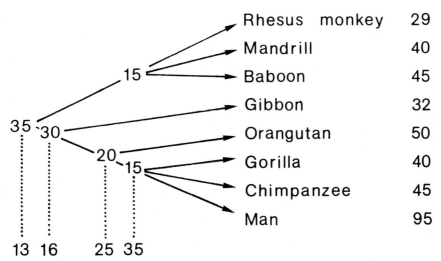

Fig. 2.2. The evolutionary development of various primates (adapted from Cutler, 1976a). The figures at the branching points of the evolutionary tree are the accepted geological dates in millions of years at which each genus evolved. The figures to the right of the diagram represent the present MLP values for each genus, whereas the figures at the bottom represent the estimated MLPs at each appropriate branch point.

whereas those species which had emerged during the last million years showed a broader, flatter distribution. This increasing tendency to longevity is associated in primates (Cutler, 1975, 1976a, b) and in other mammals (Hart and Setlow, 1974) with a corresponding increase in those processes which protect DNA from faulty synthesis and are capable of initiating repair, when damage as the result of u.v. irradiation, for instance (Hart and Setlow, 1974), has occurred. Attempts to extrapolate these observations to human subjects, i.e. to assess whether body size, brain size or a complex function of both may be used to predict life-span for an individual has not proved possible. This is as might be expected from the shapes of the distribution curves of MLP values reported by Cutler (1979) (*Fig.* 2.3). As man has evolved from his primitive forebears the definitive relationship between MLP and EQ has been lost. Mean values still place him ahead of other mammals, but there is no direct relationship at the individual level.

2.7 Somatic Mutation Theory

Changes in the germ during evolution are usually regarded as being the driving force behind evolutionary development. These alterations which provide daughter cells with a different genetic make-up from their parents' ova and sperm provide the changes, which, if they can withstand the pressures of the body's internal and external milieu, provide new characteristics in future generations. Ageing effects cannot be passed on in this way because, in effect, the germ cells are rejuvenated every time fertilization occurs. Curtis (1963, 1966), Szilard (1959) and Failla (1957)

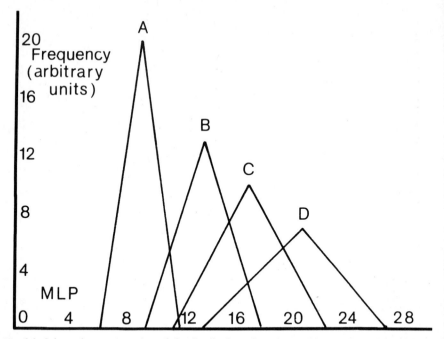

Fig. 2.3. Schematic representation of the distribution of maximum life-span potential (MLP) in the evolutionary development of the ungulates (derived from Cutler, 1979). Cutler's hypothetical gaussian distributions for ten species in each epoch have been simplified and are represented by a series of triangles. A, archaic; B, paleogene; C, neogene, and D, recent species of ungulants. The relative heights of the triangles demonstrate the fall in MLP with evolutionary development, their breadth records the way in which the actual values have assumed a broader spread. The likelihood of extinction has proved to be inversely proportional to the degree of dispersion (breadth of triangle).

have, however, suggested that the organism's somatic cells can also suffer spontaneous mutaton with resulting alterations in function. A variety of factors have been postulated as being effective in this type of reaction such as radiation and cross-linking by intracellular mutagenic substances. Maynard-Smith (1982) has pointed out, however, that for somatic mutations to be regarded as primary mechanisms of ageing, they should occur randomly both in terms of time and cellular location. This might be true of radiation damage, but the accumulation of mutagenic substances within the cell might be due to faulty secretion across the cell membrane and if this were so then the fundamental change in membrane permeability would have to be regarded as the true age-related phenomenon. Much of the evidence in favour of somatic mutation has arisen as a result of a study of chromosome abnormalities which can be observed in many peripheral tissues (*Fig.* 2.4). Crowley and Curtis (1963) showed, for instance, that regenerating mouse liver cells contained between 3·3 and 4 times as many bridged and fragmented chromosomes at 24 months as they did at 2 months. The rate of development of chromosome abnormalities was greater in the short-lived animals than in the ones which lived longer, an observation which was later confirmed (Curtis, 1966) when a strain of intermediate longevity was shown to develop

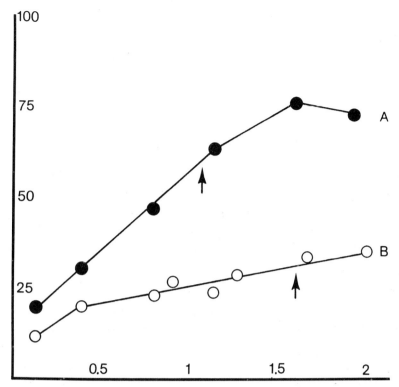

ig. 2.4. The increasing number of chromosome aberrations in cells from the livers of inbred strains of
nice: A, A/IIE's; B, $C_{57}BL/6$ (adapted from Crowley and Curtis, 1963). The former is a shorter-lived
train than the latter; the two arrows indicate the points of median life-span for the two strains.

aberrations at a rate intermediate between the other two. Curtis (1971) and Curtis
and Miller (1971) later extended their studies to include other species and showed
that, in general, longevity was inversely related to the rate at which chromosome
abnormalities developed. Certain deviations from this relationship, however,
cannot be overlooked, especially that concerning F_1 hybrids. Many first generation hybrids live longer than either of their inbred parent strains (see p. 30), but
develop chromosome faults at a rate intermediate between those of their parents.
Schofield and Davies (1978) comment on the difficulties which accompany
attempts to rationalize the observations made by Curtis and his colleagues,
pointing to the lack of statistical analysis in their studies and the problems
associated with the actual measurement of chromosome aberrations.

2.8 Immunological Theories of Ageing

Many workers (Burnet, 1959; Comfort, 1964; Walford, 1962, 1969, 1974; Makin-
dan and Adler, 1975; Burch, 1968) have proposed that the ageing process may

represent the accumulation of 'prolonged minor grade histo-incompatibilit reactions' (Walford, 1969).

Age changes in the immune system occur first in the thymus, which loses it function of promoting T-cell differentiation at a relatively early age (*see* p. 212) The thymic cortex begins to atrophy from puberty onwards (Andrew, 1952 Pantelouris, 1972) and the number of T-cells starts to decrease shortly afterward (Kay, 1978) falling to a level which is only 70% of its early adult value by th seventh decade (Augener et al., 1974). These changes in the thymus are mirrored b a reduction in T-cell mediated immune responses as in the development of disease such as lupus erythematosus and multiple sclerosis and the spread of carcinomas That these conditions are directly related to thymic involution can be deduce from the results of experimental thymectomy. Thymectomized mice develop variety of immunodeficiency diseases and age more rapidly. These changes can b reversed by transplanting thymus cells from young animals (*see* p. 213).

It has been pointed out that while the immune system of the body is undergoin a process of atrophy, alterations occur in the response of the immune system to th tissues of the body. Under ideal circumstances, in young subjects, the immun system recognizes the tissues of the body as self and does not react to them Walford (1969) and Burch (1968) have suggested that at least some of the ag changes observed in the tissues of the body may be due to a progressive failure o this recognition process whereby the immune system increasingly regards the tissu proteins as *non-self*. Burch has pointed out that the changes which induce the bod to recognize its own tissue as foreign will be unlikely to occur in the target cells o tissues themselves, since this would imply that numerous alterations in th structure of such tissues would have to occur in exactly the same way at variou sites in the body. A far more reasonable suggestion would be that the change take place at the central organ from which such cell-bound immune factors originate Thus, in agreement with Burnet (1959) he suggested that the development o autoimmune response is brought about by a mutation in the stem cell line fron which the lymphocytes differentiate (*see* p. 213).

It is something of a paradox that these stem cell mutations which may contro the autoimmune process develop at the same time that the overall immun response of the body is declining. This may explain in part at least how the livin organism is capable of maintaining its metabolic integrity in the presence of a autoimmune reaction which is potentially capable of destroying importan peripheral tissues. The decline in general immune activity minimizes the effect o the autoimmune response and makes it possible for the body to maintain it function even though there is an increasing reaction between elements of th central immune system and peripheral target tissues.

2.9 Age Theories Related to Control Mechanisms

The control of physiological function within the body is dependent on th maintenance of adequate neuronal and hormonal systems to provide the necessar

ansfer of information from organ to organ. (Comfort, 1979) has pointed out that
)r any organism to retain its physiological integrity it is necessary for it to remain
1 actively operative system, and that to understand the way in which such a
/stem may change with age, it is necessary to take a holistic view. The function of a
ven group of cells or tissues may be modified by mutation or cross-linkage but
1e function of the organism as a whole will depend on how the individual organs
·e able to maintain communication with one another. The science of communi-
1tion and the interaction of different elements of a system with one another is
:fined as *cybernetics*. It is useful to use some of the terminology of communicat-
·n technology to describe the sorts of change in message transfer and control
hich occur in an ageing organism.

There are a number of prerequisites for the successful transfer of information
om a transmitter to a receiver. The two must be linked by a suitable communica-
ons channel either for the transport of coded impulses or for the transmission of
iscrete packages of information. The transmitter must have either enough power
) bridge the distance to the receiver or must be in a position to emit the packages
f information in a form which permits their transport to the receiver. Coded
iformation may require amplification during transmission, not only to ensure
1at the signal, when it reaches the receiver, is adequately loud for reception but
so to raise it above the level of any 'noise' which might be introduced alongside
1e signal during transmission. The receiver, as well as being able to decode the
1essage, must be able to differentiate meaningful elements of the code from the
1ndom elements of the 'noise'. This applies to packaged information as well as
)ded messages, since the receiver must be able to discriminate between slight
ifferences in the structure and content of the package.

These definitions from communication techniques are equally applicable to
hysiological information transfer if one assumes that the coded information is
1rried on the neurones and the packaged information is in the form of hormones.
.s the organism grows older, its ability to transmit meaningful information by
ther of these processes deteriorates. The transmitters become less effective, the
·erve conduction rates decrease, the structure of the hormones may be affected and
1e receptors, whether they be neuronal or hormonal, become less capable of
:acting appropriately to the incoming impulse or molecular message. Noise also
ecomes amplified and tends to drown out the meaningful message. All these
1ctors react to reduce the efficacy of the intercellular and interorgan information
·ansfer and hence to lower the efficiency of the organism as a whole.

In the central nervous system both structural and functional changes occur with
ge. Both of these factors reduce the effective transmission of information (*see* p.
93). Alteration in the complexity of the dendrites of neurones in the brain results
1 an impoverishment of communication between cells since the individual
·anches provide, in youth, receptors for intercellular transmissions. Neural
1formation channels are not continuous throughout the body, being divided into
1dividual neurones separated by synapses. The transmission of information
cross the synapse necessitates the secretion of substrates and enzymes to produce
ctive molecules which can pass across the gap, where they interact with a specific

receptor to pass on the 'information' to the acceptor neurone. Age-induce alterations in substrate, enzyme or receptor may be assumed to bring about t bodily dysfunction associated with advancing years.

The other form of information transmission by means of molecular messenge carried in the circulation—the hormones—also suffers deterioration with increa ing age (*see* Chapter 6). Blood levels of the various hormones are determined I rates of cellular synthesis and secretion, concentrations of carrier proteins and t effectiveness of degradation processes. Alterations in any or all of these factors ca control the transmission of information by this pathway.

2.10 The Concept of an Ageing Centre

Many of the important hormones are synthesized and secreted by cells of t hypothalamic–adrenocortical axis and acceptance of their potential involvement the ageing process has led to the development of a generalized theory of ageir which postulates the existence of a centre lying between the brain and t hypothalamus which acts as a control centre for hormonal synthesis. It suggested that this centre may receive impulses from the brain, from t gastrointestinal tract and possibly from other sensory centres. The conseque activation or repression of pituitary activity would control the provision hormones which might then determine the activity of cells throughout the boc and precipitate 'ageing' phenomena.

2.11 Programmed Ageing

The concept of an ageing process which is programmed implies that t inevitability of age change is built into the life pattern of all living things. As a organism passes from stage to stage in its life certain events occur in a preordaine pattern. There is considerable evidence that this sort of hypothesis is able to answ many of the questions which spring to mind as one considers the way in whic human subjects and other animals age and die. Evidence in favour of programmed theory has arisen from a variety of levels of age research such a studies of longevity, the effects of twinning and parental age on survival, t genetic control of biochemical systems and the development of increased su ceptibility to external factors with increasing age. Each of these will be dealt with detail below, and this section completed by an assessment of these circumstanc for which the programmed theory is incapable of offering a suitable explanatio

2.12 Survival Curves

Because of the difficulties which have been observed in the estimation of optimu ages for caged or wild animals, or individual members of human populations,

s proved more appropriate to study survival curves which not only provide
idence for the longevity of a species, but also characterize the way in which the
·pulation ages in the various phases of life before death.

Various factors such as size, rate of living, diet and, of course, genetic structure
ay have a role to play in determining the difference in life history of mouse and
an. If, however, one compares different strains of the same species many of these
ctors are eliminated (*Fig.* 2.5). A major difference between different types of dog

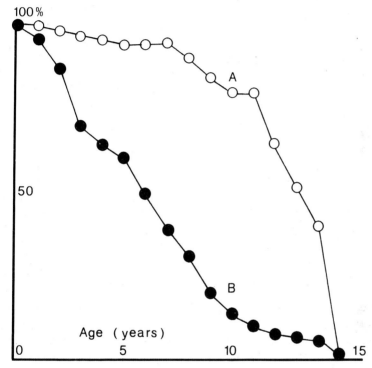

. 2.5. Survival curves for two breeds of dog: A, Spaniels; B, Wolfhounds, demonstrating the different
: profiles of smaller and larger breeds, and the inverse relationship between size and survival,
›ecially at intermediate ages. The survival curves of larger breeds are similar in shape to those of
imals which do not demonstrate any degree of age-specific ageing (cf. *Figs.* 3.9 and 3.10). Comfort
•60) had demonstrated similar relationships between the survival curves of Pekingese and Mastiffs.

size, a characteristic which is without doubt under genetic control. Within
ysical limitations, they are capable of cross fertilization indicating a close genetic
›mology. The shapes of their survival curves (Comfort, 1960), however, show
arked differences, 50% survival times being inversely proportional to size. Also
ɔrthy of note is the fact that the larger dogs show little sign of senescence, the
rves for Mastiffs and Wolfhounds being more nearly typical of populations with
constant rate of mortality. On a completely different time scale, the effect of
ɪerbreeding has been studied in the case of *Drosophila subobscura* (Clarke and
aynard Smith, 1955) (*Fig.* 2.6). The two inbred strains have almost identical

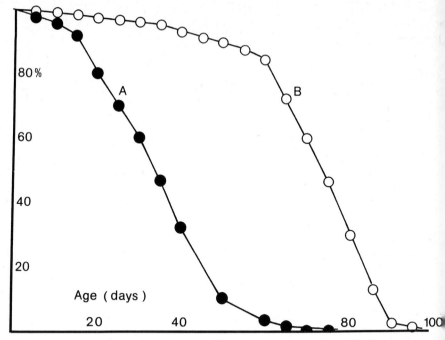

Fig. 2.6. Survival curves for two inbred strains of *Drosophila subobscura*, B and K. Curve A represen
the mean values for the two inbred strains. At no point are values for identical percentage surviv
separated by more than 6 days. Curve B represents the mean values for hybrid strains obtained
cross-breeding B-males and K-females and *vice versa*. Once again, the two derived F$_1$ strains gi
virtually the same shaped curves. The mean age for 50% survival is increased by hybridization fro
c. 32 to *c.* 65 days. (Adapted from Clarke and Maynard Smith, 1955.)

survival curves with a 50% survival point for both B and K strains at 30 day
Reciprocal hybrids exhibit the phenomenon of hybrid vigour with both cross-br
strains, B/K and K/B, retaining 50% of their populations until 68 days. T
combination of genetic elements from the two strains results in the prevention
death in mid life (between 15 and 50 days) but the subsequent mortality rate
virtually unchanged at approximately 2% loss/day. The reverse effect, in whi
repeated cross-breeding from old females concentrates those genetic factors whi
are associated with senescence, has been studied by Lansing (1952) using a strain
the rotifer *Philodina citrina*. The parent strain exhibited an almost rectangul
survival curve with virtually all deaths occurring between 20 and 30 days (the la
third of the optimum life-span). The curve for the F$_1$ generation was le
rectangular; that for the F$_2$ generation showed that nearly 40% of this populati
had died before 20 days had elapsed, and the accumulation of senescence facto
was so great that none of the third inbred generation survived for more than o
day.

One of the most characteristic genetic factors is the division of populations
many metazoa into male and female sexes. In man the genes controlling t
significant sexual differences are located on a single chromosome. In less high

eveloped animals with greater tendencies towards hermaphroditism they may not
e so well separated. There is, however, evidence that even in house flies (*Fig.* 2.7)
Rockstein and Lieberman, 1958) more females survive into 'later life' than males,

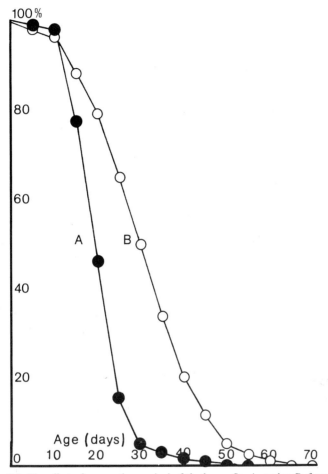

Fig. 2.7. The effect of sex on the survival of the house fly. A, males; B, females.

a phenomenon similar to that which has intrigued research workers in human
ageing for many years (*Fig.* 2.8). In both these instances, the effect is most
pronounced in the third quartile of the life-span. There is no evidence for greater
optimum life-span, merely for a larger number of females surviving over that
period during which mortality pressure is greatest in the male. If the curve relating
expected age at death to chronological age is plotted for human males and females
see *Fig.* 3.7) it can be seen that the two curves converge above 50 years of age and
that by the time the average old man or old woman has survived to age 90 their
chances of living an extra two or three years are identical.

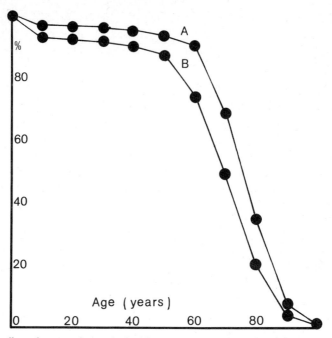

Fig. 2.8. The effect of sex on the survival of human subjects, A, males; B, females. The figures are
derived from the figures provided by the Office of the Registrar-General for the year 1971-1972.

2.13 Effect of Parental Age

It is well known that chromosomal damage such as is reflected in the development
of Down's syndrome is more prevalent in the offspring of elderly mothers, rising
from a risk factor of 1 : 2300 in mothers under 20 years of age to one of over 1 : 4!
at ages above 45. Children with Down's syndrome do not usually survive for more
than three decades, but there is little evidence for any direct effect on life-span
without associated mongoloid involvement. In animals, however, there is some
evidence that maternal age has a direct effect on the life-span of offspring, although
in the case of some of the animals studied it would be difficult to separate such
pathological changes from the direct effects of ageing. Rockstein (1959) for
instance, has observed that flies bred from 4-day-old mothers lived 45% longer
than those from 27-day-old mothers. The same could be observed with the
mealworm (*Tenebrio molitor*).

Similarly, the lethal genes accumulated in the rotifers studied by Lansing (1952
which eliminated the strain after three generations of inbreeding were present in
elderly mothers and could be eradicated by the introduction of a generation of
young females. At higher levels of evolutionary development, however, similar life
shortening effects could not be observed in the progeny of elderly mice (Suntseff e
al., 1962) and brood mares (Comfort, 1959).

Paternal age at conception does not appear to have anything like as great importance in the life expectancy of the offspring at any point in the evolutionary hierarchy.

2.14 The Ageing of Twins

The factor which determines whether the ageing of an organism is programmed or not is its genetic make-up. Each individual differs from every other individual in its genetic make-up, but one group shows an appreciable degree of interpair similarity. This is the case of monozygous twins where both individuals arise from the fertilization of a single egg. Studies on the longevity of twins carried out by Galton (1876), Kallman and Jarvik (1957) and Hauge et al. (1963), have shown a considerable similarity between the ages at death of pairs of monozygous twins. This is not apparent in the case of dizygous twins or other pairs of siblings although Kallmann and later Jarvik et al. (1960) have shown that the difference between the two pairs of twin types decreases the longer they live. However, many geneticists have some reservations about the effectiveness of twin studies, dizygous twins being indistinguishable from other pairs of siblings since their cellular origins are equally dissimilar. In fact, the results for dizygous twins lie midway between those of monozygous twins and other pairs of non-twin siblings, perhaps because they have shared a common intrauterine environment and have, in most instances, been brought up after birth in a more closely similar environment than that experienced by siblings whose birth dates are separated by a year or two.

Kallman and Sander (1949) in 58 pairs of twins who had already completed their full life-span, showed that the mean life-spans of dizygous twins differed by either 78·3 months for same-sex pairs or 126·6 months for opposite-sex pairs, whereas the mean differences between monozygous twins were significantly ($P < 0.05$) lower at 36·9 months. A further group of over 1600 twins age 60 and above have been subjected to longitudinal studies over the period 1946–1973, by the end of which period full survival statistics had been obtained for 96% of the individuals.

The incidence of age-related diseases such as cancer, hypertension, ulcers, etc. was recorded for these pairs of individuals. Jarvik and Falek (1961, 1962) reported a concordance of 25% in the incidence of cancer in the monozygous twins and only 4·3% in dizygous pairs, observations which were in agreement with four earlier studies (Busk et al., 1948; Harvald and Hauge, 1956, 1958; von Verschuer and Kober, 1956; Nielsen and Clemmesen, 1957). This led Jarvik to conclude that the susceptibility to cancer was under some form of genetic control. Since Burch has shown that the age-specific incidence of various forms of cancer with respect to age, conforms to the same equation as that which is applicable to the incidence of a variety of more closely age-related conditions and to the age-specific death rates for these conditions, it would seem likely that Jarvik's twin studies confirm the existence of a genetically controlled ageing process.

Using Wechsler–Bellvue (Wechsler, 1944) and a variety of other digit symbol, vocabulary, and hand and eye tests, Jarvik et al. (1957, 1962) showed that a greater similarity could be observed between the scores of monozygous than of dizygous twins, even when they were over 60 years of age.

Jarvik and Kato (1970) examined the relationship between chromosome number in leucocytes and showed that there was no evidence for a greater degree of aneuploidy in monozygous than in dizygous twins. In fact, the intrapair differences were less in monozygous pairs.

The general nature of the results of this massive longitudinal study suggest that whilst hereditary factors determine the mean longevity of a twin-pair, certain stress variables of exogenous origin over-ride the similarity in survival potential, making it possible to predict the longer-lived twin on the basis of applied stress. Studying the 28 survivors in 1976, Bank and Jarvik (1976) were unable to discover any evidence of such suppression of the hereditary effect by environmental factors, thus indicating how important hereditary factors are in determining survival.

2.15 Genetic Factors at a Molecular Level

If the controlling factors for senescence considered above are apparent at the population level it should be possible to identify related changes at a molecular level controlling the ageing process in individual organs or indeed in individual cells. If cellular function is to change with age this would involve the repression and de-repression of areas of the genome at various points in time. In morphogenesis the genes controlling the synthesis of components of individual biochemical reactions are expressed at certain well-defined stages of development, taking over from genes whose function is by then redundant. If ageing is programmed at the level of the genome it might be expected that similar repression and de-repression will occur to tone down the activity of certain cell strains and to create new senile pathways.

Another possibility is that the gene products mRNA, tRNA, rRNA and ultimately protein are only produced in limited quantity in early life. The concentration of these elements in the synthesis of biochemically active systems is reduced throughout life as individual molecules are lost through accident or turned over irreplaceably as a function of use. This will result in suboptimal amounts of the necessary species of macromolecule and a consequent reduction in the specific activity associated with that particular pathway.

If either of these two possibilities is in fact operative, it should be possible to identify changes in the protein end products even though difficulties might arise in assessing changes in the intermediate RNA molecules. From the nature of the repression of protein synthesis and from a study of whether one protein system merely decreases in amount or is replaced by another, it should be possible to indentify which of the processes is operative.

Evidence for repression and de-repression is available both for structural and for enzymic protein species. The various types of collagen (see Chapter 4) differ so markedly from one another that it is unlikely that a single gene is involved, even though there is evidence that some of them may be synthesized under the control of genes located on the same chromosome (p. 92).

If the differences between the primary structures of the types of collagen were restricted to the non-helical telopeptide regions, it might be assumed that a common precursor could be synthesized using a common mRNA molecule as a template and that subsequent post-translational changes could convert this into one or other of the collagen species. However, the amino acid composition and the α-chain distribution is so varied, and polymorphism occurs not only in the telopeptide but also in at least two regions of the helical portion of the molecule and it is apparent that no amount of post-translational modification could convert one type of collagen into the other, or either from a common precursor.

Further evidence for the switching on of a specific gene and the switching off of another comes from studies of the content of lactic acid dehydrogenase (LDH) in the heart and skeletal muscles of rats of various ages (Kanungo, 1975). LDH exists as five different isoenzymes, H_4, H_3M, H_2M_2, HM_3, M_4, composed of varying amounts of two non-identical subunits H and M. These two differ in amino acid composition and their synthesis has been shown to be under the control of two separate genes (Shaw and Barto, 1963). The H_4 isoenzyme and those containing high concentrations of the H subunit are present in largest amounts in heart muscle and oxidize lactic acid preferentially in aerobic conditions. The M_4 and other M subunit-rich isoenzymes are present in the skeletal muscles and prefer anaerobic conditions. Singh and Kanungo (1968) observed that the concentrations of *both* H-LDH and M-LDH rise initially with age in rat heart and rat skeletal muscle, falling subsequently as the rats become senescent. Of one calculates the ratio of H-LDH to M-LDH for the two tissues (*Fig.* 2.9) it can be seen that the ratio rises in both tissues as age increases. The graphs in *Fig.* 2.9 have been normalized to a value of 1

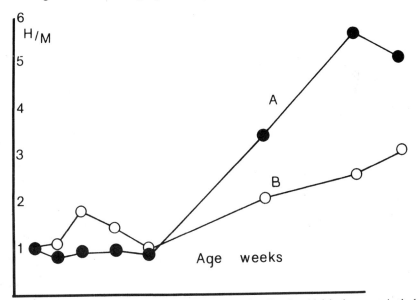

Fig. 2.9. The effect of age on the ratio of the H and M subunits of lactic acid dehydrogenase in the heart and skeletal muscles of the rat. Individual values for each curve have been calculated as multiples of the values for the ratio H/M at birth (calculated from the data of Kanungo, 1980, *see* references for Chapter 5).

at birth since the two curves would otherwise have such dissimilar slopes (the values for H-LDH for heart muscle, which is rich in H-LDH, rise from 1·16 to 7·69 throughout life, whereas the values for the same ratio for skeletal muscle which is relatively less rich in H-LDH only rise from 0·25 to 0·86). As the animal grows older, the changing synthesis of LDH molecules appears to constrain the enzyme to prefer to work under aerobic conditions. If one performs the jump from rat to human, it can be seen that under conditions in which, due to faulty pulmonary and cardiac activity, the carriage of oxygen through the body is restricted, the genetic control of enzyme synthesis is such as to provide the less effective of the two forms of the enzyme. The body is apparently programmed to exacerbate some of those phenomena of ageing which are induced by other physiological changes.

Consideration of the way in which such genetic control manifests itself in the organism has provided the basis for much speculation over the years. Weismann (1891) regarded senescence as an essential concomitant of life in metazoa arising by chance as the result of mutations but retained as a useful product of natural selection because 'worn out individuals are ... valueless to the species'. According to this theory, therefore, genes specific for the degeneration of the organism (such as those which provide for the synthesis of a functionally less effective form of collagen and an LDH molecule which adjusts less appropriately to changes in the anaerobic nature of the internal milieu) become operative as age increases. However, he did not consider how these disadvantageous genes came to be expressed at certain specific stages in life. Williams (1957) suggested that the existence of pleiotropic genes which changed their function as age progressed could explain this sequential effect. Medawar (1952) on the other hand postulated that the expression of newly active genes at any stage during senescence might be under the control of special *modifier genes*. Other theories have involved the concept of gene redundancy (Medvedev, 1967; Calow, 1978) in which it is postulated that a progressive loss of information from the genome results in an imbalance of gene expression, 'turning on' appropriate genes as the activity of others regresses.

The *operon* theory of Jacob and Monod (1961) provides yet another and possibly a more logical explanation of sequential gene expression. Devised to explain the induction of enzyme synthesis, it can also be applied to any gene controlled synthesis. Monod and his colleagues suggested that a *regulator gene* could produce a *repressor* which interacted with an inducer of enzyme synthesis to control the transcription of the *structural gene*.

The application of this theory to the sequential transcription of the different genes for the various types of collagen would appear to be a rational development (Hall, 1981) (p. 144).

2.16 The Error Catastrophe Theory

2.16.1 *Cell Health and Ageing*

Hayflick and Moorhead (1961) observed that the life-span of human diploid fibroblasts in culture is limited. Hayflick later (1965) advanced the hypothesis that the fact that such cells could only suffer a finite number of passages before death may be related to the development of ageing processes within the cell. Martin et al. (1970), in an extensive study of donor age, tissue of origin and genotype, confirmed Hayflick's findings regarding the changes which can be observed in a human cell line as it ages and its relationship to the age of the donor. Cell growth in culture is triphasic. An initial lag phase (Phase I) is followed by an essentially linear phase (Phase II) during which the relative number of cells increases rapidly. This is followed by a third involutionary phase (Phase III) during which the cells suffer 'senescence' and the culture ultimately dies. Alterations to the cell strain may occur at any time during Phase II to produce 'immortal' cell lines which never pass into Phase III but continue to multiply indefinitely. These abnormal cell lines do not age but continue to produce, in culture, cells with all the characteristics of cells from earlier doublings. Hayflick reported that 13 human embryo fibroblast strains died out between 35 to 65 doublings and Martin showed that on average 0·2 potential doublings were lost for every year of life of the donor tissues. The number of possible doublings also depended on the source of the cells. Lung and skin cells could undergo more doublings before death than could cells from kidney, muscle, heart, thymus, thyroid and bone (Hayflick and Moorhead, 1961; Martin et al., 1970).

There was a considerable difference between the doubling capacity of cells from comparable aged donors (*Fig.* 2.10). In fact, although there is a definite age regression of division potential, some of the doubling capacities of cells from the oldest individuals were still higher than those of the lowest values of strains from the youngest tissues (Hayflick, 1965). Goldstein et al. (1969) demonstrated that the effect of diabetes mellitus was also to reduce the number of possible passages before death. It is of interest to observe that *in vivo* ageing can be seen to accompany diabetes. The collagen fibres in the connective tissues of human

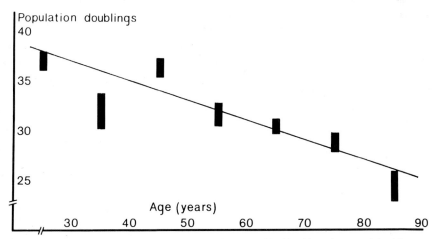

Fig. 2.10. Mean cumulative population doublings of human skin fibroblasts (±s.e.m.) for 10 year age groups of donors. The regression line (method of least squares: $P < 0.001$) for all 95 observations over the full age range shows that the doubling potential of the cells falls by 1·8 doublings per decade.

diabetics (Hamlin et al., 1975) and alloxan diabetic experimental animals (Behera and Patnaik, 1979, 1981) are one or two decades 'older' on the basis of solubility and collagenase susceptibility than might be expected from the chronological age of the patients.

Patients suffering from Werner's syndrome (Epstein et al. 1966) also showed a marked decrease in doubling potential, only a few passages being possible before death occurs. Holliday et al. (1974) have shown that there are marked changes in the enzymic make up of such cells, a high proportion of the glucose-6-phosphate dehydrogenase for instance being inactive.

Hayflick's original findings and the subsequent observations on growth limitation have led to the suggestion that the control of doubling potential is controlled by changes occurring within the cell. Other workers, however (Hay and Strehler, 1967; Ryan et al., 1974), have suggested that culture media may become deficient; interaction with other cells is essential for normal development of a culture (Franks, 1970) and contamination of the culture by viruses or mycoplasma may prove lethal. The concept of limited *in vitro* survival is, however, generally accepted and efforts have been made to define the intrinsic changes which bring it about.

2.16.2 *The Accumulation of Errors*

Orgel (1963) suggested that cellular misfunction and ultimately cell death could originate from the accumulation of random errors in protein synthesis. If it so happened that the erroneously programmed proteins produced by such faulty synthesis were enzymes with intracellular function, a process of positive feedback would amplify and accelerate the build-up of cellular damage. Over the past two decades much evidence has been provided which is in favour of such a hypothesis, but many eminent workers have also failed to obtain positive results in well designed test experiments.

To appreciate to the full the rationale behind Orgel's theory both in its original and modified forms (Orgel, 1970) it is necessary to appreciate the complexity of the processes of protein biosynthesis. The starting point of all protein synthesis is the DNA molecule, consisting as it does of discrete coded sequences of nucleotides in the genes for each protein. In the prophase of mitotic activity the nucleic acids are present in the form of a double helix, the two strands being bound together by hydrogen bonds between pyrimidine residues in one strand and complementary purine residues in the other. The pyrimidines and purines in DNA are invariably paired one with another, adenine (A) always linking with thymine (T) and guanine (G) with cytosine (C). Thus the two strands of nucleic acid are complementary to one another throughout their length and when, during the anaphase of mitosis, the chromosomes separate before reassuming their structure as strands of chromatin in the telophase they are structurally different. Under the action of DNA polymerase new nucleotides are aligned along each of the separated DNA strands, each base attracting its appropriate complementary element. Thus A attracts T, T attracts A, C attracts G and G attracts C, and ester linkages are formed between adjacent phosphate and sugar residues to form a continuous chain. Each original strand thus becomes associated with a replica of its original partner and as the cell divides into two daughter cells each contains an exact replica of the original double standard DNA, one strand of each being newly synthesized. Faulty replication, the incorporation of a wrong base or of the right bases in the wrong order usually means that the DNA helices are malformed. The cell has repair mechanisms to deal with such an event. An endonuclease breaks the linkages between the nucleotides on either side of the faulty section, stripping out the misplaced bases and then a synthetase (DNA polymerase) catalyses the insertion of the correct components. Failure to accomplish such a repair resulting in the maintenance of an abnormal DNA chain means that the genetic structure of the daughter cell is altered and a mutation has occurred (see p. 23). Since the triplet coding on the nucleic acid molecules is ultimately read from one end of the molecule, errors inserted down the length of the chain can have greater or less effect on the final message. The introduction of one or two faulty nucleotides in place of the correct ones will only affect that region of the message in which they are incorporated. The removal or addition of a base, however, will alter the whole of the subsequent message since a hypothetical series .... TTCTTCTTC.... would translate to an mRNA molecule UUCUUCUUC (see below) and would be read by the cytoplasmic ribosomes as poly-phenylalanine. If, however, the initial thymine was omitted, the series would read TCTTCTTCT and the mRNA molecule UCUUCUUCU would be read as polyserine. If both initial thymines were omitted the resultant protein would be polyleucine. Clearly greater confusion would arise if the trinucleotides were not repetitive as in this hypothetical instance, since so-called *nonsense* triplets and triplets for chain termination could be possible. If the latter are present in the mRNA, short lengths of polypeptide rather than complete proteins are produced.

The information contained in the DNA code is transcribed onto RNA molecules. Almost all the DNA content of the cell occurs in the nucleus whereas most of the RNA is present in the cytoplasm. There are three major differences between DNA and RNA. First, the sugar molecule in RNA is ribose rather than deoxyribose. Secondly, one of the two pyrimidines present in DNA, namely thymine, is replaced by uracil. This pyrimidine forms a hydrogen bonded pair with adenine just as thymine does in DNA. Finally, the RNA molecules are single stranded but can form double helices by folding back on themselves. This is especially true of transport RNA which carries activated amino acids to the site of protein synthesis on the fibrosomes. In these molecules there are at least three looped regions with varying function which are produced by the alignment of three relatively short regions of the overall RNA molecule in a double helical structure.

RNA polymerase takes instructions from a DNA template in exactly the same way that DNA polymerase does. In this instance, however, the template function is restricted to one single strand of DNA, not to both of them. Faulty RNA molecules can result from erroneous transcription and under normal circumstances such errors will be eliminated by the action of an appropriate endonuclease and resynthesis of the correct polynucleotide. DNA polymerases faced with the initial synthesis of DNA or the repair of erroneous or damaged strands test the correctness of the preceding base pair before forming the next phosphodiester bond. RNA polymerases do not test the previous structure in this fashion, hence the error rates of RNA polymerases are some orders of magnitude greater than those of DNA polymerases. In fact, genetic analyses of DNA synthesis by *E.coli* indicates that the error rate of DNA synthesis is only of the order of 1 in 10^{10}. RNA synthesis may be in error on 1 in 10^7 occasions, one thousand times more frequently.

RNA molecules have more than one role in protein synthesis. The coded message indicating the order in which amino acids are to be introduced into the protein is transcribed from a portion of the DNA molecule to form messenger RNA (mRNA).

Other nucleotides are combined together to provide transport RNA (tRNA) whilst yet a third form of RNA is synthesized to provide a portion of the ribosome (rRNA) by which the code carried on the mRNA is read.

Amino acids present in the cellular pool are activated for incorporation into nascent protein by coupling to the 2′ or 3′ hydroxyl group of the ribose component of the terminal adenosine of a specific tRNA. This is catalysed by the enzyme aminoacyl tRNA synthetase acting in the presence of adenosine triphosphate. The first stage of the reaction is the synthesis of an aminoacyl adenylate. The same enzyme then catalyses the transfer of the aminoacyl group from the adenosine to the tRNA molecule. There is at least one aminoacyl tRNA synthetase for each amino acid. The fidelity of the ultimate protein synthesis depends to a considerable extent on the incorporation of the activated amino acid on to the appropriate tRNA molecule and is hence dependent on the specificity of the aminoacyl tRNA synthetase. The tRNA molecules have many common secondary structural features and also contain a number of nucleosides not found in mRNA molecules. These include inosine, pseudouridine, dihydrouridine, ribothymidine and methylated derivatives of guanosine and inosine. Of these nucleosides, one in particular, inosine, frequently occurs in that portion of the clover leaf structure of the tRNA molecule containing the anticodon through which the tRNA recognizes the appropriate codon on the mRNA molecule. Inosine is more catholic in its choice of complementary base pairs than any other purine or pyrimidine. It can, in fact, form pairs of stable hydrogen bonds with cytidine, adenosine and uridine.

The genetic code of nucleotide triplets is degenerate in that more than one codon is available for certain amino acids. The presence of inosine in certain anticodon sequences of tRNAs therefore permits a single anticodon to read more than one codon. Thus, alanine tRNA which contains the anticodon IGC recognizes the three codons GCU, GGC and GCA i.e. three out of the four possible codons for this amino acid.

The sequence of events which occur on the ribosome is determined by the existence of two sites on the ribosomal structure associated with the location of the nascent peptide and the recognition of the newly arrived aminoacyl tRNA. After recognition of the incoming amino acid complex, the nascent protein chain is elongated by transfer of the existing peptide structure to the new amino acid with the formation of a peptide link through the carboxyl group of the former and the amino group of the latter. The tRNA is then released and the ribosome moves along one codon, in effect therefore transferring the elongated protein to the second site and vacating the recognition site for the acceptance of the next aminoacyl tRNA complex.

This complex reaction is the one which Orgel (1963) suggested was likely to suffer irreparable damage due to the accumulation of errors at one or more point in the sequence of events (*Fig.* 2.11). The effects of some errors would be so gross as to be lethal, killing the parent cell immediately, others could result in the production of faulty proteins which the defence mechanisms of the body would recognize immediately as foreign and would hence remove. Certain errors, however, would not be in either of these categories and would modify the function of the cell in a subtle fashion accumulating and being amplified by positive feedback acting at other points in the synthetic pathway. These would be the errors which, according to Orgel, resulted in a reduction in optimal cell functioning and finally to cell death.

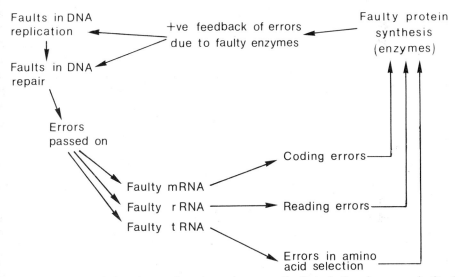

Fig. 2.11. The accumulation of errors, first suggested as a causative factor in the aging process by Orgel (1963). If the faults in protein synthesis involve enzymes implicated in nucleic acid synthesis or repair, the positive feedback loop will amplify the error.

There are at least two important predictions which arise from the Orgel hypothesis. The first is that senescence should be accompanied by an increase in the amounts of aberrant protein accumulating in cells or secreted by cells. Secondly, experimental treatment of cell lines in such a fashion as to produce increasing amounts of aberrant protein should simultaneously induce changes in the cells which mimic those of the normal ageing process.

The first of these two predictions lays itself open to experimental proof in a number of ways, all of which have been exploited during the past two decades. First, it should be possible to observe changes in the ratio of activity to protein mass—i.e. specific activity—as faulty enzyme molecules accumulate at the expense of ones with normal activity. Further, preparations of enzyme proteins isolated from ageing cells might be shown to contain increasing proportions of molecules which differ from those of normal enzymes in that they have altered physico-chemical properties—solubility, stability, etc. Measurements of specific activity can be made in a variety of ways, but the one which has proved most effective in studies of ageing is that which is based on the measurement of biological activity in the intact cell or total cell extract, using the normal substrate appropriate to the particular enzyme and measurement of total enzyme protein using antibodies raised against purified preparations of the enzyme. Since the first of these measures activity whilst the second measures total protein their quotient provides a value for specific activity. The validity of this method is dependent on the near identity of the active and inactive forms of the enzyme. Thus it has to be assumed that any change in the biologically active centre of the enzyme must be without effect on that part of the molecule which combines with the antibody. This may not be true of all the examples which have been tested and hence is as yet unproven and thus casts a degree of doubt on the assumption made. Until other methods are derived for comparison which are universally applicable these have to suffice. Gershon and Gershon (1970) observed a reduction in the specific activity of isocitrate lyase in ageing populations of the nematode *Turbatrix aceti* (later confirmed by Reiss and Rothstein, 1974, 1975) and Zeelon et al. (1973) demonstrated that fructose-1,6-diphosphate aldolase activity also decreases with advancing age whilst the inactive form of the aldolase increases. Bolla and Brot (1975) also observed inactive forms of elongation factor-1 in senescent nematodes. Bozcuk (1972) has also employed less highly developed animals for the experimental testing of Orgel's theory, pointing out that in *Drosophila* there is no somatic cell division during adult life, so that cellular selection such as has been suggested by Maynard-Smith (1962) as a possible explanation of changes in the activity of cellular enzymes, cannot occur during this period. Experiments by Harrison and Holliday (1967), however, involved the administration of amino acid analogues (which might be expected to shorten life-span if they interfered with the synthesis of normal protein) to *Drosophila* larvae and thus were not fully protected by Bozcuk's suggestion.

Lewis and Holliday (1970) also reported on experiments with the fungus *Neurospora crassa*. The mutant *leu 5*, which has a modified leucyl tRNA synthetase, incorporates a number of faulty amino acids into proteins (Printz and Gross, 1967) and grows at a constant rate at 35 °C for between 3 and 4 days, equivalent to about 36–48 doublings, after which it dies. Towards the end of this period the proportion of altered glutamic acid dehydrogenase (GDH) molecules increases dramatically. This is as would be expected on the basis of the error catastrophe theory since the accumulation of errors would be exponential in type. Holliday (1969) also observed a similar accumulation of altered GDH molecules in another mutant strain of neurospora, natural death (nd).

At higher levels in the evolutionary hierarchy, Gershon and Gershon (1973) were able to repeat their observations on fructose-1,6-diphosphate aldolase using mouse liver cells. Although they were unable to observe age-related changes in the specific activity of mouse skeletal muscle aldolase the increased level of aldolase protein in the muscles of very old animals was taken as indicating a 30–40% increase in inactive or only partially active enzyme molecules. Although Bozcuk's comment on *Drosophila* may not apply to mammals, it is worth commenting that Gershon and Gershon compared very young and very old animals. It is possible that developmental changes in cellular type could occur between 2 months (their younger age group) and 'middle-aged' animals (say 18–20 months) which were not tested. Baird et al. (1975) note that a more apposite comparison might be between such 18–20-month-old animals and the 30-month-old group which they examined.

Reiss and Gershon (1976) have observed decreasing levels of specific activity in rat liver superoxide dismutase (SOD) and an increased level of inactive lactic acid dehydrogenase in the same organ. Mennecies and Dryfus (1974) have shown that inactive aldolase and glucose-6-phosphate dehydrogenase (G-6-PD) accumulate considerably in ageing human and rabbit erythrocytes.

Other studies (Oliveira and Pfuderer, 1973; Rothstein, 1975; Yagil, 1976) have not shown similar accumulations of inactive molecules in ageing tissues *in vitro* or *in vivo*. Schofield and Davies (1978) point out that certain enzymes—they quote as an example prolyl hydroxylase which catalyses the hydroxylation of peptide-bound proline during the biosynthesis of collagen—occurs in fibroblasts in either active or inactive forms. The inactive form is converted into the active form by the association of four of the single subunits in which the inactive form occurs. These two forms appear to be in equilibrium and the balance is displaced in the direction inactive → active during growth and maturation.

Although these workers were not mainly interested in any age effect, it could be inferred that the reverse of this change, i.e. dissociation, could occur with increasing senescence without any new inactive molecules being synthesized. Hence not all cases in which inactive enzymes accumulate can be ascribed unequivocally to the accumulation of errors in protein synthesis.

The production of enzyme molecules which are different from those of the normal species produced by young cells has again been reported by Holliday and Tarrant (1972). They observed that glucose-6-phosphate dehydrogenase (G-6-PD) from young cultures of fibroblasts (up to 22 passages) lost its activity linearly with time when heated to 59 or 60 °C. The line relating enzymic activity to time of heating could be extrapolated to zero time when it appeared to pass through the 100% point on the y-axis (*Fig.* 2.12) indicating that all the enzyme was in the active form before heating. If the action of heat on the enzyme present in cells from cultures of fibroblasts which had undergone 61 passages was compared with its effect on that from young cultures it could be seen that the regression line of enzymic activity on time of treatment was parallel to that for the young culture after about 5–7 minutes but significantly below it. Extrapolation of this line produced an intercept on the activity axis appropriate to an initial percentage of G-6-PD activity of 82%. Hence it would appear that as the cell culture approaches death after the finite number of passages characteristic of this strain, the G-6-PD produced is modified so as to be thermally labile at temperatures below 59–60 °C. Other workers have either been able to identify age-related

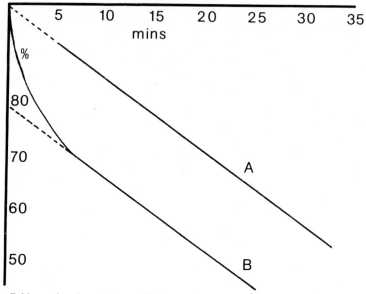

Fig. 2.12. Evidence for the existence of abnormal enzyme molecules in cultures of cells when approaching their maximum number of possible doublings before the extinction of the culture. The enzyme (glucose-6-phosphate dehydrogenase) when isolated from an ageing culture (curve B, 61 passages) is equally susceptible to thermal denaturation at 59 °C as the enzyme from a younger culture (Curve A, 22 passages), but the lowered position of the curve reveals extrapolation that approximately 20% of the enzyme is already denatured at temperatures below 59 °C.

increases in thermolabile enzymes (Harding, 1973; Wulf and Cutler, 1975; Schofield and Hadfield, 1978) or have completely failed to do so (Yagil, 1976).

If amino acid analogues are administered to cells which are actively engaged in protein synthesis, it might be expected that they would be incorporated into the nascent proteins and might modify their activity if they were enzymic in nature. This artificial production of altered enzymes should therefore induce errors in cell activity and ultimately cell death and life shortening due to an error catastrophe (Harrison and Holliday, 1967). These workers fed a mixture of amino acid analogues to *Drosophila melanogaster* larvae and observed that the mean life-span of the adults was shortened. As mentioned earlier, however, Dingley and Maynard-Smith (1969) and Bozcuk (1972) questioned their deduction from these results that their experiments confirmed Orgel's hypothesis. Later studies by Holliday and his colleagues (Holliday, 1969; Lewis and Holliday, 1970) using different experimental models—*Podospora ansering* and *Neurospora crassa*—appeared to confirm Orgel more unequivocally, since both species became senile earlier than normally would be the case and altered proteins accumulated. Ryan et al. (1974) were unable to discover evidence for ageing effects due to cells treated with amino acid analogues. Moreover they showed that the proliferation of cultures of normal cells and of apparently immortal transformed cell lines were equally affected by the administration of analogues of normally occurring amino acids.

Lewis and Tarrant (1972) demonstrated to their own satisfaction that old cells were less capable of discriminating between amino acid analogues. Growing cultures of fibroblasts in the presence of the two amino acids, methionine and ethionine, they demonstrated that whereas young cultures incorporated only the normally occurring methionine into protein, older cultures incorporated either indiscriminately. They were also able to show that changes in discriminatory power could be induced in young cells by tampering with the synthesis of RNA. Cells grown in the presence of 5-fluorouracil were initially able to discriminate between methionine and ethionine, but after 6 days culture, in the presence of this abnormal pyrimidine the degree of discrimination rapidly fell from a mean value of c.83% effectiveness to c.20% (*Fig.* 2.13). Kurtz (1975) used cell-free preparations of protein-synthesizing microsomes to study the validity of Orgel's hypothesis. He stimulated mouse liver microsomes with polyuridylic acid to synthesize polyphenylalanine and measured the incidence of incorporation of leucine residues. This could occur through the misreading of -UUU- -UUG- or -CUU-.

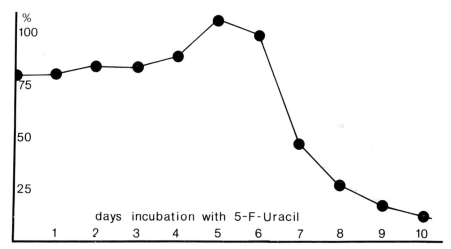

Fig. 2.13. The production of age-type changes in cultured cells by nucleic acid modification. The incubation of fibroblasts with 5-F-uracil for 6 days brings about a sharp reduction in the capability of the tRNA to differentiate between the two similar amino acids—methionine and ethionine. Such failure of differentiation is typical of cells from ageing cultures.

Kurtz reported errors of this type which rose between 1 and 14 months but not between 14 and 31 months. Because there was no evidence of an exponential increase in error with increasing age, it has been assumed that Kurtz's observations are not in agreement with Orgel's hypothesis. The amplification of error production postulated by Orgel presupposed a positive feedback if enzymes which were involved in DNA or RNA synthesis were produced in a faulty state. Polyphenylalanine is in the main secreted by the cell and even if it is retained will not effect the pathways of protein synthesis at earlier stages. Hence it would not necessarily be expected that the administration of polyuridylic acid would either affect or be affected by the ageing process.

It can be seen from these observations that the results of experiments designed to test Orgel's hypothesis have been very varied. Some workers, namely Holliday and his colleagues, have obtained evidence which would on the face of it require that Orgel's hypothesis be retained at least as a working proposition. Other groups of workers (Baird et al., 1975; Gershon and Gershon in later papers, 1976; Bozcuk, 1972) are overtly critical not only of Orgel's original hypothesis, but also of Holliday's interpretations of his own efforts to confirm Orgel's proposal. However, as mentioned above, some at least of these criticisms cannot themselves stand up to judgement, and there is still a shortage of concrete evidence on which to refute the error hypothesis. It is always easy to obtain negative results to any experiments, but less easy to obtain meaningful positive ones. Until such time as the full story of enzyme production, both for internal and external use, has been elucidated for a considerable number of cell types, it will be necessary to accept both pro and contrary findings at their face value, but at the same time to weigh them according to their individual validity. As things stand at the present time, the positive findings for Orgel's hypothesis carry more weight than the negative findings of those opposed to it.

2.17 Can we Integrate these Theories?

Sanders (1968) attempted an integration of a number of the theories of ageing at that time under consideration, basing his concept on the idea of a cybernetic control of the homeostatic factors in the body. Hall (1978) reviewed programmed and error catastrophe theories and concluded that both were tenable working hypotheses. His view of integration was based on the assumption that programmed ageing controls certain aspects of ageing, notably the species-specific differences which can easily be observed, whereas the accumulation of errors determines how intraspecies differences arise. A useful analogy can be obtained from a study of the trajectory of a stone thrown into the air (Hall, 1979).

When a projectile is thrown at an angle through the air, the height it reaches and the ultimate distance travelled before it returns to earth is dependent on a number of factors (*Fig.* 2.14). First, the force and angle at which it is projected. A factor which is continuously operative throughout flight is gravity, acting on the mass of the projectile and possibly contrary winds. At its peak when it is moving upwards at its slowest speed and the forward component of its motion is most effective, it can come under the influence of changing atmospheric conditions and friction which may become very important if the projectile begins to disintegrate—if for instance the casing of a tennis ball becomes detached from the underlying structure. If it manages to traverse its trajectory without being affected by these factors it will reach the earth again at a predictable point dependent solely on force, angle and gravity. If the parabola is equated with the life path of an organism the species-specific life-span can be identified with the distance the projectile travels in the model. This is then controlled, in the ideal biological situation, by those factors which start the organism off on its passage through life, on its genetic vital force and on those factors which are operative, like gravity, throughout its passage.

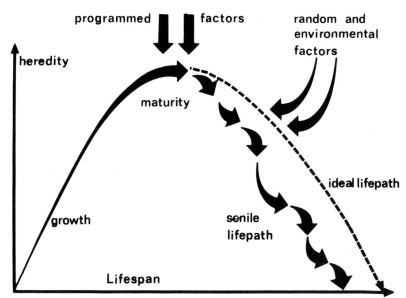

Fig. 2.14. The comparison of life-span modulation by internal and external factors to the flight path of a projectile, demonstrating the composite effects of programmed and random ageing processes (Hall, 1981).

These again are of genetic origin; differentiation and growth and any ageing factors which are directly under genetic control. Still considering the ideal situation, all individuals with identical genetic make-up should travel the same ideal pathway and have the same life-span. In the second half of life, environmental and endogenous changes, disease, pressure of living, and faulty metabolism induced by errors in protein synthesis will cause the organism to deviate from the ideal pathway and may well result in a shortened life-span. In *Fig.* 2.14 this abnormal life path is indicated by a series of curved arrows destroying the symmetry of the parabola and bringing its descending limb back to the base line earlier. Extraneous factors, whether environmental or intrinsic, will detract from life-span by inducing senescence in this period of the life path.

The integration of theories proposed by the present author, therefore, consists of the superimposition of accumulating errors on a programme. The programme is predictable, whereas the errors, being stochastic cannot be. This can, therefore, explain how, although all mice and all men live out their respective life-spans which differ manyfold, each mouse and each man remains an individual, ageing in his own peculiar way, being more or less senescent than the mean, and dying his own particular number of weeks or years before the end of the maximum specific life-span for his species.

Recommended Reading

J. D. Schofield and I. Davies's 'Theories of Ageing' in J. C. Brocklehurst's *Textbook of Geriatric Medicine and Gerontology*, Churchill Livingstone (1978) and B. J. Merry and J. G. Phillips's '*Basic Gerontology*' in M. Green's *Clinics in Endocrinology and Metabolism*, Saunders (1981) are both good reviews of present knowledge regarding ageing theory.

References

Acharya P. V. N. (1972) The isolation and partial characterization of age-correlated oligo-deoxyribo-ribo-nucleotide with covalently linked aspartyl-glutamyl-polypeptides. *John Hopkins Med. J.* Suppl. **1**, 254.

Alexander P. (1957) Accelerated ageing—A long term effect of exposure to ionizing radiation. *Gerontologia* **1**, 174.

Amici D., Gianfranceschi G. L., Marsili G. et al. (1974) Young and old rats: ATP, alkaline phosphatase, cholesterol and protein levels in the blood: DNA and RNA contents of the liver—Regulation by an aqueous thymus extract. *Experientia* **30**, 633.

Andrew W. (1952) *Cellular Changes with Age*. Springfield, Ill., Thomas.

Augener W., Cohnen G., Reuter A. et al. (1974) Decrease of T-lymphocytes during ageing. *Lancet* **1**, 1164.

Baird M. B., Samis H. V., Massie H. R. et al. (1975) A brief argument in opposition to the Orgel hypothesis. *Gerontologist* **21**, 57.

Bank L. and Jarvik L. F. (1976) The effect of stress on longevity of twins. *Abst. 29th Ann. Meet. Gerontol. Soc.* New York.

Behera H. N. and Patnaik B. K. (1979) *In vivo* and *in vitro* effects of alloxan on collagen characteristics of bone, skin and tendon in Swiss mice. *Gerontology* **25**, 255.

Behera H. N. and Patnaik B. K. (1981) Increased stability of collagen following alloxan diebetes in Swiss mice. *Gerontology* **28**, 163.

Bjorksten J. (1974) Cross-linkage and the aging process. In: Rockstein M. (ed.) *Theoretical Aspects of Aging*. New York, Academic Press, p. 43.

Blackett A. D. and Hall D. A. (1981) Tissue vitamin-E levels and lipofuchsin accumulation with age in the mouse. *J. Gerontol.* **36**, 529.

Bolla R. and Brot M. (1975) Age-dependent changes in enzymes involved in macromolecular synthesis in *Turbatrix aceti. Arch. Biochem. Biophys.* **169**, 227.

Bozcuk A. N. (1972) DNA synthesis in the absence of somatic cell division associated with ageing in *Drosphila subobscura. Exp. Gerontol.* **7**, 147.

Bradley M. O., Erickeson L. C. and Kohn K. W. (1976) Normal DNA strand rejoining and absence of DNA cross-linking in progeroid and aging human cells. *Mutat. Res.* **37**, 279.

Brody S. (1945) *Bioenergetics and Growth*. New York, Reinhold.

Burch R. P. J. (1968) *An Inquiry Concerning Growth, Disease and Ageing*. Edinburgh, Oliver & Boyd.

Burnet F. M. (1959) *The Clonal Selection Theory of Acquired Immunity*. Cambridge, Cambridge University Press.

Busk T., Clemmensen H. and Nielson A. (1948) Twin studies and other investigations in the Danish Cancer Registry. *Br. J. Cancer* **2**, 156.

Calow P. (1978) *Life Cycles*. London, Chapman & Hall.

Clarke J. M. and Maynard-Smith J. (1955) The genetics and cytology of *Drosophila subobscura* XI. Hybrid vigour and longevity. *J. Genetics* **53**, 172.

Comfort A. (1959) The longevity and mortality of thoroughbred stallions. *J. Gerontol.* **15**, 126.

Comfort A. (1960) Longevity and mortality in dogs of four breeds. *J. Gerontol.* **15**, 216.

Comfort A. (1964) *Ageing—the Biology of Senescence*. Edinburgh, Churchill Livingstone.

Comfort A. (1979) *The Biology of Senescence*. Edinburgh, Churchill Livingstone.

Crowley C. and Curtis, H. (1963) The development of somatic mutation in mice with age. *Proc. Natl Acad. Sci. USA* **49**, 626.

Curtis H. J. (1963) Biological mechanisms underlying the ageing process. *Science* **141**, 686.

Curtis H. J. (1966) *Biological Mechanisms of Ageing*. Springfield, Ill., Thomas.

Curtis H. J. (1971) Genetic factors in aging. *Adv. Genet.* **16**, 305.

Curtis H. J. and Miller K. (1971) Chromosome aberrations in liver cells of guinea pigs *in vivo. J. Gerontol.* **26**, 292.

Cutler R. G. (1973) Redundancy of information content as a protective mechanism determining ageing rate. *Mech. Ageing Dev.* **2**, 381.

Cutler R. G. (1975) Evolution of human longevity and genetic complexity governing aging rate. *Proc. Natl Acad. Sci. USA* **72**, 4664.

Cutler R. G. (1976a) Nature of aging and life maintenance processes. *Interdiscip. Top. Gerontol.* **9**, 83.

Cutler R. G. (1976b) Alteration of chromatin as a function of age in *Mus* and *Peromyscus* rodent species. *Abst. 29th Ann. Meet. Gerontol. Soc.* New York.

Cutler R. G. (1978) Alteration with age in the informational storage and flow system of the mammalian cell. *Birth Defects* **14**, 463.

Cutler R. G. (1979) Evolution of human longevity: a critical overview. *J. Clin. Invest.* **57**, 694.

Deane H. W. and Fawcett D. W. (1952) Pigmented interstitial cells showing brown degeneration in the ovaries of old mice. *Anat. Rec.* **113**, 247.

Dingley F. and Maynard-Smith J. (1969) Absence of life-shortening effects of amino acid analogues in adult *Drosophila. Exp. Gerontol.* **4**, 145.

Epstein C. J., Martin G. M., Schultz A. L. et al. (1966) Werner's syndrome. *Medicine* **45**, 77.

Failla G. (1957) Consideration bearing on permissible accumulated radiation doses for occupational exposure. The ageing process and carcinogenesis. *Radiology* **69**, 23.

Franks L. M. (1970) Cellular aspects of ageing. *Exp. Gerontol.* **5**, 281.

Furth J., Upton A. C., Christenberry K. W. et al. (1954) Some late effects in mice of ionizing radiation from an experimental nuclear detonation. *Radiology* **63**, 562.

Galton F. (1876) The history of twins as a criterion of the relative powers of nature and nurture. *J. Roy. Anthropol. Inst. G.B. and Ire.* **6**, 391.

Gedick P. and Fischer R. (1959) Uber die Entstehung von Lipopigmente in Muskelfasern unter Untersuchungen beim Experimentellen Vitamen E-Mangel der Ratte und an Organen des Menschen. (Concerning the alterations in lipid pigments in muscle fibres in experiments with vitamin E on rats and human organs.) *Virchows Arch. Pathol. Anat. Physiol.* **332**, 431.

Gershon H. and Gershon D. (1970) Studies on aging nematodes. I The nematode as a model organism for ageing research. *Exp. Gerontol.* **5**, 7.

Gershon H. and Gershon D. (1973) Altered enzyme molecules in senescent organisms: Mouse muscle aldolase. *Mech. Ageing Dev.* **2**, 33.

Gershon D. and Gershon H. (1976) An evaluaton of the 'error catastrophe' theory of ageing in the light of recent experimental results. *Gerontology* **22**, 212.

Goldstein S., Littlefield J. W. and Soddner J. S. (1969) Diabetes mellitus and aging: diminished plating efficiency of cultured human fibroblasts. *Proc. Natl Acad. Sci. USA* **64**, 155.

von Hahn H. P. and Fritz E. (1966) Age-related alterations in the structure of DNA III. Thermal stability of rat liver DNA related to age, histone content and ionic strength. *Gerontologia* **12**, 237.

Hall D. A. (1978) The ageing process—two theories explained. *Mod. Geriatrics* **8**, 60.

Hall D. A. (1979) The biochemical background to current theories of ageing. In: Stevenson I. H. and Crook D. (ed.) *Drugs and the Elderly.* London, Macmillan, p. 3.

Hall D. A. (1981) The ageing of collagenous tissues: genetic and random effects. *J. Clin. Exp. Gerontol.* **3**, 201.

Hamlin C. R., Kohn R. R. and Luschin J. H. (1975) Apparent accelerated aging of human collagen in diabetes mellitus. *Diabetes* **24**, 902.

Hamperl H. (1934) Die Fluorescenzmikoskopie menlischer Gewebe. (Fluorescent microscopy of human tissues.) *Virchows Arch. Pathol. Anat. Physiol.* **292**, 1.

Harding J. J. (1973) Altered heat-lability of a fraction of glutathione reductase in aging human lens. *Biochem. J.* **134**, 995.

Harman D. (1956) Aging: a theory based on free-radical and radiation chemistry. *J. Gerontol.* **11**, 298.

Harrison B. J. and Holliday R. (1967) Senescence and the fidelity of protein synthesis in Drosophila. *Nature* **213**, 990.

Hart R. W. and Setlow R. B. (1974) Correlation between deoxyribonucleic acid excision-repair and lifespan in a number of mammalian species. *Mech. Ageing Dev.* **5**, 67.

Harvald B. and Hauge M. (1956) Catamnestic investigation of Danish twins: preliminary report. *Dan. Med. Bull.* **3**, 150.

Harvald B. and Hauge M. (1958) Catamnestic investigation of Danish twins: survey of 3100 pairs. *Acta Genet. Stat. Med.* **8**, 287.

Hauge M., Harvald B. and Degnbol B. (1963) Hereditary factors in longevity. In: Geerte S. J. (ed.) *Genetics Today. Proc. 11th Internat. Congr. Genet.* London, Pergamon.

Hay R. J. and Strehler B. L. (1967) The limited growth span of cell strains isolated from the chick embryo. *Exp. Gerontol.* **2**, 123.

Hayflick L. (1965) The limited *in vitro* lifetime of human diploid strains. *Exp. Cell Res.* **37**, 614.

Hayflick L. and Moorhead P. S. (1961) The serial cultivation of human diploid cell strains. *Exp. Cell Res.* **25**, 585.

Holliday R. (1969) Errors in protein synthesis in clonal senescence in fungi. *Nature* **271**, 1224.

Holliday R., Porterfield J. S. and Gibbs D. D. (1974) Premature ageing and occurrence of altered enzyme in Werner's syndrome fibroblasts. *Nature* **248**, 762.

Holliday R. and Tarrant G. M. (1972) Altered enzymes in ageing human fibroblasts. *Nature* **238**, 26.

Jacob F. and Monod J. (1961) Genetic regulatory mechanisms in the synthesis of proteins. *J. Mol. Biol.* **3**, 318.

Jarvik L. F. and Falek A. (1961) Cancer rates in aging twins. *Am. J. Hum. Genet.* **13**, 413.
Jarvik L. F. and Falek A. (1962) Comparative data on cancer in aging twins. *Cancer* **15**, 1009.
Jarvik L. F., Falek A., Kallmann F. J. et al. (1960) Survival trends in a senescent twin population. *Am. J. Hum. Genet.* **12**, 170.
Jarvik L. F., Kallman F. J. and Falek A., (1962) Intellectual changes in aged twins. *J. Gerontol.* **17**, 289.
Jarvik L. F. Kallman F. J., Falek, A. et al. (1957) Changing intellectual functions in senescent twins. *Acta Genet. Stat. Med.* **7**, 421.
Jarvik L. F. and Kato T. (1970) Chromosome examinations in aged twins. *Am. J. Hum. Genet.* **22**, 562.
Jerison H. J. (1973) *Evolution of the Brain and Intelligence.* New York, Academic Press.
Jones H. B. (1956) A special consideration of the ageing process, disease and life expectancy. *Adv. Biol. Med. Phys.* **4**, 281.
Kallman J. F. and Jarvik L. F. (1957) Data on genetic variations in resistance to tuberculosis. In: *Genetica della Tuberculosi e dei Tumori,* Torino, Analecta Genetica, p. 15.
Kallman F. J. and Sander G. (1949) Twin studies in senescence. *Am. J. Psychiatry* **106**, 29.
Kanungo M. S. (1975) Regulation and induction of enzymes as a function of age of the rat. *Proc. 10th Internat. Congr. Gerontol. Jerusalem,* p. 35.
Kay M. M. B. (1978) Cells, signals and receptors. The role of physiological autoantibodies in maintaining homeostasis. In: Oota K., Makinodon T., Masami I. et al. (ed.) *Ageing Phenomena.* New York, Plenum Press. p. 171.
Kunze (1933) *Forschn Fortschr.* **9**, 25. quoted by Bürger M., In: *Altern und Krankheit* (Age and Disease) 2nd ed. (1954) Leipzig, Georg Thieme. p. 17.
Kurtz D. I. (1975) The effect of aging on *in vitro* fidelity of translation in mouse liver. *Biochem. Biophys. Acta* **407**, 479.
Lansing A. I. (1952) In: Cowdry E. V. (ed.) *Problems of Aging.* Baltimore, Williams & Wilkins.
Lewis C. M. and Hollday R. (1970) Mistranslation and ageing in *Neurospora. Nature* **228**, 877.
Lewis C. M. and Tarrant G. M. (1972) Error theory and ageing in human diploid fibroblasts. *Nature* **239**, 316.
Lindop P. and Rotblatt J. (1959) Aging effects of ionizing radiation. *Prog. Nucl. Energy* **6 (2)**, 58.
Lindop P. and Rotblatt J. (1961a) Long term effects of a single whole-body exposure of mice to ionizing radiations. I. Life-shortening. *Proc. R. Soc. Lond. (Biol.)* **154**, 332.
Lindop P. and Rotblatt J. (1961b) Long term effects of a single whole-body exposure of mice to ionizing radiations. II. Causes of death. *Proc. R. Soc. Lond. (Biol.)* **154**, 350.
Lorentz E., Jacobson L. O., Heston W. E. et al. (1954) In: Zirkle R. E. (ed.) *Biological Effects of External X and Gamma Irradiation.* New York, McGraw-Hill. p. 24.
Makinodan T. and Adler W. H. (1975) The effects of aging on the differentiation and proliferation potentials of cells of the immune system. *Fed. Proc.* **34**, 153.
Marinesco G. (1934) Nouvelle contribution à l'étude du mecanisme de la vieillesse. *Bull. Acad. Natl Med. (Paris)* **111**, 761.
Martin G. M., Sprague C. A. and Epstein C. J. (1970) Replicative lifespan of cultivated human cells: effect of donor's age, tissue and genotype. *Lab. Invest.* **23**, 86.
Maynard-Smith J. (1962) The causes of ageing. *Proc. R. Soc. Lond. (Biol.)* **157**, 115.
Medawar P. B. (1952) *An Unsolved Problem of Biology.* London, Lewis.
Medvedev Zh. A. (1967) Molecular aspects of ageing. *Symp. Soc. Exp. Biol.* **21**, 1.
Mennecies F. and Dryfus J. C. (1974) Molecular aging of fructose bi-phosphate aldolase in tissues of rabbit and man. *Biochim. Biophys. Acta* **364**, 320.
Milch R. (1963) Studies of collagen tissue aging. Interaction of certain intermediary metabolites with collagen. *Gerontologia* **7**, 129.
Mole R. H. and Thomas A. M. (1961) Life shortening in female CBA mice exposed to daily irradiation for limited periods of time. *Int. J. Radiat. Biol.* **3**, 493.
Neary G. J., Munson R. J. and Mole R. N. (1957) *Chronic Irradiation of Mice by Fast Neutrons.* Oxford, Pergamon.
Nielson A. and Clemmesen J. (1957) Twin studies in the Danish Cancer Registry. 1942–1955. *Br. J. Cancer* **11**, 327.
Oliviera R. J. and Pfuderer P. (1973) Test for missynthesis of lactate dehydrogenase in ageing mice by use of a monospecific antibody. *Exp. Gerontol.* **8**, 193.
Orgel L. (1963) The maintenance of accuracy of protein synthesis and its relevance to aging. *Proc. Natl Acad. Sci. USA* **49**, 517.
Orgel L. (1970) The maintenance of the accuracy of protein synthesis and its relevance to aging: a correction. *Proc. Natl Acad. Sci. USA* **67**, 1476.
Pantelouris E. M. M. (1972) Thymic involution and aging: a hypothesis. *Exp. Gerontol.* **7**, 73.

Pearl R. (1928) *The Rate of Living: being an Account of some Experimental Studies on the Biology of Life Duration*. New York, Knopf.

Printz D. S. and Gross S. R. (1967) An apparent relationship between mistranslation and an altered t-RNA synthetase in a conditional lethal mutant of *Neurospora crassa. Genetics* **55**, 451.

Reiss U. and Gershon D. (1976) Rat liver superoxide dismutase: purification and age-related modifications. *Eur. J. Biochem.* **63**, 617.

Reiss U. and Rothstein M. (1974) Heat-labile isozymes of isocitrate lyase from aging *Turbatrix aceti. Biochem. Biophys. Res. Commun.* **61**, 1012.

Reiss U. and Rothstein M. (1975) Age-related changes in isocitrate lyase from the free-living nematode *Turbatrix aceti. J. Biol. Chem.* **250**, 826.

Reubner M. (1908) Probleme des Wachstums und der Lebensdauer. (Problems of growth and life-span.) *Mitt. Gesell. inn. Med. Wien* **7**, 58.

Rockstein M. (1959) The biology of aging insects. In: Wolstenholme G. E. W. and O'Connor M. (ed.) *Ciba Foundation Coll. on Ageing* Vol. 5, p. 247. London, Churchill.

Rockstein M. and Lieberman H. M. (1958) Survival curves for male and female house-flies (*Musca domestica*. L). *Nature* **181**, 787.

Rothstein M. (1975) Aging and the alteration of enzymes. *Mech. Ageing Dev.* **4**, 325.

Rudzinska M. A. (1952) The influence of amount of food on the reproduction rate and longevity of a suctarian (*Tokophyra infusorium*). *Science* **113**, 10.

Růžička, V. (1924), Beiträge zum Studium der Protoplasmahysterethehen Vorgange (Zur Kausalitat des Alterns). *Arch. Mikr. Anat.* **101**, 459.

Ryan J. M., Duda G. and Cristofalo V. J. (1974) Error accumulation and aging in human diploid cells. *J. Gerontol.* **29**, 616.

Sacher G. A. (1956) On the statistical nature of mortality, with special reference to chronic radiation mortality. *Radiology* **67**, 250.

Sacher G. A. (1959) Relation of lifespan to brain weight and body weight in mammals. In: Wolstenholme G. E. W. and O'Connor M. (ed.) *Ciba Foundation. Coll. on Ageing* Vol. 5, p. 115. London, Churchill.

Salser J. S. and Balis M. E. (1972) Alterations in DNA bound amino acids with age and sex. *J. Gerontol.* **27**, 1.

Sanders H. J. (1968) Aging, an integrated theory. *Chem. Eng. News* **July** 13.

Schofield J. D. and Davies I. (1978) Theories of aging. In: Brocklehurst J. C. (ed.). *Textbook of Geriatric Medicine and Gerontology*. Edinburgh, Churchill Livingstone. p. 37.

Schofield J. D. and Hadfield J. M. (1978) Age-related alterations in the heat-lability of mouse liver glucose-6-phosphate dehydrogenase. *Exptl Gerontol.* **13**, 147.

Shaw C. R. and Barto E. (1963) Genetic evidence for the sub-unit structure of lactic acid dehydrogenase iso-enzymes. *Proc. Natl Acad. Sci, USA* **50**, 211.

Singh S. N. and Kanungo M. S. (1968) Alterations in the lactic acid dehydrogenase of the brain, heart, skeletal muscle and liver of rats of various ages. *J. Biol. Chem.* **243**, 4526.

Stubel H. (1911) Fluorescenz tierscher Gewebe in ultraviolettem Licht (Fluorescence of animal tissues in ultraviolet light). *Arch. Gesamte Physiol.* **142**, 1.

Sulkin N. M. (1955) The occurrence, distribution and nature of PAS-positive substances in the nervous system of the senile dog. *Assoc. Gerontol. 3rd Cong.* 1954, p. 156.

Suntseff V., Cowdry E. V. and Hixon B. B. (1962) Possible maternal influence on longevity of offspring in mice. In: *Biological Aspects of Ageing*. New York, Columbia University Press.

Szilard L. (1959) A theory of ageing. *Nature* **184**, 956.

Tappel A. L. (1968) Will antioxidant nutrients slow aging processes? *Geriatrics* **23**, 97.

von Verschuer O. V. and Kober E. (1956) Tuberkulose und Krebs bei Zweillingen. *Acta Genet. Stat. Med.* **6**, 106.

Verzar F. (1963) *Lectures on Experimental Gerontology*. Springfield, Ill., Thomas.

Walford R. L. (1962) Autoimmunity and Aging. *J. Gerontol.* **17**, 281.

Walford R. L. (1969) *The Immunologic Theory of Aging*. Copenhagen, Munksgaard.

Walford R. L. (1974) The immunologic theory of aging: current status. *Fed. Proc. Fed. Amer. Soc. Exp. Biol.* **33**, 2020.

Warthin A. S. (1929) *Old Age: the Major Involution*. New York, Hoeber.

Weschsler D. (1944) *The Measurement of Adult Intelligence*. Baltimore, Williams & Wilkins.

Weismann A. (1882) *Uber die des Lebens* (Concerning Lifespan). Jena, Fisher.

Weismann A. (1891) *Essays Upon Heredity and Kindred Biological Problems*. London, Oxford University Press.

Williams G. C. (1957) Pleiotropy, natural selection and the evolution of senescence. *Evolution* **11**, 398.

Wulf J. H. and Cutler R. G. (1975) Altered protein hypothesis of mammalian aging processes. Thermal stability of glucose-6-phosphate dehydrogenase in C₅₇BL/6J mouse liver. *Exp. Gerontol.* 1₵ 101.

Yagil G. (1976) Are altered glucose-6-phosphate dehydrogenase molecules present in aged liver cells *Exp. Gerontol.* **11**, 73.

Zeelon P., Gershon H. and Gershon D. (1973) Inactive enzyme molecules in aging organism Nematode fructose-1-6-diphosphate aldolase. *Biochemistry* **12**, 1743.

3   The Effect of External Factors on Longevity

.1   Ageing and Longevity

These two terms are often confused by the man in the street. He tends to use the term *ageing* to describe the *fact of growing old*, that is being longevous or long-lived, whereas its use should more properly be restricted to a description of the *process of growing old*. There is no direct relationship between the two, since the fact of growing old only records a measurement of time, whereas the process of ageing involves an assessment of all the physiological changes which precede the terminal point of the life-span. It is, however, possible to use information gained in studies of longevity to provide the background against which the ageing process occurs. This is especially true if studies are performed not only on the maximum longevity of man or of assorted species of experimental animals under the influence of various external factors, but also on those proportions of the population attaining both this maximum value and other intermediate ages.

3.1.1   *Historical Longevity*

Studies of survival and age at death have loomed large in man's investigations of the ageing process for many thousands of years. In the Bible, reference is made to a mean life-span of three score years and ten, but a number of individuals are ascribed ages vastly in excess of this statutory seventy years. This obsession with the exceptionally long-lived is also apparent in the legends of numerous other cultures as well and in nearly all cases the supercentenarians are represented as the

53

leaders of their respective clans or national groups and are obviously greatly respected, as much for their age as for their deeds. Even these legendary subjects however, are relatively few and the majority of normal mortals are recorded as having enjoyed shorter, more typical, life-spans.

Passing from legend to fact, studies made on the admittedly sparse material available from prehistoric burial grounds have shown that over the past tens of millenia, after the initial prevalence of death at ages below 14 years which was common before the beginning of recorded history, mean values for age at death have hardly risen at all (*Table* 3.1). The small numbers of cases available for study

Table *3.1.* **Estimated mean life-span of early populations**

	Years
Neanderthal	29·4
Upper paleolithic	32·4
Mesolithic	31·5
Bronze	38
Classic Greece	35
England after Black Death	38

and the fact that assessment of age had to be based on methods of bone measurement which are strictly only applicable to present-day populations makes these results very suspect. It is not until the beginning of the present era that sufficient numbers of burials are available for meaningful statistical analyses to be attempted, and only from the end of the eighteenth century are there full census figures for even one or two countries. Comparison of these more recent observations with those obtained from the earlier studies is not easy, partly because of the different numbers available and partly because two different methods have had to be employed to display the results. Results based on burial statistics record the numbers of individuals *dying at a given age*, whereas census figures refer to the *age distribution of a population at a given moment in time*. The latter distribution is most usually expressed in the form of an age distribution pyramid in which the numbers (or proportion of the total population) present in successive 5- or 10-year age groups is recorded horizontally for males and females to give a histogram which in the case of a primitive culture is essentially triangular, but which becomes distorted into a bee-hive outline as the population assumes a more highly developed state (*Fig.* 3.1). Such census figures, are of necessity cross-sectional measuring as they do an age distribution on one single day, but the deviations of such histograms from either true triangles or smooth, bell-shaped curves may reflect the previous history of the population. Thus the age pyramid for France for 1956 shown in *Fig.* 3.2 reflects by its various indentations the effect recorded on an instantaneous population cross-section that two World Wars and an inter-war depression have had on death rates (especially of males in World War I and of both sexes in World War II) and on the consequent birth rates of both sexes.

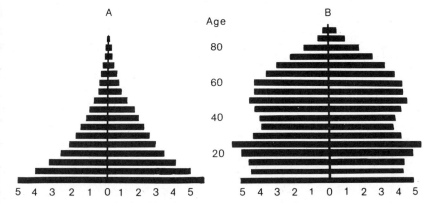

Fig. 3.1. Age distribution 'pyramids' for A, Costa Rica, 1967, and B, Sweden, 1967. The left-hand side of each diagram records the male population in 5-year age groups, the right-hand side the female population. The units are arbitrary, differing from one country to the other since the populations differ markedly: Costa Rica c.2 million, Sweden c.8 million.

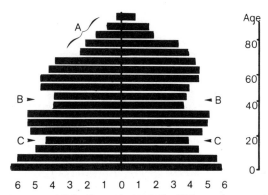

Fig. 3.2. Age distribution 'pyramid' for France in 1956. The difference between the male (left side) and female (right side) population, apparent at ages above 65 is exacerbated by the loss of males (A) due to deaths during World War I. The losses for both male and female lives during World War II (B) and the reduced birth rate consequent on the latter war (C) can clearly be seen.

3.2 The Quantification of Ageing Parameters

A more objective assessment of the relationship between survival and age is obtained by a longitudinal study of a single cohort taken throughout life (*Fig.* 3.3). Actual measurements are difficult in the case of human subjects because of the length of time taken to follow the population through growth, maturity and senescence to death. Such curves are of course more easily obtainable for shorter-lived animals, for which meaningful survival curves can be obtained (*Fig.* 3.4). It is, however, possible to calculate from raw human census data life tables which are more closely comparable with those obtained by cohort analysis by making use of the age distribution and the number and age of all people dying during the year of the census ($d_x = 1_x - 1(x-1)$). 1_x represents the number of individuals alive at the

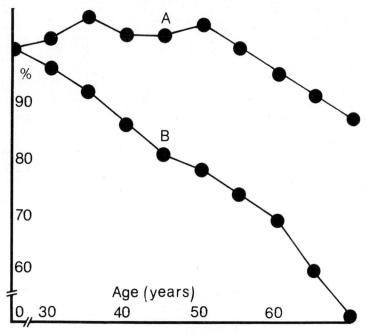

Fig. 3.3. A comparison of (A) cross-sectional and (B) longitudinal studies of word fluency.

commencement of the year x and 1 (x − 1) the number in the previous year (x − 1) (these figures are derived from death certificates signed during this period). From these two sets of data the age-specific death rate (conventionally ascribed the symbol q_x) can be calculated, $q_x = d_x/l_x$. It can then be assumed that the appropriate age-specific death rate acts on a theoretical cohort of 100 000 people for each successive age interval.

These figures are, however, still based on cross-sectional evidence and do not provide the same type of information that can be obtained from a true cohort analysis since, for a human cohort born in 1901 the latter would provide age specific death rates for all 1-year-old individuals in 1902, 2-year-olds in 1903, etc. In the former, however, these values are distorted due to the fact that an appreciable number of 80-year-olds are still alive, and this distortion becomes more apparent the younger the age group under consideration. The two types of life table will only be identical in the unlikely occurrence that the age structure and environmental conditions remain constant over long periods of time. The semi-log graph of the relationship of q_x and age for the periods 1910–1912 and 1960–1962 (*Fig.* 3.5 shows that although the force of mortality is lower in the more recent figures at all ages, the difference is greatest between 10 and 40 years of age, i.e. where accidental deaths are of greatest importance.

A further element in all life tables, which can be calculated from the age-specific death rate and the number of survivors at that age is the expectation of life (e_x) For non-ideal populations of human subjects and many animal species, the

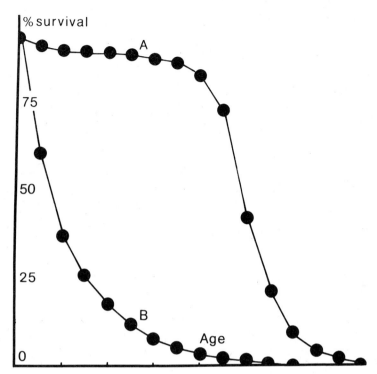

Fig. 3.4. Longitudinal studies of the survival of two types of animal. A, a species in which, above a certain threshold age, ageing and death are age-related and B, a species in which the likelihood of ageing or death occurring, is equal at all ages.

calculation of e_x from l_x and d_x is not possible since values for d_x are changing continuously. The *age structure* of the population is, therefore, defined as the number of individuals alive during the age interval x:

$$Lx = \int_{x}^{x=1} l_x d_x$$

and this can be summated to describe the total number of animal years (or months in the case of shorter-lived animals) still to be lived by that part (T_x) of the original population alive at the start of the period x:

$$Tx = x + L(x+1) + L(x+2)\dots Lj$$
$$= \sum_{x}^{J} Lx.$$

Hence the total expectation of life of the population is $T_x a$, where a represents the size of the time interval. The individual expectation of life of each of the l_x subjects alive at the beginning of the period x is defined by the formula:

$$e_x = \frac{T_x a}{l_x}.$$

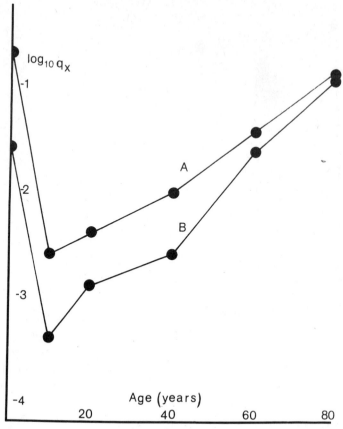

Fig. 3.5. The change in the relationship between the age-specific death rate (qx) over a 50-year period. A, 1910–1912; B, 1960–1962.

This value e_x can be calculated for a value of $x = 0$ to give the total expectation of life at birth (e). e_0 varies from country to country (*Table* 3.2) and from year to year (*Fig.* 3.6) and incidentally from sex to sex. When the expectation of life at any age (e_x) is added to that age (x) this effectively provides a figure for the expected age at death (*Fig.* 3.7), and if these values are plotted against age the curves for the two sexes can be seen to be separated at age $x = 0$ by the difference in e_0 for that particular population and to maintain the difference for the first 30–40 years of life. Thereafter when both curves start to rise as the anticipated age at death begins to increase, the male curve rises more rapidly than the female one until at age 90 + the two are indistinguishable. The difference in e_x for the two sexes is considered in detail below, suffice it to say at this point that whatever advantages may be derived from some female factor in early life is lost by the time advanced age is reached.

There have been appreciable changes in e_x over the past 20 years (*Fig.* 3.8) but these have been most apparent before 60 years of age, decreasing quite rapidly thereafter.

Table 3.2. **Life expectancy (e₀) of various developed and developing countries**

	e_0
Guinea	25–35
Togo	30–40
Gabon	25–45
Mongolia	30
Haiti	35–45
Pakistan	45
Iran	45
Morocco	50–55
Egypt	50–55
Turkey	50–60
South Africa (Black and White)	50–60
Guatemala	50–60
Mauritius	58–65
Ceylon	62
Portugal	64
Venezuela	65–70
Finland	69
Austria	70
USA	71
France	71
UK	71
Australia	71
Israel	72
Norway	73
Netherlands	74
Sweden	74

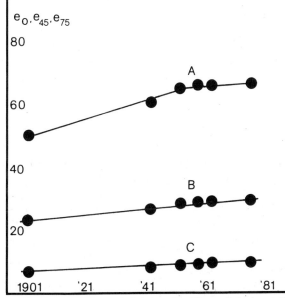

Fig. 3.6. Changes in life expectation at (A) birth (e_0) and at (B) age 45 (e_{45}) and (C) age 75 (e_{75}) during
the present century.

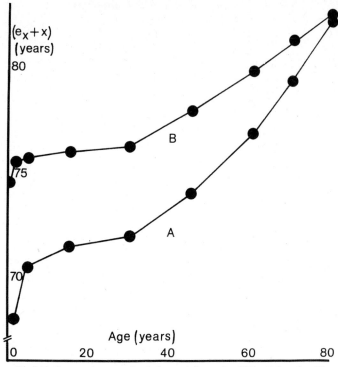

Fig. 3.7. Expected age at death (e_x + x) for males (A) and females (B).

It has been assumed up to now that all animal populations age in a fashion which is similar to that which occurs in human populations. In fact, this is not the case in relatively simple animals such as *Hydra* (Comfort, 1979) nor in other animals which are subject to a considerable degree of predation and environmental hazard (*Fig.* 3.9). Lamb (1977) reports on the survival of ringed nestlings in flocks of lapwings (*Vanellus vanellus*) where the curve relating survivors (e_x) to age is exponential (*Fig.* 3.10) due to a constant age-specific mortality which is not age related. Because of this the life expectancy for these birds also remains constant at between 2·2 and 2·6 years throughout the first 9 years of life. Senescence plays no part in the degeneration of these populations, because neither harsh environmental conditions nor predators take notice of an animal's age, culling all age groups equally. A hawk will attack and kill a 3-year-old lapwing just as easily as a 1-year-old. Nestlings are, of course, more susceptible to attack than those able to fly, but here the outstanding maternal protectiveness of birds such as the lapwing has a major role to play in the reduction of infantile mortality.

Primitive human populations (*Fig.* 3.11; Hall, 1981) also show exponential survival curves, presumably due to the large number of possible reasons for death at all ages. It is only the exceptionally old who are less capable of protecting themselves who will be subjected to an age-related mortality. This explains the sigmoid

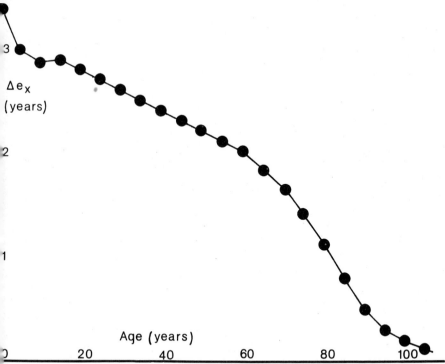

Fig. 3.8. The change in life expectation throughout life, Δe_x, over the period of 20 years between 1951 and 1971 demonstrating that the effect diminishes progressively with increasing age.

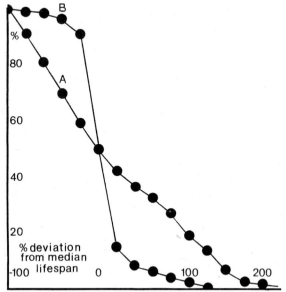

Fig. 3.9. Survival curves for (A) Hydra—no age-related ageing effect, and (B) Drosophila—with a pronounced age dependency for ageing and death. The ages of the two species are expressed in terms of their median life-span in order to accommodate both on the same graph.

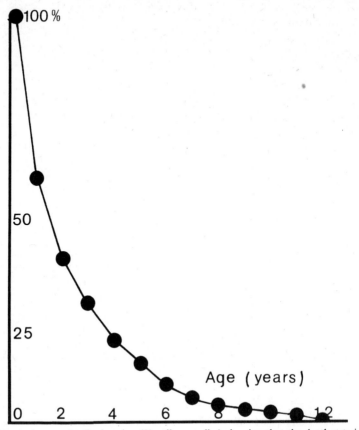

Fig. 3.10. Survival curve for the lapwing (*Vanellus vanellus*) showing that the death rate is not age related.

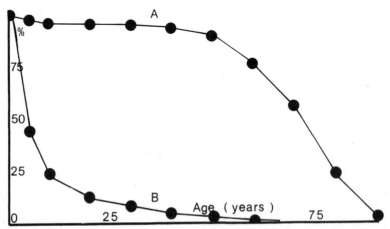

Fig. 3.11. A comparison between survival curves for a developed and a primitive society. A, Great Britain, 1971; B, the Yamomana—an Amazonian tribe still maintaining a Stone Age culture.

nature of the survival curve for the Yamomana at ages above 70, although he small numbers alive at this age detract from the credibility of such an observation. Hufeland, without the benefit of official statistics and relying solely on his personal estimates (1798) reported a similar survival curve (*Fig.* 3.12) for the population of North Germany in 1787. This can be compared with a curve for the same region 117 years later (Vischer, 1947) which, after a marked fall due to the degree of infant mortality still prevalent at that time, assumes a sigmoid form, demonstrating that, even allowing for faulty assessment by Hufeland, there was a marked change in age-specific mortality during the nineteenth century.

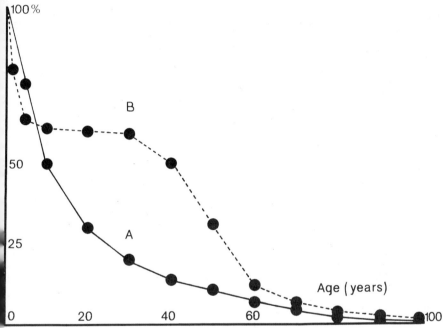

Fig. 3.12. Survival curves for N. Germany (A) estimated figures from Hufeland (1798). (B) Census figures for 1910. Both curves represent mean values for males and females combined.

In 1825 Gompertz propounded a formula to describe the effect of age on the age-specific death rates of human populations. He demonstrated that this function (μ_x) increased exponentially with age from about 35 years of age onwards:

$$\mu_x = \frac{1}{n}\frac{d_n}{d_x} = \mu_0 e^{\alpha x}$$

where n = the number of individuals surviving at time t and d (which defines the slope) and μ_0 (a hypothetical value for mortality at x = 0) are constants. Theoretically, therefore, a plot of the logarithm of the age-specific mortality (μ_x) against age should be linear (*Fig.* 3.13). These plots for the male and female populations of the United Kingdom for the year 1975 are essentially linear over the

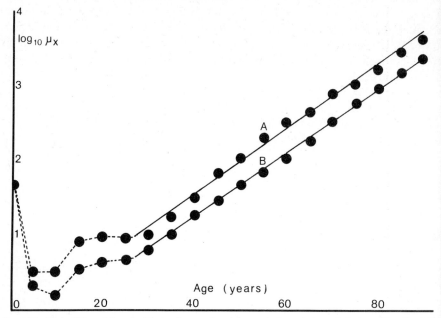

Fig. 3.13. Male (A) and female (B) death rates for the population of Great Britain, 1975. (Data from Office of Population Censuses and Surveys.)

age range 30–85. A similar plot for *Drosophila melanogaster* (Lamb, 1977), owing presumably to the smaller population, is more variable but is essentially linear over the period 15–40 days. Curves in which age-specific deaths due to single pathological condition have been plotted against age have been discussed in some detail by Burch (1968) (*Fig.* 3.14). He demonstrated that the age-specific death rates of many conditions conformed to a complex series of exponential relationships expressed in the general form:

$$\frac{dP}{dt} = S(1 - e^{-kt^r})^n$$

where S represents the proportion of the population at risk, r and n define the number of 'incidents' required to initiate the condition and k is the kinetic constant (*see* Chapter 9).

3.4 Longevity in the Animal Kingdom

Between 1920 and 1934 Pearl and Pearl (1934) instituted a massive study of longevity in man. They calculated a 'total index of ancestral longevity' (TIAL) based on the sum of the ages at death of parents and four grandparents divided by 6. They observed a higher than average value for TIAL for those subjects who had either died aged 90 or over, or were still surviving into their tenth decade, and

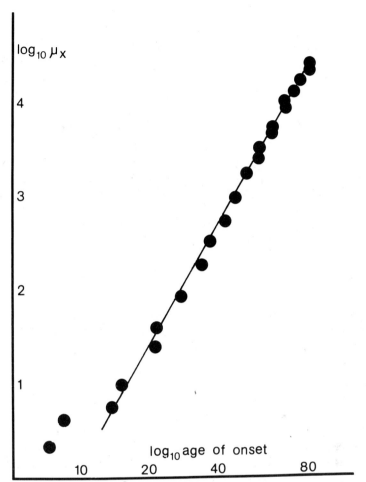

Fig. 3.14. The linear relationship between the logarithm of the age-specific death rate due to coronary artery disease and the logarithm of its age of onset (Burch, 1968). The line represents Burch's calculated expression:

$$dP/dt = 6kt^5 \exp(-kt^6).$$

The data points are for males and females combined. To superimpose both sets of data on the calculated line, it is necessary to correct male values by a latent period of 10 years and female values by a latent period of 20 years.

predicted that a value for TIAL of over 75, indicating a high degree of survival in the previous two generations, might indicate a high chance of long life in the present generation. Murphy (1978) has criticized these earlier results on the basis that the 'controls' of the Pearls' survey including individuals presenting at a clinic with tuberculosis, a condition which might well have cut short the lives of their parents or grandparents. However, at the end of a long and well-controlled survey during the 1960s (Abbott et al., 1974) Murphy reached the conclusion that familial longevity *had* a role to play in determining the longevity of children, but this might only be as low as 1 added year for every 10 years of parental survival. The saying that 'the best way to ensure that you live to a ripe old age is to choose long-lived grandparents' would, however, still appear to make sense.

The mouse lives on average for a period of 2–3 years, the human individual for from 70 to 90, with individuals surviving for one or two decades above this upper limit. Other animal species survive for periods ranging from 1 or 2 days (*Coleoptera sp.*—beatles; Comfort, 1979) to 152 + years (*Testudo sumerii*—Marion's tortoise; Flower, 1937).

Figures for maximum age, especially for very long-lived species are, however, of doubtful significance depending as they often do on recordings which may be faulty. Comfort (1979) mentions that the Royal Tongan tortoise which died in 1966, and was reputed to have belonged to Captain Cook, and hence might be assumed to have been at least 180 years old, died without benefit of a birth certificate and its age cannot therefore be authenticated. Comfort also reports a so-called long-lived guinea pig (Rogers, 1950) aged 7 years 7 months. The present author, however, has personal experience of a guinea pig which died in 1966 aged 8 years 6 months. Clearly one is as likely to obtain true records of animal longevity from the *Guinness Book of Records* as from scientific journals. As for human longevity, numerous claims have been made over the years for the existence of supercentenarians. Some like Old Parr who is reputed from the inscription on his tomb in Westminster Abby to have lived through three centuries (1483 to 1635) a total of 152 years, have been exposed as having no worthwhile documentation. Similarly, Walter Williams who, when he died at the supposed age of 117 in 1959, claimed to be the only survivor of the American Civil War, could not be identified on any army list.

On the other hand, Charles Smith who claims to have been brought to the United States as a child of about 12 in 1854, survived his early years of slavery and was still alive in 1972 at the supposed age of c.130, a claim which was acceptable to the American Medical Association.

Some areas of the world abound with claims for longevity, notably those parts of the Himalayas inhibited by the Hunza people, the Abkhasia and Azerbaijan regions of the Caucasus and certain villages and small towns in the Loja district of Ecuador (Nikitin, 1954; Davies, 1975; Leaf, 1975; Halsell, 1976). Comfort (1979) reports Professor C. A. Pitzkhelauri of Tbilesi University as being reasonably convinced that there are a number of individuals alive today in Abkhasia who are over 130 years of age. Berdishev and Stavikov (1960) note, however, that the proportion of centenarians in the Yakutsk and Altai regions of Siberia, where the overall numbers are 32 and 20 per 100 000 as apposed to under 1 per 100 000 elsewhere in Russia, is far greater in the villages that in the towns. A similar observation has also been made about the inhabitants of the township and the environs of Vilcabamba in Ecuador (Davies, 1975; Hall, 1977) (*Table* 3.3). Hall has suggested that although the isolation in which these groups have lived for many generations may have consolidated a variety of genetic characteristics such as longevity—the even greater longevity experienced by village dwellers rather than

Table 3.3. *A comparison between the age distributions in the male population of the rural area of Vilcabamba and the whole male population of Ecuador. The proportion of the population aged over 50 is twice as great in Vilcabamba as in Ecuador as a whole*

Age group	Percentage of total population	
	Vilcabamba	Ecuador
0–9	32	36
10–19	21	22
20–29	11	13
30–39	12	10
40–49	9	7
50–59	8	5
60–69	5	3
70+	7	2

Values for females are similarly greater at advanced age in Vilcabamba.

town dwellers may indicate the importance of some particular environmental factors.

3.5 The Effect of Diet on Longevity

Leaf (1981) reported studies by Russian workers that the exceptionally long-lived inhabitants of the Caucasus do not consume more than 1700–1900 calories per day, a value which is appreciably less than that recommended for elderly subjects by the Russian Central Institute of Nutrition. Similarly, adult male members of the Hunza tribe in the Himalayas on average only take in 1923 calories per day, whilst the supercentenarian inhibitants of Vilcabamba in Ecuador consume a diet providing only 1200 calories. Osborne and his co-workers (1915, 1916) and later McCay et al. (1934, 1939, 1952, 1956) showed that experimental extension of the life-span of in-bred rodents was possible if their calorie intake was restricted, especially during the early years of life. Shock (1970) has confirmed these observations with lower animals (rotifers and Daphnia). Segall and Timiras (1975, 1976) and Segall (1979) have, however, demonstrated that the restriction of diet may be more selective than being merely related to an overall reduction in calorie intake. Reduced availability of tryptophane results in lowered serotonin levels (Oaka, Segall and Timiras, 1978) and this may depress physical and reproductive development. It is, therefore, of interest to note that in two out of the three groups of supercentenarians mentioned by Leaf (1981), the Ecuadorans and the Hunza tribesmen, the protein intake is only between 50 and 70% of the normal requirement of 70 g per day. Although these observations on 'naturally' longevous subjects do, therefore, appear to correlate reasonably well with the results of animal experimentation, there is no direct experimental evidence that longevity can be induced in man by dietary restriction alone. Unfortunately, other factors always confuse the issue. Thus there is no evidence of a greater age at death in the case of those individuals who survived the dietary restrictions associated with incarceration in concentration camps during World War II, or in displaced person camps in the immediate post-war years. This might not be unexpected since the majority of those who have already reached an age at which there is the greatest probability of death will have been in the camps during early adulthood rather than during infancy. It will not be until the early years of next century that the effects of early dietary restriction during the period 1939–1945 may be apparent when those who have suffered perinatal and infantile dietary restriction will have reached a critical age for selective survival. Even then survival may not be enhanced to any great extent since the starvation suffered by such individuals was more far reaching than that experienced by experimental animals; vitamins and trace elements also being restricted and the 'experiment' invalidated by simultaneous mental and physical trauma.

Similar difficulties arise when attempts are made to correlate survival and diet in the case of those social groups who lead abstemious existences. Closed societies of nuns or monks may have dietary peculiarities, but they also differ from their fellow men and women in the outside world in many other aspects of their lifestyle and attempts to restrict observations to a study of dietary variation alone has not proved possible.

3.6 Geographical and Physical Factors

The regions of the world in which hyperlongevity appears most prevalent are in the main located in mountainous regions and hence are isolated. The high valleys of the Himalayas, the Caucasus and the Andes contain small pockets rich in supercentenarians. The actual ages claimed for individual inhabitants of these regions are hard to justify since in such isolated regions records of births were not compulsory, universal, or indeed common over 100 years ago. This is, however, immaterial since although there may be little firm evidence that a particular individual is 120 or 149, as has been claimed, there is considerable evidence for a greater proportion of supercentenarians in these rather than in other comparable regions (*Table* 3.4). The isolation experienced by these mountain tribes will have

Table 3.4. Centenarians (per 100 000) in various regions of USSR with other east and west European regions for comparison

Geographical region	Year	Nos. per 100 000
Abkhasia	1926	3500
Yakutsk	1960	32
Altai	1960	20
USSR (whole)	1961	10
Yugoslavia	1948	10
Yugoslavia	1971	30
Great Britain	1951	3·5

tended to ensure that a considerable degree of inbreeding will have taken place. Hence any genetic factor (*see* p. 34) which might predispose towards longevity will have been preserved and amplified. This could explain why longevity is not universal in all mountainous districts. The relatively thin atmosphere present 4000–6000 metres above sea level cannot adequately protect the inhabitants against cosmic ray showers. This may well result in a greater incidence of mutation than is apparent at sea level. Assuming that the genetic factors which may induce longevity in certain tribes have been produced at some stage in their history by favourable mutation(s), it can equally well be expected that mutations resulting in the opposite effect may have occurred elsewhere. Isolation, due to unfavourable terrain would then have amplified such traits, leading to poor survival in these regions.

Although hyperbaric oxygen has been prescribed as a therapeutic aid in geriatric medicine (Jacobs et al., 1969) the low oxygen tension which accompanies the overall reduction in atmospheric pressure will slow down the metabolic processes especially in the prepubertal period and may well have the same effect on survival as dietary restriction has.

The nature of the terrain may also have other effects on the survival of mountain dwellers. Small groups living alone tend to be very non-specialized in their activities, everyone having to take their share of work on the land, either in the scattered patches of arable land or herding livestock. The very nature of the land makes it necessary for pockets of semi-fertile ground to be sown and harvested wherever they may lie in respect to the village. Davies (1975) has reported that many of the very elderly inhabitants of the valley of Vilcabamba in Ecuador have to ascend and descend up to 500 metres two and three times a day to till their land. It is, therefore, not surprising that there is in this valley a greater number of elderly inhabitants in the outlying districts where the land is precipitous than in and near to the village itself where fields lie closer to hand. Such exercise cannot but affect the fitness of the individual mountain dweller (*see* p. 132) and may well have some influence on the proportion of the population who are in the upper age bracket (*Table* 3.5).

Table 3.5. **Distribution of population by age between the village and surrounding countryside in Vilcabamba**

Age	Village	Countryside
5–20	200	121
21–40	83	85
41–60	60	75
61–80	21	35
Over 81	13	24

The difference between the age distributions in the village and in the surrounding districts, in an area which overall has a higher proportion of elderly than Ecuador as a whole, led the present author (1977, 1979) to consider another factor which might have an important role to play in determining the degree of longevity experienced by such isolated groups—namely, population density.

3.7 The Effect of Population Density on Longevity

It has long been appreciated that the inhabitants of the massive conurbations of the world are less likely to live as long as their compatriots in the surrounding countryside, all other factors remaining unchanged. For instance, in the 25 largest cities of Great Britain, the mean recorded value for that proportion of the population which reaches the age of 75 is 4·4% as apposed to 8·3% for the rural and ubran populations taken as a whole (*Table* 3.6). Moreover, it has usually been assumed that this differential applies to all rural communities and that all country dwellers have an identical capability for survival, the operative factor being that they do not live in a city. However, the marked differences between the numbers of the very elderly in the countryside surrounding the village of Vilcabamba and in the village itself, indicate the possibility that a similar differential could exist between the survival capabilities of regions of differing population density outside closely packed cities.

Table 3.6. **The percentage of the total populations of the 25 major cities in Great Britain who, in 1971, were over 75 years of age**

Standard region	No. of cities	% 75 +
SW and S England	4	5·25
Greater London	1	4·8
Wales	1	4·7
Scotland	2	4·5
Yorkshire and Humberside	4	4·45
N Ireland	1	4·3
Lancashire	2	4·25
NE England	3	4·20
Midlands	7	4·05
Total for UK for comparison	—	8·3

Initial attempts to identify a population of similar structure to that in the Vilcabamba valley for which adequate demographic information was available led to an examination of the historical data provided in Sinclair's *Statistical Account of Scotland* (1831–1845). Sir John Sinclair obtained the information for his report from each parish priest and although in places the data are very scanty, in the main sufficient detail is provided for an adequate picture of the life-style of the parishioners to be built up. It can be deduced for instance that the inhabitants of the highland regions of Scotland, in the period prior to the development of easy communication between villages and small towns, lived a relatively austere life with an adequate but limited diet, and few social activities other than those associated with the church and the ale house, whether their homes were situated in an outlying croft, a small clachan or hamlet, or a nucleated village. Although

Sinclair's 'reporters' varied greatly in their interpretation of what was required of them in preparing a full account of their individual parishes, they must have been provided with some directions as to the form that these reports should take. Thus nearly all those who submitted details of the numerical analysis of their parishioners provided figures relating to the following age groups: 0–15, 15–30, 30–50, 50–70, and 70 + . Surprisingly, very few provided details of the distribution of the sexes among these age groups.

Some parishes contained larger than average numbers of children, a sign of a vigorous community, whereas others were essentially societies in decay with few children and the majority of the inhabitants in the upper age groups. Obviously the presence of children, providing as they do an important investment for the future, might have some sociological or psychological effect which could assist in the maintenance of a high degree of survival of the elderly section of the population, but conversely a large 0–15 age group would have a dramatic effect if the proportion of the population surviving to upper age groups were to be calculated. Therefore, to obtain a figure which was comparable from parish to parish, a 'survival index' was calculated as follows:

$$\text{Survival Index (SI)} = \frac{\text{Number of inhabitants over age 70}}{\text{Number of inhabitants aged between 15 and 50}} \times 100$$

$$= \frac{\text{Very elderly}}{\text{Reproductive age groups}} \%.$$

Many of the parishes on the west coast of Scotland at the beginning of the 19th century were so dispersed that most were only populated at a mean density of less than 0·2 individuals/hectare. In the nucleated villages of the north and east, however, there was a broad range of densities ranging from 0·036 to 1. Over the range 0·1–1 the value for SI falls with increasing values of population density. Below 0·1 this negative correlation appears to fall off. If instead of plotting SI against density it is plotted against the reciprocal of density—living space—it can be seen that in fact the relationship between SI and density (or living space) peaks at a density of 0·1 individuals/hectare (mean living space of 10 hectares per individual) (*Fig.* 3.15). Similar relationships are apparent in the case of the parishes of the west coast with dispersed populations although here, because of the typically lower densities, the peak can be demonstrated most readily by plotting the values of SI against density. It may be assumed from these observations that the effect of a reduction in population density in the parishes of early 19th century Scotland was to increase the likelihood of greater longevity until the density reached 0·1/hectare. Reduction of the density below this value decreased the probability of survival. Apparently, although an undue degree of proximity to their neighbours lowered the possibility of survival, a certain degree of 'neighbourliness' was necessary. This presumably took the form of aid in the normal tasks of everyday living at that time: harvesting, fishing, etc. and aid when illness struck. Absence of this degree of help mitigated against survival.

It did not appear possible that such a biphasic correlation between survival and

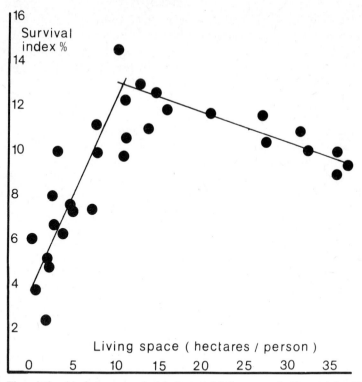

Fig. 3.15. The relationship between survival indices and living space (both sexes) for 30 nucleated parishes in the north and north-east of Scotland for the period 1790–1810. (Calculated from data presented in the Statistical Account for Scotland. Sir John Sinclair, 1820–1840.)

population which was apparent in relatively primitive regions such as mid-20th century Ecuador and early 19th century Scotland could apply to the rural areas of more highly developed countries such as late 20th century England. However many of the 22 countries of England (pre-1974 classification) which have a mean population density of less than 1·0/hectare do show similar biphasic relationships between SI and density (*Fig.* 3.16) for their individual parishes; peaking between 0·1 and 0·5 persons/hectare.

The mean values for each county do not show this type of relationship since the inter-parish differences tend to reduce the number of very low values. The 22 counties do, however, show not only a highly significant negative regression for SI against density (*Fig.* 3.17) but may also be divided into three groups, each of which has a comparable regression coefficient. The uppermost curve includes all the 'retirement counties', such as Devonshire, Dorset, Somerset, etc. and shows that the 32% of counties in this category have values for SI which are roughly 6 units higher than those of the majority (45% of the total 22 counties). Finally, there are five counties (Westmoreland, Cumberland, Rutland, the Holderness district of Lincolnshire and Huntingdonshire) which have, on average, SIs which are 4 units below the main group of counties at all density levels. The elevated levels for the

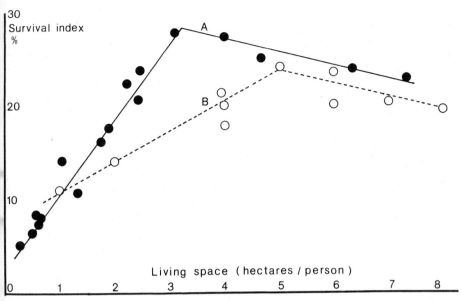

Fig. 3.16. The relationship between survival indices and living space for males in individual rural parishes in (A) the West Riding of Yorkshire, and (B) Northumberland. (Calculated from data recorded for the 1971 census (the two counties are as constituted prior to local government reorganization in 1974).)

'retirement counties' is easily explained since the incidence of immigrant retirees will raise the level appreciably. The reason for the five counties having a lowered SI is difficult to explain. They are not counties with excessively large military establishments or universities which could provide numbers of young people whose inclusion could bias the observations. Nor are they likely to be adversely affected by the proximity of large conurbations in adjacent counties. Therefore, although in general the negative regression of survival on density can justify the assumption that density may be of importance in determining the degree of longevity enjoyed by a given community, the displacement of these five counties indicates that population density cannot be the only factor involved.

At least one other factor which may determine indices of survival in large population groupings and might also be responsible for the displacement of the five counties listed above, must also be mentioned.

3.8 Financial Status and Longevity

A measure of the material circumstances of a country can be obtained from a study of its gross national product (GNP) and the per capita value of the GNP indicates the mean wealth of each individual inhabitant. Since food intake, housing, sanitation, medical facilities and many other factors which may affect a person's ability to survive into old age are wealth-dependent, it might be expected that

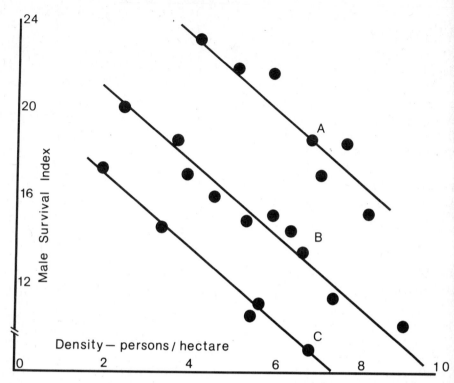

Fig. 3.17. Mean values for male survival indices for the rural parishes of each of the 22 pre-1974 English counties with rural population densities lower than 1 person per hectare. The upper group for which the regression line A has been drawn includes all those counties such as Devonshire, Somerset, Cornwall, etc. with high concentrations of elderly attracted there in their retirement. Group B constitutes the main body of counties (45%), whereas group C consists of five counties: Cumberland, Westmoreland, Rutland, the Holderness district of Lincolnshire and Huntingdonshire. The three regression lines are parallel. No geographical reason can explain the lower position of group C. They are, however, the group with the lowest rateable value.

survival would be dependent on the mean per capita GNP over the range of values which this parameter can assume from the poorest third world nation to the most wealthy western country. Although there is an overall positive relationship between e_0 and GNP in the relationship of life expectancy at birth to the log of the per capita GNP for most countries, there is also a considerable degree of variation. For groups of countries of similar GNP, for instance those between $75 and $100 or between $400 and $600, there may be between 25 and 30% variation in e_0 about the mean value. Once again although the GNP represents a parameter, variations of which can affect the mean longevity of the population of a country, it cannot be the only factor involved. Incidentally the five counties of England which show abnormally low correlations with population density in the previous section are among the bottom few in the league table of per capita rateable values, a figure which at a local level is comparable to the GNP at national level.

3.9 Conclusions

Although it has been shown that ageing and longevity are most probably dependent on intrinsic factors, it is fully apparent that numerous external factors have an important role to play in the way these intrinsic factors operate on the organism. This is most apparent when one considers one or other of the estimates of longevity or age potential. Certain factors such as diet, overcrowding and financial status all apparently have a role to play, but no single factor is all important.

Recommended Reading

Much of the available information about the demographic analysis of ageing is scattered throughout the literature, but M. J. Lamb has a very informative chapter in her book *Biology of Ageing* (1977) which is couched in relatively non-technical terms.

References

Abbott M. H., Murphy E. A., Bolling D. R. et al. (1974) The familial component in longevity. A study of offspring of nonagenarians. II Preliminary analysis of the completed study. *John Hopkins Med. J.* **134**, 1.

Berdishev G. D. and Stavikov N. M. (1960) Longevity in Siberia and Far Eastern Russia. *2nd Conf. Gerontol. Geriatr. Moscow Natural Soc.* p. 25.

Burch R. P. J. (1968) *An Inquiry Concerning Growth, Disease and Ageing.* Edinburgh, Oliver & Boyd.

Comfort A. (1979) *The Biology of Senescence.* 3rd ed. Edinburgh, Churchill Livingstone.

Davies D. (1975) *The Centenarians of the Andes.* London, Barrie and Jenkins.

Flower S. S. (1937) Contributions to our knowledge of the duration of life in vertebrate animals. III Reptiles. *Cairo Sci. J.* **10**, 1.

Gompertz B. (1825) On the nature of the function expressive of the law of human mortality and on a new mode of determining life contingencies. *Philos. Trans. R. Soc. Lond. (Ser. A)* **115**, 513.

Hall D. A. (1977) Longevity—facts and fables. *General Pract.* July 1977, p. 14.

Hall D. A. (1979) The biochemical background to current theories of ageing. In: Stevenson J. H. and Crook D. (ed.) *Drugs and the Elderly.* London, Macmillan, p. 3.

Hall D. A. (1981) The ageing of collagenous tissues: genetic and random effects. *J. Clin. Exp. Gerontol.* **3**, 201.

Halsell G. (1976) *Los Viejos.* Emmaeus, Pa., Rodale Press.

Hufeland G. W. (1798) *Makrobiotik, oder der Kunst das menschliche Leben zu verlangern.* Jena Trans. The Art of Prolonging Human Life. 1829. quoted by Comfort A. (1979).

Jacobs E. A., Winter P. M., Alvis, H. J. et al. (1969) Hyperoxygenation effect on cognitive functioning in the aged. *N. Engl. J. Med.* **281**, 753.

Lamb M. J. (1977) *Biology of Ageing.* Glasgow, Blackie.

Leaf A. (1975) *Youth in Old Age.* New York, McGraw-Hill.

Leaf A. (1981) Effects of environmental factors and life patterns on lifespan. Discussion. In: Danon D., Shock N. W. and Marois M. (ed.) *Aging, a Challenge to Science and Society.* Geneva, Institute de la Vie and WHO p. 218.

McCay C. M. (1952) In: Lansing A. I. (ed.) *Problems of Ageing.* Baltimore, Williams & Wilkins.

McCay C. M. and Crowell M. F. (1934) Prolonging the lifespan. *Sci. Mon.* **39**, 405.

McCay C. M., Maynard L. A., Sperling G. et al. (1939) Retarded growth, lifespan, ultimate body size and age change in the albino rat after feeding diets restricted in calories. *J. Nutr.* **18**, 1.

McCay C. M., Pope F. and Lunsford W. (1956) Experimental prolongation of the lifespan. *Bull. NY Acad. Med.* **32**, 91.

Murphy E. A. (1978) Genetics of longevity in man. In: Schneider E. L. (ed.) *The Genetics of Aging.* New York, Plenum. p. 261.

Nikitin V. N. (1954) Longevity. *Sci. and Life (Moscow)* **8**, 27.

Ooka H., Segall P. E., and Timiras P. S. (1978) Neural and endocrine development after chronic tryptophan deficiency in rats. II, Pituitary–thyroid axis. *Mech. Ageing Dev.* **7**, 19.

Osborne, T. B. and Mendel L. B. (1915) The resumption of growth after long-conditioned failure to grow. *J. Biol. Chem.* **23**, 439.

Osborne, T. B. (1916) Acceleration of growth after retardation. *Am. J. Physiol.* **40**, 16.

Pearl R. and Pearl R. D. (1934) *The Ancestry of the Long-lived.* Baltimore, John Hopkins Univ. Press.

Rogers J. B. (1950) The development of senility in the guinea pig. *Anat. Rec.* **106**, 286.

Segall P. E. (1979) Interrelations of dietary and hormonal effects with aging. In: *Conference on the Endocrine Aspects of Aging*, Bethesda, MD.

Segall P. E. and Timiras P. S. (1975) Age-related changes in the thermoregulatory capacity of tryptophan deficient rats. *Fed. Proc.* **34**, 83.

Segall P. E. and Timiras P. S. (1976) Pathophysiologic findings after chronic tryptophane deficiency in rats. *Mech. Ageing Dev.* **5**, 109.

Shock N. W. (1970) Physiologic aspects of ageing *J. Am. Diet. Assoc.* **56**, 491.

Statistical Account of Scotland (1820–1840) Sinclair J. (ed.), Edinburgh, Sir John Sinclair.

Vischer A. L. (1947) *Old Age, its Compensations and Rewards* London, Allen & Unwin.

4

Ageing of Connective Tissues

4.1 Introduction

Knowledge of the structure and function of connective tissue and its various components has, over the past quarter of a century, developed alongside related research into the ageing process as expressed in connective-tissue changes. Workers in both fields have provided data on which their colleagues have built. Research into the changes which occur with age in the physical properties of collagen fibres have on the one hand provided the basis for a search for intra- and intermolecular cross-links whereas on the other it has proved possible, for instance, to explain the deterioration which occurs with increasing age in the resilience of articular cartilage on the basis of recently acquired knowledge concerning the structure of the glycosaminoglycans which make up the major portion of the cartilage.

It can, however, be seen from a study of the literature, especially that dating from the late '60s and early '70s, that some gerontologists have been so carried away by their belief that the chronological changes in connective-tissue components are true ageing effects, that their appreciation of the relative effects of maturation and ageing has become very distorted. More recently, the overall picture has been rationalized and those factors which can be truly regarded as relating to ageing have been separated from those which merely improve the function of the tissue during periods of growth and development.

Early studies on connective tissues were bedevilled by the even earlier belief that this constituent of the body in all its forms was virtually metabolically inactive, merely performing the functions associated with its title; namely those of connection, location and protection. Although Neuberger and his colleagues

(1951) employed relatively sophisticated methods of analysis, entailing measurements of the degree of incorporation of radioactive amino acids into collagen, they did little to dispel this belief. They reported that collagen was essentially metabolically inert, basing their observations on the incorporation and retention of radioactively-labelled leucine into rat tail tendon. Their choice of tissue was, however, unfortunate since had they examined the half-life of collagen from many other connective tissues they would have observed a far greater degree of metabolic activity. For instance, the turn-over time of gingival ligaments is only two days, as compared with that of various tendons, which is far closer to a value indicating that once laid down collagen remains unchanged for the rest of the life of the animal. Other evidence which appeared to indicate a marked degree of permanence in adult collagen could be found in the observation that the amount of hydroxyproline appearing in the urine was markedly reduced after puberty (Kivirikko, 1970). Although a high proportion of all collagenous tissues is remodelled during growth and this results in a consequently high output of degradation products in the urine, some retain a marked degree of lability throughout life and hence do not age whereas others, such as tendon, become stabilized and are thus capable of undergoing the processes of ageing.

Another difficulty which has interfered with studies of connective-tissue ageing, especially with respect to changes in function and physical properties is the varied and complex structure of each tissue. In some tissues the major fibrous component, collagen, plays a leading role in determining its tensile properties, in others this is modified either by the complex arrangement of the collagen fibres or by the presence of elastic fibres and/or by the nature of the amorphous matrix in which the fibres are bathed. Since each or all of these components can suffer age changes, most probably occurring at different rates and to different degrees, the extent of any age-induced malfunction in the tissue as a whole can be seen to be quite variable.

Many workers in the field of connective-tissue ageing have tended to concentrate either on physical or chemical changes. As will be shown later, these two facets are interrelated and for a full appreciation of the age changes it is essential that they be studied simultaneouly. This, however, complicates matters since the complex nature of the individual tissues ensures that biochemical measurements on tissue samples of size appropriate for physical determinations only provide mean values for the various components which are present. On the other hand, dissection or chemical separation of individual constituents, in many instances, interferes with the topography of the tissue and renders impossible a direct correlation between chemical and physical properties.

The final factor which makes difficult the assessment of ageing *per se* is the fact that many connective tissues are subject to considerable alteration throughout life due to the simultaneous presence of various pathological conditions which may themselves be unrelated to ageing but are induced by a variety of age-related factors. Thus, studies of the ageing of arterial tissue are closely bound up with studies of atherosclerosis and those of bone changes with osteoporosis. Attempts have been made by numerous workers to separate 'physiological' from 'pathological' ageing (Craciun, 1974). The two are, however, so interrelated as to make these attempts relatively abortive. It would be far more relevant to accept the existence of a continuum of ageing phenomena stretching across both these areas, with conditions which may be regarded as pure ageing at one extreme and pure pathology at the other, but with a considerable grey area in between in which both are operative and interact with one another. This provides a more complex situation for analysis, but one which is more closely related to reality than either extreme.

To enable this synthesis to be accomplished it is essential that the following aspects of connective-tissue research be dealt with initially: structure, function, age changes and pathology. Their interrelationship can then be appreciated more fully.

4.2 Overall Structural Changes in Connective Tissues

Connective tissues vary greatly in structure depending on the site which they occupy and hence the function which they perform. They differ from most other tissues in being relatively deficient in cells, most of their mass being taken up with intercellular matrix. Such cells as are present are of various types: fibroblasts, which synthesize collagen and elastin and other components of the intercellular matrix in specialized tissues; mast cells, macrophages and, in certain tissues, such as the choroid of the eye and corium of dark-skinned races, pigment-forming cells.

Measurement of cell number and its change with age is not easy because of their scarcity but DNA determinations which give upper limits for cell content, including as they do dead cells as well as those which are viable, can demonstrate reductions in the initially small cell content as age increases. Hilz et al. (1963) have, for instance, shown an 80% reduction in the DNA content of rat aorta during the first year of life followed by a relatively small fall thereafter. Silberberg and Lesker (1973), on the other hand, have observed an initial rise of 45% in the DNA content of guinea pig articular cartilage followed, at the end of 12 weeks, by an 88% fall during the rest of the first year of life. To assess changes in the number of viable cells it is necessary to measure some metabolic function of the tissue. Here, however, the difficulty arises that individual cells may suffer a loss in activity which will appear to exacerbate any apparent reduction in cell number (*see* p. 37). This cannot, however, explain the observation by Silberberg and Lesker that a group of enzymes involved in glycosaminoglycan metabolism in guinea pig cartilage cells increased in activity by between 700 and 1200% between 3 and 36 months of age. As will be seen elsewhere, these increases in cellular activity may be due to the untypical changes which take place in load-bearing regions of the skeletal system.

With this exception, the age changes in the cellular components of connective tissue are similar to those which occur in the cells of other organs, due account being taken of the difference in cell distribution. It is, however, in the intercellular matrix that most of the typical changes associated with age occur. The nature of these changes depends on the distribution of the individual components within this matrix. They consist in most instances of varying amounts of three major constituents, collagen, elastin and glycosaminoglycans. The first two components being fibrous in nature contribute to the tensile properties of the tissue. Collagen fibres are virtually inextensible and hence act as reinforcing structures for the various tissues of which they form a part. In most tissues, however, collagen fibres form either a random three-dimensional network or a series of layers with fibres in adjacent layers aligned at a fixed angle to one another. When a load is applied to such a system, the fibres rotate relative to one another, either singly or in bundles, until they approach a parallel alignment. Hence the tissue as a whole, although composed of inextensible fibres can extend relatively freely during the application of the first portion of the increasing load (*Fig.* 4.1). As the fibres become

Fig. 4.1. A network of collagen fibre bundles in tissues such as the skin in which the bundles are aligned at an angle to one another. The application of a load, either horizontally or vertically (as indicated by the pairs of arrows) will distort the network until the fibre bundles assume a parallel array. When the load is removed the network resumes its open structure, probably due to the elastic fibres which are schematically indicated by the bindings at the intersections of the collagen bundles.

increasingly more parallel to one another, more of them come under tension and the curve relating load to extension becomes steeper. In tissues of this type some system is required to return the structure to its resting state once the load is removed. In the artery wall this factor may be the recoil of the elastic lamellae and the finer elastic fibres which extend between the lamellae, or the contraction of the smooth muscle cells. In the skin it is almost certainly the elastic fibres which are intertwined round the collagen bundles (Hall, 1976). As the tissue ages its ability to

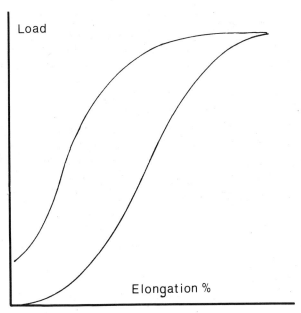

Load

Elongation %

Fig. 4.2. Load/extension curve for a sample of connective tissue such as the dermis (lower curve). When the load is removed the dimensions of the piece of tissue return towards their initial values ('upper curve'). Some irreversible extension occurs, and at the condition of 'no load' a small but finite degree of extension still remains.

return to a resting state is reduced (*Fig.* 4.2). It is not easy to identify collagen fibres in the media of the aorta, because the whole of each interlamellar region stains with the same intensity. However, the return of the collagen fibres to their relaxed non-parallel state results in the crumpling of the fine elastic fibres which lie in between them and hence these fibres, which stain quite intensely with Weigert's resorcinol fuchsin stain, can be seen to be very contorted. This, however, is only true for fetal or very young subjects. As age increases the elastic fibres in a relaxed section of aorta can be seen (*Fig.* 4.3) to be straighter and less convoluted thus indicating that the collagen fibres between which they lie have also not returned to their normal youthful non-parallel state. Roach and Burton (1969) have shown that this topographical evidence for structural ageing is mirrored in an analysis of the physical properties of the tissue. The slopes of the load extension curves for rings of aortic tissue (*Fig.* 4.4) become steeper and have smaller 'toes' as age increases. These 'toes' represent the phase of extension during which the collagen fibres are being rotated relative to one another, and hence during which appreciable extension can occur without the application of much load. If the values for load are differentiated twice against extension (*Fig.* 4.5) it can be seen that young and old tissues differ markedly. The area under each curve, which is proportional to the number of collagen fibres under tension, is greater in the case of the older tissue. Moreover the position of these peaks, i.e. the degree of extension at which this proportion of the fibres come under tension is much lower in the case of the older

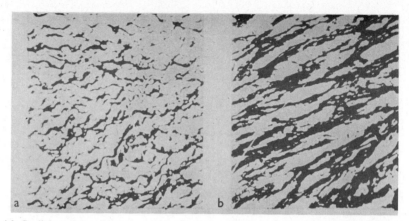

Fig. 4.3. Radial sections of human aorta stained for elastin. *a*, Fetal tissue, *b*, Tissue from elder subject. These two demonstrate that whereas the elastic lamellae in the fetal aorta become contorted when the tension exerted by the blood flow is withdrawn, those in elderly tissue are retained in a extended form, even after removal from the body.

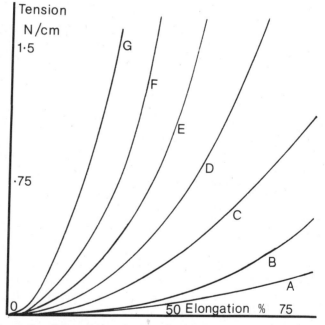

Fig. 4.4. The elongation of rings of tissue cut from the aortas of subjects aged A, 5 years; B, 10 years; C, 20 years; D, 30 years; E, 50 years; F, 70 years; and G, 90 years.

subject. The typical curves in *Fig.* 4.5 show that one-and-a-half times as many collagen fibres are under tension when a ring of aortic tissue from a 90-year-old subject is extended by 30% as when tissue from a 30-year-old is extended by as much as 75%. This indicates that with increasing age the collagen fibre network remains in an extended state even when the distension due to each successive pulse

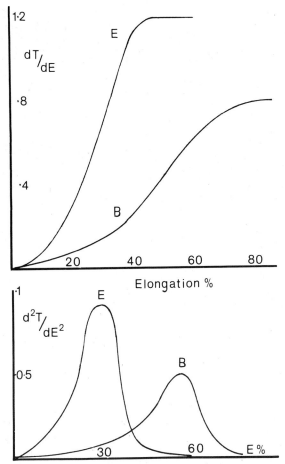

Fig. 4.5. Mathematical proof of the concept that as age progresses, increasing numbers of interlamellar collagen fibres in the aortic media come under tension as a load is applied. The upper diagram of the rate at which tension changes with elongation (the changing slopes of the curves in *Fig.* 4.4) records values for the curves B, 10 years old and E, 50 years old. The lower diagram in which the data in *Fig.* 4.4 has been differentiated a second time shows, from the position of the peaks and the areas under the two curves, that when the younger tissue is extended by nearly 60% only half of the collagen fibres are under tension, whereas over 80% of the fibres are under tension when the older tissue is extended by only 30%. Adapted from Roach and Burton, 1959.)

has been removed. This is in close agreement with the anatomical observations of Wellman and Edwards (1950) who showed that the diameter of the aortic lumen continued to increase in size long after the organ might have been expected to cease increasing in size, i.e. when total bodily growth had ended (there is in fact a seven-fold enhancement of cross-sectional area over 9 decades). The functional implications of such a change in resilience of the aortic wall are considerable and explain the lack of compliance which occurs in the elderly aorta. When these age changes are coupled with atherosclerotic degeneration of the wall and ultimately with calcification, it is not surprising that impairment of the circulation ensues.

In the skin, inability on the part of the collagen bundles to return to a nor
parallel state after the removal of an applied force results in the appearance o
sagging and wrinkled tissue. This may be due to a reduction in the elasti
properties of the elastic fibres which are required to return the collagen meshwor
to its random state. There are, however, other factors such as the degeneration o
the collagen fibres themselves, which are dealt with elsewhere, which may add t
these effects. Elastic fibres are present in a number of different connective tissues i
a variety of forms. Elastic tissue appears in the vascular wall as a series o
concentric cylinders around the lumen of the vessel and in between these lamella
and in most other sites in the body in the form of elastic fibres. As its name implies
it is essentially the elastic element of connective tissues. It is in fact possible t
extend an elastic structure, whether it be in fibrous or laminar form, by up to 100%
without rupture and with almost complete return to its original dimensions. Th
tissue which has been used as type tissue, being the one which contains the highes
proportion of the protein elastin—the major protein constituent of elastic tissue, i
the ligamentum nuchae of bovine species such as the domestic cow. The fibres i
ligamentum nuchae lie essentially parallel to one another and account for abou
80% of the dry weight of the tissue. However, Wood (1954) demonstrated that a
the animal ages the linear array of elastic fibres becomes more wavy. Apparentl
an opposite effect occurs in this tissue to that which is apparent in the aortic media
In youth, the minor collagenous component which lies between the elastic fibres i
the ligament is not in any way attached to the elastin. Hence when a load is applied
along the axis of the elastic fibres, they extend and move past the collagen fibres
When the load is removed the collagen and the relaxed elastic fibres reassume their
original spatial relationship. In older tissues, however, some linkage between o
essential adhesiveness of collagen fibres to elastin (probably due to the presence o
increased amounts of fibronectin) prevents the elastic fibres from returning to their
straight unstretched condition when the load is removed and they appear
contorted when in the relaxed state.

Although it is more difficult to observe this type of interaction in tissues such as
the skin, where the elastic fibres are not initially arranged parallel to one another, i
may well be that this same type of reaction affects the alignment of the elastic fibres
relative to the collagen bundles in old age and hence prevents the elastic fibres from
exercising their normal function of returning the tissue to its relaxed state after the
removal of a load. The fibrous components of connective tissue also vary in their
concentration relative to one another. As mentioned earlier, the amounts o
collagen and elastin present in tissues vary markedly from site to site (Table 4.1). In
tendon there is very little if any elastin present, whereas in the ligamentum nuchae
the pre-eminent component is elastin. Other tissues have various intermediate
contents of the two proteins. Over the years many workers have estimated the
amounts of these two fibrous proteins by a variety of methods and have extended
their observations so as to record the changes which occur with increasing age.
Unfortunately, differing methods of analysis have been employed and this has
resulted in marked variations in the relative amounts of collagen and elastin being
reported. Collagen can be dissolved by alkali and the amount extracted estimated

Table 4.1. *Collagen and elastin content of various tissues*

| | (g/100 dry weight) | | |
	Collagen	Elastin	Partially degraded collagen (pdc)
mineral-free cortical bone	88	—	—
achilles tendon	86	Trace	—
cornea	68	—	—
cartilage	46–64	2–5	—
ligamentum nuchae	17	56–70	—
aortic media	12–24	19–50	+
lung	10	4–13	—
liver	4	—	—
dermis	99	1–4	+

by measuring the hydroxyproline content of the solution. Theoretically, this would leave elastin as the major proteinaceous residue, but unfortunately many older tissues contain, in addition to pure collagen and elastin, degradation products which are not so clearly defined by their alkali solubility. Thus, the degradation product of collagen—also known as pseudoelastin (Hall, 1969) retains the ability to be dissolved by alkali (Hall, 1976). Theoretically it should be possible to utilize the specific enzymes collagenase and elastase to determine the amounts of collagen and elastin present in a tissue and Banga (1966) employed this technique. However, the partial degradation of collagen which occurs with advancing age both reduces the tissue's susceptibility to collagenase and renders it more susceptible to elastase (Hall, 1971). Therefore, methods employing these enzymes do not necessarily give a true estimate of the amounts of unchanged collagen and elastin. It is, however, possible to combine the results from alkaline extraction and elastase treatment of two separate tissue samples to obtain meaningful values for the amount of partially degraded collagen (pdc) and, hence, when this is combined with estimations of total protein, total alkali, soluble and collagenase-digestible protein, it can provide values for collagen, elastin and pdc (*Table* 4.1). From this it can be seen that initial increases in collagen content are followed by a maintenance of the ratio of elastin to collagen plus partially degraded collagen, although as age progresses the ratio of partially degraded to intact collagen increases. As its alternative name, pseudoelastin, suggests, pdc mimics some of the properties of elastin. Not only is it extensible but it also assumes an amorphous appearance in the electron microscope similar to elastin and takes up elastica stains, such as Weigert's resorcinol-fuchsin, Verhoff's acid orcein and Masson's trichrome, etc. (Hall, 1959). Therefore, changes in the relative amounts of intact and degraded collagen alter the appearance and the physical properties of collagenous tissues. These changes may in part explain why the aortic wall of elderly subjects extends to a greater extent than might be expected from the presence of collagen fibres in the interlamellar spaces in the media.

4.3 Post-translational Changes in Collagen

4.3.1 *Maturation*

Collagen is synthesized on polyribosomal clusters in connective-tissue fibroblas
(*Box* 4.1) secreted from the cells and stabilized by the formation of cross-linkag
which vary in permanence from hydrogen bonds to covalent linkages.

Once the structure has been initially stabilized by the formation of the hydrog
bonds, the terminal extension peptides are redundant and are removed
procollagen peptidases acting near to or actually at the cellular membrane. T
tropocollagen which passes into the extracellular space forms the structural bas
of the connective tissue of which its parent fibroblast formed a part. These pur
synthetic reactions cannot be regarded as being directly related to the agei
process, but their completion determines the subsequent metabolic reactivity of t
collagen and determines how the fibres develop within the tissue. Duri
childhood and adolescence the amount of collagen synthesized is greatly in exc
of the body's requirements, even allowing for the massive amount of tiss
building which is required. Since neither hydroxyproline nor hydroxylysine can
incorporated into collagen during ribosomal synthesis but must be produced in t
nascent protein by enzymic hydroxylation, neither acid is recycled into the ami
acid pools which supply the cells with suitable building material for further prote
synthesis. They therefore pass to the kidneys and are excreted (*Table* 4.2). T
hydroxyproline content of urine rises four-fold from birth to puberty and suffers
marked reduction thereafter. Kivirikko (1970) has suggested, however, that t
figures for 24-h hydroxyproline excretion should be normalized to account for a
changes in body mass. If this is carried out (plotting 24-h output f
hydroxyproline/m^2 of body surface against age) the apparent prepubertal rise ca
be ascribed solely to increasing body size. The changing level of excretion implies
falling rate of collagen degradation/unit mass of collagenous tissue as the bo
ages. It is highest immediately after birth, falling with age, only to rise aga
around puberty. The postpubertal, or more specifically postmaturation, fall
urinary hydroxyproline cannot be ascribed to any change in body size, howeve
and must indicate that as tissues age they become more stable and less likely
suffer endogenous degradation. A high proportion of the hydroxyproline excret
in the urine of infants is in the free form (Woolf and Norman, 1957; Jagenbur
1959; O'Brien et al., 1960) whereas the smaller amounts excreted by the elderly is
peptide form. Since hydroxyproline cannot be synthesized except from proli
already in peptide form this must imply either that enzyme systems present
young subjects are capable of breaking the linkages on either side of t
hydroxyproline residue whereas those present in elderly subjects are not, or th
the collagens which are over-produced in early life are different in compositic
from those synthesized later. Although there is evidence for differences in collag
type at different ages (*see* p. 90) the various types do not differ markedly in t
amount of hydroxyproline they contain nor is there evidence for major differenc
in the triad arrangement of amino acids. It appears likely, therefore, that eith
collagenases with different specificities are available for collagen degradation

OX 4.1

simplistic scheme for the synthesis of the collagen fibril. The individual procollagen α-chains are
nthesized on ribosomal clusters in the fibroblasts. The chain lengths of these polypeptides are
ppreciably greater than those of α-chains as finally incorporated into collagen macromolecules, due to
e presence of N and C terminal peptides. Cysteine residues permit disulphide cross-linkages to be
rmed between adjacent pro-α-chains. These locate the pro-α-chains in such a way that the optimum
umber of inter-chain hydrogen bonds are formed. This would not be possible if these covalent linkages
ere not formed. (It would be rather like trying to plait three pieces of string without knotting them
gether first—a rather difficult task!) In the diagram a typical Type I procollagen is indicated with two
o-α$_1$- chains and one pro-α$_2$-chain. Hydroxylation of proline and lysine to form hydroxyproline and
droxylysine, for neither of which is there an RNA-borne code, can only occur after the synthesis of
e procollagen structure. Only some of the available proline and lysine residues are hydroxylated and
ain only some of the hydroxylated residues are subsequently substituted with sugar residues. At the
embrane through which the nascent collagen molecules pass to reach the external milieu, the
tension peptides are removed enzymically to leave short lengths of non-helical peptide—the
lopeptide—at each end of the chain. The triple helical structure, tropocollagen, formed in the case
Types I, IV and V collagen, of two α$_1$-chains and one α$_2$-chain and in Types II and III of three
entical α$_1$-chains, is soluble but can align itself with other similar molecules to form fibrils with the
pical 64 nm cross-striations typical of collagen from most connective tissues. The cross-striations
d other micro-periodicities are the result of the stacking of adjacent tropocollagen molecules with a
arter stagger between laterally adjacent molecules and a gap between longitudinally adjacent
olecules. As the connective tissue matures, covalent cross-links are formed between lysine and
droxylysine residues in the telopeptide regions of one molecule and similar residues elsewhere in
jacent molecules. These covalent linkages are permanent and resist hydrolysis. The only subsequent
st-translational change which can occur in ageing tissue is the fission of peptide linkages in the α-
ains themselves resulting in a conversion of the rigid collagen structure to the more flexible, elastic
ucture defined in the text as pdc (partially degraded collagen) which because of its properties has in
e past been referred to as pseudoelastin.

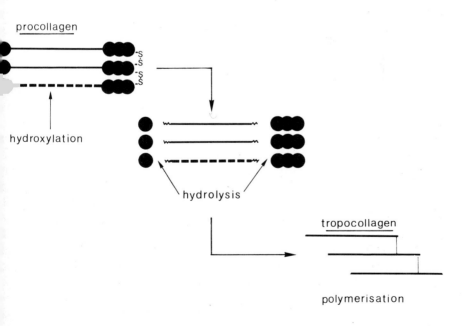

Table 4.2. *Changes in urinary output of hydroxyproline with age (mg/24 h)*

Age range (years)	Hydroxyproline
0–1	37·5
1–5	42·5
6–10	67·0
11–15	122·5
16–21	46·0
Over 21	16·5

youth, or the activity of the same collagenases, which are present throughout life, augmented by other proteolytic enzymes which are only secreted in youth.

4.3.2 *Solubility*

The tropocollagen molecules formed within the cell pass into the extracellula matrix in a form which is soluble in neutral salt solution (0·17 M NaCl). Much c the collagen which is present in old tissues, however, is neither soluble i physiological saline, nor even in stronger salt solutions. The strength of sodiu chloride solution required to extract a given proportion of the collagen in an tissue increases with increasing age (*Table* 4.3) but all the soluble collagen can b

Table 4.3. *Percentage extractability of collagen from skin tissue of varying age by sodium chloride solutions of increasing ionic strength*

Age (years)	Molarity of sodium chloride solutions		
	0·17	0·5	2·0
Fetal	1·0	15·1	21·0
27	4·0	12·9	16·4
16	2·0	7·7	8·0
30	2·0	6·5	6·9
67	1·1	2·9	3·5

extracted with 2 M NaCl. A further fraction can be extracted with dilute acid an even more with hot decinormal alkali. There is, however, a limit to the amour which is extractable, and this proportion decreases with increasing age. Fc instance, the amount of collagen extractable with 2 M NaCl from human ski decreases with increasing age to c.16 µg/mm² at 80 years of age (Hall et a 1974). The expression of these findings in terms of µg collagen/mm² of ski surfaces refers to a column of the full thickness of the dermis beneath 1 mm² c epidermis. By expressing it in this way (Shuster and Bottoms, 1963), account taken not only of changes in collagen concentration (which would be expressed a µg/g tissue) but also of changes in skin thickness (µm/mm). Coupled with chang in solubility are alterations in the total amount of collagen in the skin (*see Fig* 4.21). Not only does the amount of newly-synthesized soluble collagen decreas with age, but the total amount of collagen (soluble and insoluble combined) decreases. This fall is in part due to the decreased synthesis of collagen and partly to a reduction in the amount of mature, insoluble, cross-linked collagen which also occurs with increasing age. Since the level of skin collagen is maintained by a balance between synthesis and degradation, a lower level of total collagen coupled with a lower level of newly-synthesized collagen must imply that the rate of degradation increases or at least remains constant throughout life.

4.3.3 Skin Thickness

Changes in collagen content of the dermis are mirrored by changes in skin thickness. Measurement of this latter parameter is often used to determine the amount of subcutaneous fat, but if readings are taken for a fold of skin on the dorsum of the hand, the skin can be lifted free from any underlying fat and the value obtained is solely dependent on changes in the dermis itself. The very low values which can be observed in the thickness of the skin of elderly subjects have led various workers to suggest that this fall in advanced age is merely the final stage of a progressive change which is continuous throughout life. Hall et al. (1981) measured the skin-fold thickness of over six hundred supposedly normal subjects aged 5 months to over 80 years of age, and showed that far from being a continuous process, the loss of thickness was in fact triphasic in nature (Fig. 4.6). From infancy to maturity (20 years of age) there is a sharp fall, the curve for females being steeper than that for males. From 20 to 60 years of age the values for skin thickness falls only slightly, with the curve for females remaining below that of males throughout, whilst at ages above 60 both curves fall dramatically. This rapid loss of skin thickness in old age is not, therefore, the continuation of a change which had started earlier in life. The suggestion was made that the the three separate phases may, in fact, be due to different factors which, although overlapping, are each predominantly effective in one of the three successive phases (Fig. 4.7). The initial massive fall in youth may be due to dehydration, the slight fall during the middle phase to a reduction on collagen synthesis, and the final rapid fall in old age to the degradation of the collagen which remains.

   If it can be assumed that:

   a. the skin thickness is constant over the whole surface of the body; and

   b. any changes with age occur equally at all points on the body surface,

it should be possible, from values for total skin collagen expressed as $\mu g/mm^2$ skin surface, to calculate the total amount of collagen lost per day. Although neither assumption is likely to be completely correct, it can be seen from such a calculation that the maximum amount of skin collagen lost per day is well below the level of 16·5mg/24 h quoted in Table 4.2. Thus a reduction in the collagen content by 87%, which at first sight appears to represent a considerable loss, but which can, in fact, occur under certain conditions (p. 111), is insufficient to account for the observed amount of hydroxyproline excreted in adult urine in 24 h.

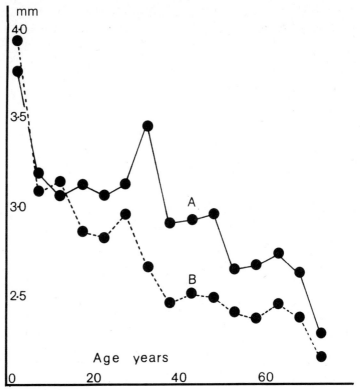

Fig. 4.6. The mean skinfold thicknesses of 5 year age groups of (A) males and (B) females.

4.4 Collagen Polymorphism

The changes in the total amount of collagen present in tissues as the subject grows older are also associated with alterations in the type of collagen (*Box* 4.2) in the tissue. Types I and III occur in both dermis and cultures of aortic smooth muscle cells (Epstein, 1974; Muir et al., 1976). In the dermis (*Table* 4.4) the Type III collagen which is present to the extent of 30% of the total collagen in fetal tissue is replaced in the adult dermis by Type I collagen, whereas the opposite appears to be the case in cultures of aortic smooth muscle. Layman and Titus (1975), Layman et al., (1977) and Reuterberg et al. (1977) have shown that there is a reduction in the ratio of Type I to Type III collagen as the age of the subject from whom the smooth muscle cells were taken for culture increases. Reuterberg and his colleagues, for instance, observed an increase in Type III collagen from 16 to 20% in 3–4-month-old fetuses to more than 30% by 9 years of age. No further variation was observed, however, up to 90 years of age. Types I and III collagen differ significantly in amino acid compostion, notably in respect of threonine, alanine, valine, methionine, phenylalanine and hydroxylysine, which are present at concentrations which are between 20 and 50% less in Type III, and in the amount of the less prevalent form of hydroxyproline, with the hydroxyl group on carbon atom 3

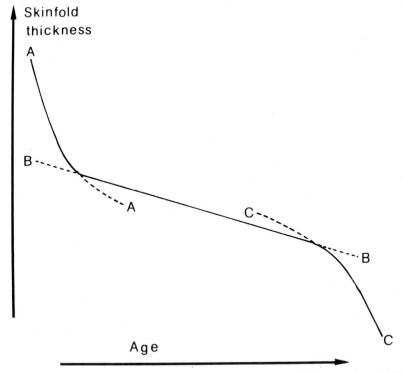

Fig. 4.7. Suggested reason for a triphasic relationship between skinfold thickness and age (Hall et al., 1981). A represents the progressive dehydration of skin during childhood and adolescence, B an age-related reduction in collagen content during mid-life and C the collagen degeneration which accompanies advanced ageing.

BOX 4.2

Collagen molecules from various tissues differ in their α-chain composition. Initially it was thought that collagen consisted of two α_1-chains and one α_2-chain, i.e. the structure to which the title Type I is now applied. The tissues in which Type I collagen occurs are those from which pure samples can easily be obtained. Subsequent studies showed that Types II and III have three identical α_1-chains, but that their amino acid analyses are markedly different from the α_1 from Type I. Types IV and V which have only recently been characterized, have a heterogeneous structure.

Type	Structure	Tissues
I	$[\alpha1(I)]_2\,\alpha2(I)$	Bone, cornea, dentine, fascia, placenta, skin, tendon, blood vessel walls
II	$[\alpha1(II)]_3$	Cartilage, intervertebral disc, vitreous
III	$[\alpha1(III)]_3$	Skin, fascia, vessel walls
IV	$[\alpha1(IV)]_2\,\alpha2(IV)$	Basement membranes
V	$[\alpha1(V)]_2\,\alpha2(V)$	Amnion, aorta, bone, cornea, muscle sheath, skin, tendon

---

rather than 4 of the pyrrole group, which is virtually absent from Type III. Probably the most significant difference between the two types is the ratio of the amounts of hydroxylysine which in Type III is only half that in Type I. This residue not only forms part of the cross-linking system but also acts as a site for

Table 4.4. **The effect of age on the distribution of Types I and III collagen in different tissues**

Tissue	Age	Type I (%)	Type III (%)
Dermis	Fetal	70	30
	Adult	100	—
Artery (smooth muscle cell)	2–4 mo (fetal)	80–85	15–20
	9 years	70	30
	67 years	70	30

glycosylation. Such substituents have been suggested as essential in promoting platelet aggregation (Beachey et al., 1979) although Shoshan (1981) has rejected this suggestion. The amino acid compositions of the two types of collagen are so different as to preclude their synthesis under the control of the same messenger RNA. Their synthesis must be under the control of two separate and distinct genes.

As age progresses the synthesis of Type I collagen in the dermis is switched on whereas the synthesis of Type III is switched off. The reverse effect occurs in smooth muscle cell cultures. Such changes in gene expression with increasing age have been ascribed to pleiotropic genes (Williams, 1957) or to the existence of regulator genes (Medawar, 1952) but Hall (1981) has suggested that Monod' theory (Jacob and Monod, 1961) is the more likely to be true. Using the operon theory of enzyme induction to explain the appearance of Type III collagen at a certain stage in the ageing of aortic smooth muscle cells (*see* p. 144) he invokes an unknown inhibitor which by combining with the repressor substance evolved by the operon gene prevents this substance from inhibiting the expression of that gene which is specific for Type III synthesis. It appears likely that the unknown inhibitory substance might well be hormonal in nature since on the one hand hormones are known to control collagen (and other protein) synthesis whilst on the other their secretion by the appropriate organ is age related (*see* p. 145).

Similar differences have been reported in the intervertebral disc (Eyre, 1979) where Type III collagen appears to be joined in the annulus by Type II as age increases (*Box* 4.2). However, such changes appear to occur mainly at the nucleus–annulus interface. Since Type II is prevalent in the nucleus, and it becomes increasingly difficult to separate the two regions of the disc cleanly as age increases, the reported appearance of Type II in the annulus may be due to an inevitable faulty dissection of elderly discs.

4.5 Cross-linkages

The changing solubility of collagen with increasing age is due to the formation of increasing numbers of cross-linkage with increasing age. The existence of cross-linkages was first predicted by Verzar (1963) when he observed that the force required to prevent the thermal contraction of collagen fibres from rat tail tendon increased with increasing age. Since then not only have other studies of the

hysical properties of collagen (*see* p. 99) confirmed these observations but
:udies of the partial hydrolysis products of mature insoluble collagen have
ermitted the isolation and identification of cross-links, increasing numbers of
√hich could produce the sorts of change observed by Verzar. Banga (1966) has, for
nstance, shown that treatment with a 40% solution of potassium iodide induces
ne contraction of collagen fibres to an extent which is age dependent (*Fig.* 4.8).

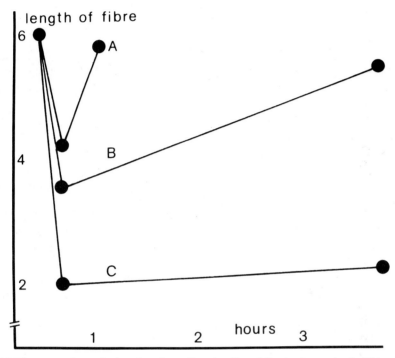

Fig. 4.8. The contraction and relaxation of rat tail tendon fibres following immersion in 40% potassium
odide, A, 2 months old; B, 7 months; C, 24–30 months old (adapted from Banga, 1966).

The subsequent relaxation of the fibre, which permits it to re-attain its original
dimensions, however, occurs more rapidly and to a greater extent in younger
nimals than in older ones. In fact, the tail tendon collagen of rats between 2 and $2\frac{1}{2}$
ears old contracts to one-third its original length when treated with 40% KI, but
does not subsequently relax over a period of many hours. The essential amino
cids for collagen cross-linkage formation are the lysines and hydroxylysines in the
non-helical telopeptide regions at the N and C termini of the molecule. Cross-
inkages are formed by the interaction of lysine and hydroxylysine aldehydes
allysine and hydroxyallysine) with hydroxylysine residues in adjacent chains.
These residues can react with one another in a variety of ways to form the different
pecies of cross-link shown in *Box* 4.3 and their concentration varies in connective
issues of different age.

BOX 4.3

The cross-links of the two structural proteins collagen and elastin originate in the lysine (an hydroxylysine in the case of collagen) residues present in these molecules. Linkages may be formed by aldol condensation of two allysine residues (cf. *Fig.* 4.15) produced by oxidative deamination of the NH_2 terminal of the lysine residue under the control of a copper-mediated amino oxidase. Other linkages may be formed through the Schiff base reaction between an allysine molecule and a unoxidized lysine residue:

$$—CH_2—CH_2—NH_2 + OHC—CH_2—CH_2— \quad \rightarrow \quad —CH_2—CH_2—N=CH—CH_2—CH_2—$$

Both aldol and Schiff's base can undergo reduction *in vivo*. This stabilizes the cross-links and provides junction which is resistant to hydrolysis. It is prior to this reductive process that drugs, such as penicillamine, react by interfering with Schiff's base formation. So-called lathyritic agents which have been claimed to inhibit the ageing process in collagen, but which, in fact, merely effect the maturation process, interfere in the initial formation of the allysine by inhibiting the amino oxidase.

Ruiz-Torres (1978) has shown that dehydrolysinonorleucine (DHLNL) increases steadily in rat tail tendon with increasing age and that this increase occurs at the expense of hydroxynorleucine (HLNL). This effect, however, is not nearly so marked or clear cut in rat skin nor are the variations in human tissue so impressive (Fujii et al., 1976). Robins et al. (1973) have studied the levels of DHLNL (HLNL) and histidinohydroxymerodismosine (HHMD) in bovine skin over a period of 6 years (*Fig.* 4.9) and have shown that the level of DHLNL, which is high in fetal skin, falls to a very low level within the first year of life. This cross-link is replaced by HLNL and HHMD which reach peak concentrations at between 2 and 4 years. The reductions in the concentration of these three cross-links are difficult to explain, those in HLNL and HHMD more so than that in DHLNL. These

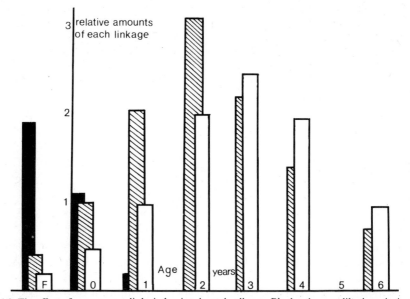

Fig. 4.9. The effect of age on cross-links in bovine dermal collagen. Black columns: dihydroxylysinonorleucine; hatched columns: hydroxylysinonorleucine; open columns: histidinohydroxymerodesmosine

cross-linkages are known to be very stable once formed but the apparent loss of DHLNL could be due to a dilution effect associated with a failure to produce this ype of cross-link as further collagen is laid down during growth. The apparent reduction in HLNL and HHMD, however, cannot be explained by a failure of further synthesis since growth has essentially ceased by the time their concentrations begin to fall. Either these cross-links are converted to other forms which have not yet been identified in the hydrolysates of the ageing tissues or, owing to excessive cross-linkage, hydrolysis itself was not complete.

4.6 Degradation of Collagen

Knowledge of the degradation of collagen has increased over the years as the results of collaborative studies by workers in a number of fields. Degraded fibres can be visualized in both the light and the electron microscopes, their mechanical properties can be measured and their chemical structures can be analysed. If the results of all lines of approach are combined a reasonably accurate picture can be obtained of what is happening during ageing (*Fig.* 4.10).

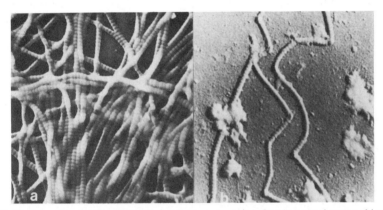

Fig. 4.10. Electron micrographs of teased material from: *a*, dermis from a normal young object, and *b*, dermis from the outer aspect of the arm of an elderly subject. The collagen fibres show evidence of partial degradation due to age and exposure.

One of the first to observe changes in collagen with increasing age and disease was the dermatologist Unna (1896) who identified at least three tissue components, *elacin, collastin* and *collacin* which had different staining properties from native collagen. Kissmeyer and With (1922) and Ejiri (1936, 1937) demonstrated that regions of dermis which had been exposed to sunlight stained heavily with elastica stains and Gillman et al. (1955) referred to this material as 'elastotically degenerate collagen'. Tunbridge et al. (1951, 1952) using teased preparations from elastica staining regions of exposed dermis for electron microscopic study, demonstrated that this elastica staining material was, in fact, partially degraded collagen (pdc) (*Fig.* 4.10). In any normal field in the electron microscope, whether it be a thin section or a teased preparation of collagen fibrils which is being viewed, it i unusual to see any cut or broken fibril ends. All the fibres extend across the complete field. In collagen preparations from old exposed skin the same is true o thin sections although some of the 64 nm cross-striations which are typical o collagen are partially obscured by layers of amorphous material. In teased preparations, however, numerous broken and bent fibrils can be seen with many ends appearing in the field. This may well be an artefact due to the mechanica disturbance associated with the preparation of the teased sample, but even if this is so, there must be an underlying difference between the older and younger tissues since teasing has no effect on the latter. It has been suggested that these changes are due to exposure rather than to age (Smith et al., 1962) but studies of the chemica changes which are associated with these structural alterations appear to indicate that at least part of the observed change in exposed elderly dermis must be age dependent.

Chemical and biochemical studies of collagen degradation have proved to be o considerable value. One of the alterations which occurs as collagen suffers degeneration of the type observed in senile skin, is a change in its susceptibility to the two enzymes collagenase and elastase. It becomes less soluble in the former and more so in the latter. Exhaustive treatment with elastase dissolves both the elastir and the degraded collagen leaving the undegraded collagen almost completely unaffected (there is, however, evidence that elastase, in common with a number of other proteolytic enzymes, can react with the non-helical terminal telepeptide regions of the molecule). If the value obtained for the elastin content of the tissue following extraction with hot alkali, which removes both intact and partially degraded collagen, is subtracted from the value obtained for the amount of pro tein extracted by elastase, the difference represents the content of pdc. Slater and Hall (1973) have shown in this way that the amount of pdc in abdominal skin rises four-fold during the period 20–80 years (*Fig.* 4.11). Even infant skin contains a finite, though small, amount of pdc but the four-fold rise during the 'ageing' period represents a pronounced effect which cannot be related to irradiation since the abdomen may be assumed to have suffered minimal exposure. Actinic changes. which are apparently additive to those of age, have also been observed in exposed sites (Slater and Hall), the pdc content of the outer aspect of the forearm of a 17- year-old being nearly $2\frac{1}{2}$ times greater than that of the abdomen (3·5% as opposed to 1·5%) whereas in the 60–70-year-old group, there is a two-fold increase in pdc between the abdomen (3·2%) and the cheek and forehead (6·5 and 7·0% respectively). These results are at variance with those of Lansing (1955) who suggested that senile elastosis was totally actinic in origin and was in fact a true elastosis and not due to the accumulation of pdc.

4.7 Physical Properties

The tensile properties of collagen fibres as they occur in tendon have been analysed by Viidik (1968) and have been shown to approximate a complex interplay of

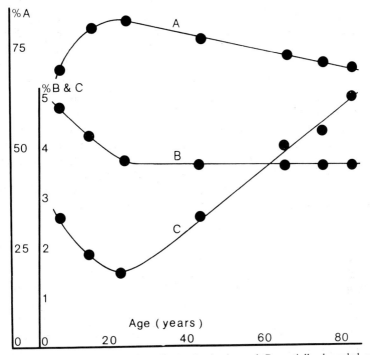

Fig. 4.11. Relative concentrations of A, collagen; B, elastin, and C, partially degraded collagen in human abdominal dermis with advancing age.

reactions which can be correlated with various theoretical tensile elements (*Fig. 4.12*). The tissue does not obey Hook's Law and the determination of values for Young's modulus is relatively meaningless unless the range of applied load is small. There are various ways in which the extension of a tissue can deviate from the Hookean form and Viidik has combined viscous elements, which are time dependent and can be represented by a function resembling a dash pot in which a piston moves in a viscous fluid, with Hookean springs both in series and in parallel to give so-called Maxwell and Kelvin elements, and with frictional factors to explain the 'plasticity' of the structure. This analytical approach enabled him to explain the major curvilinear portion of the load/extension relationship. The slope of the almost linear central portion of the curve (*Fig. 4.12*) increased with age but since it is not truly linear, direct comparisons of slope and age are difficult. Ridge and Wright (1965, 1966) overcame this by calculating an empirical formula relating extension to load:

$$E = C + KL^b$$

where E equals the extension, L the load and C, K and b are constants. They used this equation to study the effect of age on the extensibility of skin. The tissue, although complex, can be regarded essentially as an array of collagen fibre bundles which alone account for the tensile properties of the tissue once the toe of the curve

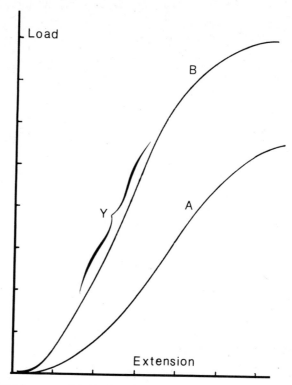

Fig. 4.12. Load/extension curves for skin from A, 20-year-old, and B, 70-year-old subjects. The region Y although not sufficiently linear to justify use for the calculation of a value for Young's Modulus, can be defined by the equation $E = C + KL^b$.

is past. The two constants C and K are dependent on the dimensions of the sample of skin under test and on the characteristics of the instrument employed to stretch the fibres, 'b' on the other hand is completely independent of the factors and appears to be related solely to the identity of the sample and hence to the properties of the collagen fibres of which it is composed. When 'b' is plotted against age it can be shown that the relationship passes through a peak for both males and females at between 40 and 45 years of age (*Fig.* 4.13).

From the rising limbs of these two curves it can be inferred that the fibres increase in stiffness with increasing age up to about 40–45 years of age and this can be correlated with the presence of increasing numbers of cross-linkages. The falling limbs of the curves, however, cannot indicate a reduction in cross-linkages since it has been shown that once formed these structural stabilizers are unlikely to suffer disruption (Bailey and Robins, 1973). Hall (1981) has suggested, therefore, that the falling away of stiffness, as indicated by lower values for the power to which the value of the load has to be raised ('b'), may be due to degradation of the main chains, presumably by an endogenous collagenolytic enzyme. Keech (1954) observed that the dermis from young and old subjects when partially digested by collagenase from *Clostridium histolyticum* was degraded to a product which could

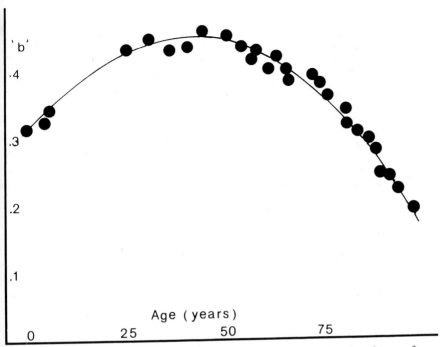

Fig. 4.13. Plot of the constant 'b' (representative of the 'stiffness' of the tissue) against age for male subjects. The female curve follows that for male subjects about 0·05 units lower throughout the whole life-span.

be converted into gelatin when heated. Dermis from middle-aged subjects, however, when treated similarly, remained in the form of an insoluble, amorphous, electron dense mass after heat treatment. Hall (1976) has suggested that all these observations may be related and that they may be explained by the existence of increasing numbers of cross-links between collagen molecules with increasing age (Fig. 4.14). Young collagen, with few if any cross-links, can be assumed to be attacked by endogenous collagenase to produce small molecular weight end products which are ultimately eliminated from the body. Old collagen which is rigidly cross-linked will also be degradable by collagenase, the individual main chains being held apart by the cross-linkages so as to permit the penetration of enzyme between them. The end products will not be as small as those which result from the digestion of the young collagen, since they will consist of small lengths of main chain joined by cross-linkages, but these may well be small enough to be eliminated through the kidneys. Where an intermediate number of cross-linkages is present in the 'middle-aged' tissues, the fission of even one or two peptides linkages in the main chain will render the structure unstable. It will collapse on itself and the presence of the limited number of cross-linkages will prevent any further penetration by the enzyme. This is the material (pdc) which is:

a. more elastic than native collagen;
b. takes up elastica stains;

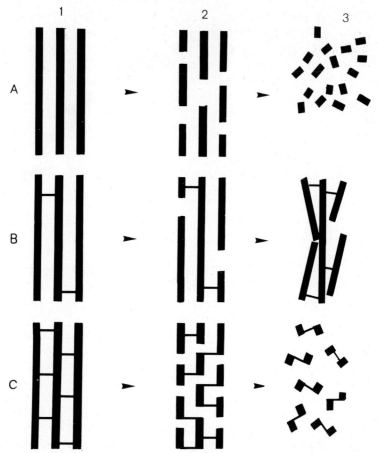

Fig. 4.14. Diagrammatic representation (phases 1, 2 and 3) of collagen degradation. Young fibres (A) are easily digested by collagenase and having no covalent cross-links are easily converted to small particles which are eliminated from the body. Old fibres (C) although fully cross-linked can also be broken down into small particles (still, however, retaining their cross-linkages) because the links hold the chain apart to permit penetration of the enzyme. 'Middle-aged' collagen fibres (B) however, being minimally cross-linked suffer initial degradation (phase 2) but the structure then collapses and, being held together by the cross-links, resists further digestion, to appear in the tissue as pdc (partially degraded collagen).

    c. is susceptible to attack by elastase;

    d. is amorphous under the electron microscope.

    Chemical analysis of pdc has not been easy since methods of extraction from tissue produce a material which is contaminated either with intact collagen or with intact elastin. In fact, there is evidence that pdc combines with elastin to form a complex which cannot easily be fractionated. Labella et al. (1960) have reported variations in the amino acid composition of 'purified' elastin and have shown that there is a closer similarity between the analyses of young (20–30-year-old) and old (60–70-year-old) elastins, than there is between those of either of these groups and the intermediate 'middle-aged' group. This middle-aged group contains larger amounts of aspartic acid (five-fold) and threonine, serine, arginine, histidine, lysine and glutamic acid (c. two-fold) and a lower value of valine (70%) than classic elastin, values which would be expected if a degraded collagen, especially pdc, from $[\alpha 1(I)]_2 \alpha 2$ were covalently attached to it.

4.8 Elastin

Much of the evidence for age changes in the elastic elements of connective tissues has arisen fortuitously from studies of intact collagen and pdc mentioned earlier. However, there are some aspects of elastin ageing which have not already been dealt with in detail.

The elastin content of essentially elastic connective tissues such as the lung, the vascular wall and the skin vary quite considerably with age. Wolinsky (1970) has stressed the importance of measuring and recording absolute rather than relative amounts of elastin. Percentages of a component expressed in tems of dry weight of tissue could lead to a serious misinterpretation of the results since the finding of a constant percentage could indicate that other components are altering in a comparable fashion. This is apparent in Fig. 4.11, where the percentage elastin content of skin appears to decrease during the years up to full maturation, but, as can be seen from the upper curve, the collagen content is, in fact increasing over this period, thus effectively lowering the proportion of elastin.

Banga (1966) measured the elastin content of aortic tissue from a variety of sources and ages using various methods. There are, however, topographical differences in distribution which add another variable factor. Harkness et al. (1957), for instance, have reported marked changes in elastin content in dog vascular tissues as the major vessels pass out of the thorax into the abdomen.

The question of changing amino acid composition of elastin with increasing age has been considered since the early 1950s when Lansing and his colleagues (Lansing et al., 1948, 1950, 1951) reported marked changes, especially in the polar amino acids which are present in relatively low concentration in classic ligamentum nuchae elastin but which assumed appreciable concentrations in the elderly human tissues which they examined. Part, at least, of this might be due to the presence of pdc but more recent studies (Kramsch et al., 1970; Kramsch et al., 1971), have shown that increases in polar amino acids are especially apparent in plaque areas of the atherosclerotic aortic wall. Kramsch et al. (1974) have observed increases in aspartic acid, glutamic acid, serine, threonine, lysine, histidine and arginine and decreased level of the cross-linking amino acids, desmosine, isodesmosine and lysinonorleucine. These changes may be more closely related to atherosclerosis than to ageing, since they invariably occur in the neighbourhood of the plaques and not elsewhere in the vascular tissue. Ageing can occur without atherosclerosis, but the full development of the atherosclerotic lesion occurs primarily at advanced age.

Elastin tissue contains two species of protein—a microfibrillar glycoprotein and amorphous elastin. In young fibres the former component represents as much as 8% of the total mass with elastin providing the remaining 92%. The glycoprotein fibrils are rich in polar amino acids and are devoid of hydroxyproline, hydroxylysine and cross-links other than cystine (present at about 0·7%). These fibrils appear to have little function in determining the underlying mechanical properties of the elastic fibres, but help to align soluble tropoelastin molecules prior to the formation of the cross-linkages which are characteristic of elastin. With advancing age, the glycoprotein content of elastic tissue increases. Robert et al. (1974) have suggested that the natural history of the elastic fibres, therefore, consists of various phases characterized by the simultaneous presence of varying amounts of the microfibrillar glycoprotein and elastin. Both are synthesized simultaneously in youth, the fibrillar glycoprotein acting as a scaffold for the alignment of the tropoelastin molecules. McCloskey and Cleary (1974) and Jacotot et al. (1973) have suggested that in addition to the glycoproteins there is a non-scleroprotein component in elastin tissue which increases in concentration with increasing age and may become closely attached to the elastic fibres in advanced age, thus altering their physical properties.

The cross-links which form between adjacent tropoelastin molecules as the elastin tissue matures are related to those occurring in collagen in that they are lysine based, but they differ in that many of the structures finally produced are more complex than the reducible linkages present in mature collagen. If lysines in adjacent chains are both oxidized an aldol condensation product is formed (*Fig. 4.15*), if only one is oxidized lysinonorleucine will result from an initial Schiff's base condensation product whereas more complex structures (desmosine and isodesmosine) (*Fig. 4.16*) result from the linkage of lysines and oxidized lysines in either three or two tropoelastin chains. It has been shown that the lysine residues which are concerned in cross-link formation lie close to regions which are rich in alanine residues (Foster et al., 1974), pairs of lysine residues which will form part of the desmosine or isodesmosine molecules being separated by two or three alanine residues (*Fig. 4.17*). The number of desmosine and isodesmosine cross-linkages is lower in elastins isolated from both aortic and pulmonary tissues from senile rather than young subjects. Some of this loss could be attributed to dilution due to the presence of greater amounts of glycoprotein, but it has also been

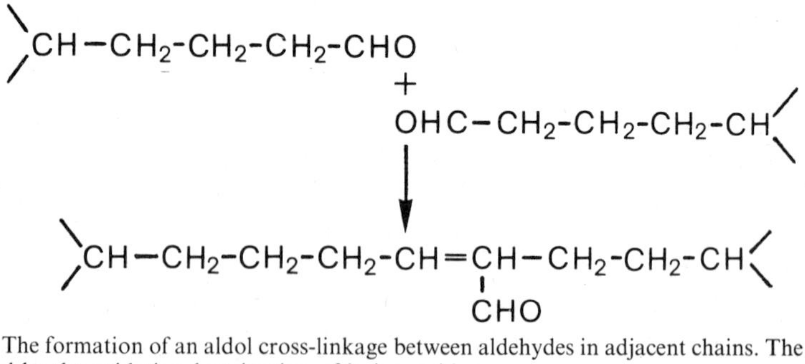

Fig. 4.15. The formation of an aldol cross-linkage between aldehydes in adjacent chains. The aldehydes are formed by the oxidative deamination of lysine residues.

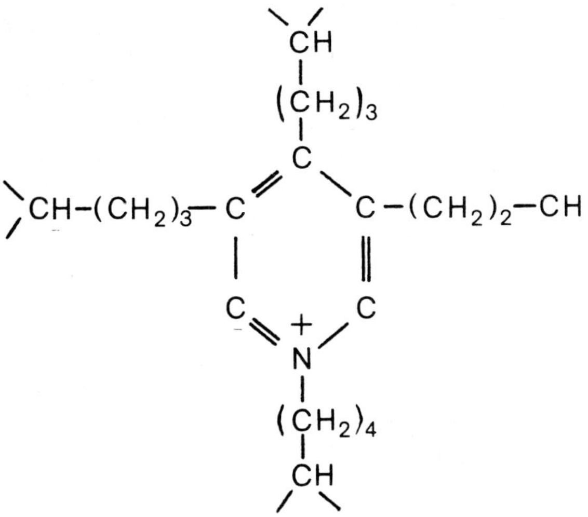

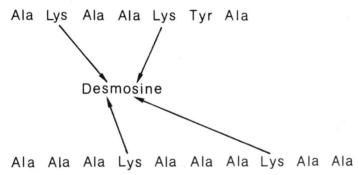

Fig. 4.16. Desmosine formed by the condensation of three aldehydes derived from lysine and one unmodified lysine. Iso-desmosine with a different distribution of substituents in the pyridine nucleus is also present in elastin. The roots of the four original lysine residues are present in two adjacent chains (cf. *Fig.* 4.17).

Ala Lys Ala Ala Lys Tyr Ala

Desmosine

Ala Ala Ala Lys Ala Ala Ala Lys Ala Ala

Fig. 4.17. The location of the lysine residues in adjacent chains which combine to provide the basis for the desmosine cross-link.

observed that fluorescent substances increase in elastin with increasing age (Banga, 1966; Kramasch et al., 1970) and it may be that they are synthesized at the expense of the desmosines.

Hall (1976) has suggested that a further form of cross-link exists in the elastin molecule and that this also is age related. Yu and Blumenthal (1960) showed that a small but finite part of the calcium present in the aorta could not be extracted even with solutions of sodium ethylene diamine tetra-acetic acid (EDTA). Hall (1970) identified this fraction of elastin-bound calcium as being bound to the protein by co-ordinate linkages to hydroxyl and carboxyl groups which had higher co-ordination constants than Ca EDTA. He showed that similarly bound calcium could also be identified in the enzyme, binding pairs of molecules together. Not all the possible sites in the elastin molecule at which calcium could be co-ordinately bound are filled, nor are all elastase molecules bound together in pairs. Since co-ordinately bound calcium appears to act as a linkage between enzyme and substrate (Hall, 1971), calcium-rich elastase dimers will react with the calcium-free centres in elastin whilst elastase monomers split calcium linkages where they occur in elastin (*Fig.* 4.18) Using preparations of elastase which were rich in either one or the other form of the enzyme, Hall et al. (1973) were able to show that the amounts of co-ordinately bound calcium in aortic media increased steadily with increasing age (*Table* 4.5). It may well be that these relatively few, co-ordinately bound calcium atoms may provide the seeds necessary for the massive deposition of calcium phosphate in those aortas which ultimately suffer calcification.

$$E-Ca-E + S \longrightarrow E + E-Ca-S$$

$$S-Ca-S + E \longrightarrow S + E-Ca-S$$

Fig. 4.18. The formation of similar enzyme-substrate complexes between calcium-rich elastase and calcium-free regions in the substrate and calcium-poor elastase and regions of the elastin molecule containing co-ordinate bound calcium.

Table 4.5. *Total amount of protein (mg) removed from 100 mg dried defatted aortic tissues of varying age by two elastase preparations*

Site	Enzyme Ca-rich	Ca-poor	2 months	21 years	47 years	75 years
Intima	−	+	−	53·5	69·8	76·0
	+	−	−	79·5	75·5	72·1
Inner media	−	+	−	60·6	73·8	82·2
	+	−	−	65·2	74·0	75·7
Media	−	+	63·9	68·2	86·8	89·1
	+	−	−	45·3	59·5	78·1
Adventitia	−	+	−	31·4	58·7	68·0
	+	−	−	—	—	—

4.9 Glycosaminoglycans

Glycosaminoglycans occur in varying amounts in different connective tissues, depending on their function. In tissues providing resilient shock absorber function between load-bearing portions of the skeletal system the proportion of glycosaminoglycan is high (*Table* 4.6) and it provides a structure which is resilient under pressure. In tissues designed to withstand extension, e.g. tendon, vascular tissue and skin, the glycosaminoglycan content provides an amorphous lubricating medium in which the collagenous fibres rotate relative to one another under load.

Because of the structural importance of glycosaminoglycans in articular cartilage, it has been this tissue which has provided most information regarding the

Table 4.6. Glycosaminoglycan content of various connective tissues

Tissue	Glycosaminoglycan content % dry wt	Change with age
Articular cartilage	60·1	CS decreases KS increases
Arterial wall	4·8	CS decreases KS increases
Skin	1·0	CS decreases KS increases DS increases

CS = Chondroitin 4 and 6
KS = Keratan sulphate
DS = Dermatan sulphate

changes which take place with advancing age. Articular cartilage contains four major forms of glycosaminoglycan, differing from one another in the amounts and position of their sulphate content. Hyaluronic acid (*Fig.* 4.19) consists of a polymer of the dimeric sugar d-glucuronyl-N-acetyl-glucosamine and is not sulphated. Two chondroitin sulphates, sulphated on carbon atoms 4 and 6 and keratan sulphate also sulphated on carbon atom 6, differ in the nature of the dimeric glycosides of which they are composed, being respectively:

CS-4   glucuronyl-$(1 \rightarrow 3)$-N-acetyl-galactosamine-4-sulphate
CS-6   glucuronyl-$(1 \rightarrow 3)$-N-acetyl-galactosamine-6-sulphate
KS   galactosyl-$(1 \rightarrow 4)$-N-acetyl-glucosamine-6-sulphate

Dermatan sulphate, present in the dermis and the menisci but absent from articular cartilage, consists of a polymer of iduronyl-1-3-N-acetylglucosamine.

The glycans do not exist in isolation in articular cartilage, but are combined with a core protein which is, itself, attached to collagen with the assistance of a linking protein (*Fig.* 4.20). The individual glycans, which are of differing molecular weight, can be separated from one another by electrophoretic techniques and differ in concentration with increasing age. Matthews and Glagov (1966) have shown that at term the total glycan content of human costal cartilage consists of equal amounts of CS-4 and CS-6. After birth during the first 40 years of life, the amounts of CS-4 and CS-6 both fall; the former decreasing three times more rapidly than the latter. Their place in the cartilage is taken by keratan sulphate. After 40 years of age, the relative amounts of the three glycans CS-4: CS-6: KS remain at 6 : 4 : 1. The ratio of CS-4 : CS-6 in human knee joint cartilage falls from 6 : 1 to 1 : 5 from birth to 80 years of age (Greiling and Bauman, 1973). Leutert and Kreutz (1964) have also observed age changes in non-load-bearing cartilage, showing that thyroidal cartilage is affected most rapidly, whilst tracheal cartilage resists age changes for an appreciable proportion of the life-span. The intervertebral disc also contains CS-4, CS-6 and KS especially in the nucleus pulposus. The ratio of CS-4 and CS-6 to KS decreases from 1 : 1 to 1 : 4 (Buddecke and Sziegoleit, 1964) and moreover there is an alteration in the CS-4 : CS-6 ratio, which falls from a value of 2 : 1 to a situation in which CS-6 represents the major chondroitin-based component. The glycoprotein content of the disc also falls with increasing age (Happey et al., 1974).

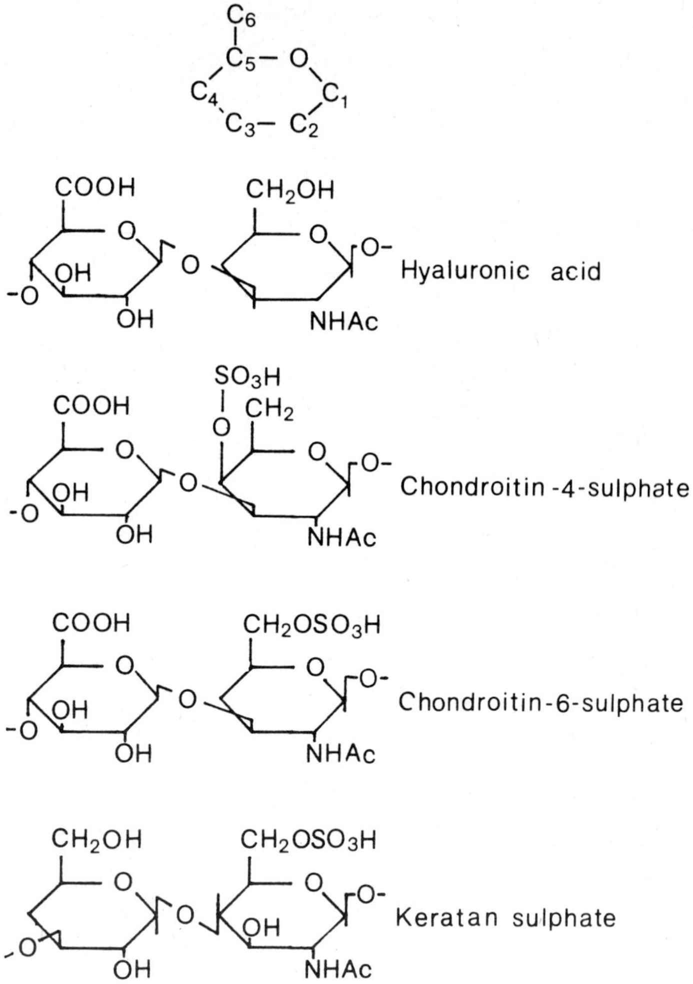

Fig. 4.19. The structures of the dimeric units of the main glycosaminoglycan constituents of connective tissues. The numbering of the carbon atoms in the individual sugar molecules is indicated in the skeleton structure at the top.

These changes provide the basis for those alterations in physical properties which can be observed on ageing. The large numbers of hydroxyl and sulphate groups in the glycan molecules provide sites to which water can become associated through hydrogen bonds, thus providing bulky space-filling molecules which are repelled by one another due to their negative changes. Compressive forces overcome these repellent forces and drive the glycan molecules closer together. Once the compressive force is removed, however, the repellent forces reassert themselves and cause the tissue to reattain its pristine shape. The chondroitin sulphate molecules in cartilage have much longer chain length than the keratan sulphate molecules and hence provide a large proportion of the resilient mass of

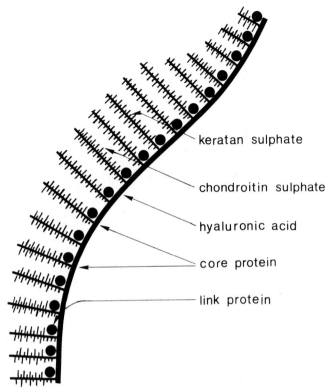

keratan sulphate

chondroitin sulphate

hyaluronic acid

core protein

link protein

Fig. 4.20. A schematic representation of the structure of a typical proteoglycan. The side chains are only shown on one side of this central hyaluronic acid backbone. They are, in fact, attached through the link proteins on all sides of the central core. The distribution of chondroitin sulphate and keratan sulphate chains varies from tissue to tissue and at various ages.

the tissue. The loss of CS-4 and CS-6 and its replacement by KS with increasing age, therefore, provides a less resilient tissue which is less effective as a shock absorber.

4.10 Fibronectin

In confluent layers of fibroblast cultures the pericellular matrix contains Types I and III procollagen, various proteoglycans and fibronectin. The cells can be removed with desoxycholate and hypotonic buffers, the procollagens with collagenase and the glycans with a mixture of chondroitin sulphatases and hyaluronidase leaving behind a material which under normal circumstances is closely associated with the collagen (Vaheri et al., 1978). *In vivo* fibronectin can be shown by immunofluorescent techniques to be closely codistributed with Type III procollagen in fetal skin (Linder et al., 1978) but cannot be demonstrated in sites where mature collagen or elastin fibres are detected by histological stains.

Kurkinen et al. (1979) have suggested that fibronectin has a role to play during the initial maturation of a tissue since it is only transitorily present alongside collagenous proteins during the organizational phase of connective-tissue growth. During corneal morphogenesis for instance, there is a massive amount of fibronectin present whereas in the mature cornea it is restricted to a thin layer in Descemet's membrane. Changes in fibronectin content can be observed even during the rapid 'ageing' processes which occur with the development of granuloma tissue where it appears before collagen, but does not remain in those regions where organized bundles of collagen fibres occur (Kurkinen et al., 1980).

4.11 Degradation of Connective Tissue

Identification and characterization of the enzyme systems responsible for the degradation of connective tissues and a study of their changes has proved of considerable importance in studies of both connective-tissue structure and its age-related degeneration. Until relatively recently exogenous collagenases had to be employed, notably those of clostridial origin, for studies of collagen degradation, since endogenous collagenases were present in such low concentration in most tissues as to be incapable of exploitation. Elastase, on the other hand, although present in certain micro-organisms is also synthesized in high concentrations in the mammalian pancreas and various other tissues and can be purified in quantities which make it easily applicable to the study of ageing. Most of the evidence for age changes in synthesis and secretion has been obtained for elastase of pancreatic origin.

Elastase was first isolated from the pancreas by Balo and Banga (1949), whilst searching for an agent capable of bringing about the degradation of aortic elastin which is observed in atherosclerosis. The major difficulty which they experienced in associating this form of human elastase with arterial degeneration was its apparent absence from the circulation. The enzyme appears to be synthesized by the δ-cells of the islets of Langerhans in the pancreas in the form of a pro-enzyme which is mainly secreted into the pancreatic duct where it is activated by trypsin and passes to the duodenum to function as a generalized peptidase with slightly restricted specificity (Hall, 1976). Acceptance of the suggestion by Balo and Banga that this essentially exocrine enzyme could degrade elastic fibres in the walls of the arteries depended on proof that part of the enzyme passes into the circulation. There is, however, a potent inhibitor of the enzyme in the α-globulin fraction of plasma which renders it impossible to measure the enzyme content of the plasma using the enzyme's normal substrate—elastin from the ligament of the ox—or certain of the artificial peptides which can be cleaved by the enzyme in the absence of plasma proteins. Hall (1966) was able to show that the modification of the enzyme's normal substrate, by the incorporation into it of the dye, Congo Red, reversed the inhibition due to the α-globulin and permitted the enzyme content of plasma to be determined. Banga and Ardelt (1967) and Geokas et al. (1967) criticized this method on account of the fact that Congo Red has a high affinity for albumin and hat, under certain circumstances, albumin can displace the dye from its complex with elastin. However, this only occurs at specific plasma : dye complex ratios, and f the conditions originally laid down by Hall are adhered to, it seems likely that the assessment of plasma elastase is valid.

Confirmation of this has recently been obtained (Elridi and Hall, 1976) by the solation of the enzyme from human plasma. Enzyme from this source can be assessed by either the classic method employing undyed elastin or using Congo Red dyed elastin as substrate.

Plasma levels of elastase have been measured by Hall and his colleagues for numerous groups of subjects of all ages, from infancy to the tenth decade (Hall, 1965; Chatterjee, 1975; Hall et al., 1980a, b, 1981). Differences were observed between males and females (*see Fig.* 5.1) but both sexes showed an overall fall in elastase levels over a major portion of their life-span. Male plasma contained increasing amounts of enzyme over the first 3–4 decades followed by a substantial fall during the next few decades. A significant increase at ages over 80 could be due to the loss through death of that proportion of the elderly population which had a lower than average level of elastase. Females, on the other hand, suffer a fall in elastase level from a value at birth which is as high as that of the male peak and which is continuous throughout life with the exception of the period between 40 and 60 years of age, around the menopause, when there is a dramatic but transitory increase (*see* p. 125).

It is well known that both age and corticosteroid therapy bring about a similar condition in human skin, namely a paper-thin appearance, pseudo-scars, bruising and increased pigmentation, either diffuse or in the form of spots. The number of thick collagen bundles is also reduced. Withdrawal of corticoid therapy results in a reversal of these changes, whereas ageing as yet has proved to be irreversible. From these observations it might be expected that either collagen synthesis is depressed or collagen degradation enhanced—or both. Depression of collagen synthesis has been reported *in vivo* and Koob et al. (1974) have shown that in culture the effect of steroids is to depress both collagen synthesis *and* collagenase production. However, there is some evidence for *enhanced* collagenase activity following corticosteroid therapy (Hall et al., 1974). The residue of mature collagen remaining after the soluble collagen has been removed from skin by extraction with 2 M sodium chloride is increasingly less susceptible to attack by collagenase of clostridial origin. After the administration of the corticosteroid prednisolone, the effect is reversed—as the age of the subject increases the amount which can be taken into solution by the action of collagenase *in vitro* increases. One explanation of this could be that part of the highly cross-linked mature collagen has been subjected to the action of endogenous collagenase *in vivo* rendering it more susceptible to subsequent dissolution *in vitro* treatment with collagenase.

The relationship between the effects of corticosteroid treatment and ageing is still very complex and as yet not fully understood. It does appear, however, that the effects are interrelated and any *in vivo* loss of connective tissue, brought about by corticosteroid therapy whether it be due to enhanced catabolism or diminished anabolism is exacerbated by age.

4.12 Clinical Manifestations of Connective-tissue ageing

4.12.1 *Introduction*

Since connective tissues, as their name implies, have a marked structural role in the body, any changes which may be due to ageing are apparent at the functional level. Because of the diverse nature of connective tissues, however, such functional changes are not restricted to those organs in which collagen plays a major structural role. Thus, although the skin, the skeleton, the cardiovascular system and the pulmonary organs show major changes with age, other organs such as the kidney, the liver and the eye also demonstrate age changes which can be attributed to alterations in their connective-tissue components.

4.12.2 *The Skeleton*

Ageing is accompanied by loss of bone from the skeleton. Such losses can be assessed by the densitometry of X-ray films, but variations in X-ray techniques render quantitative assessments difficult to correlate between institutions. Measurements of dimensions which do not necessitate the assessment of densities have proved more amenable to comparison. The majority of workers have calculated a so-called *metacarpal index* based on the measurement of the inner and outer diameter of the cortical cylinder of the second metacarpal (Gryfe et al. 1972). Various modifications of the simple difference between the outer and inner diameters (D and d) have been made to correct for the bone size of different individuals. Nordin (1971) compared cortical area to total bone area $[(D^2 - d^2)/D^2]$ while Exton-Smith et al. (1969) have introduced the length of the metacarpal into the denominator to compensate for skeletal size $[(D^2 - d^2)/DL]$. All these give reasonable correlation with post-mortem assessment of bone ash and other more complex methods of assessing changes in bone mass. There are two forms of bone loss, osteoporosis and osteomalacia. Since the bone, as a whole, may be classed as a connective tissue, in the broadest sense, both forms of bone loss could be regarded as connective-tissue changes, but there are two reasons, at least, why osteoporosis should be regarded as the typical age-related condition. First, osteoporosis, by definition, entails the loss of total bone mass—hydroxyapatite and bone matrix together, whereas in osteomalacia only the calcium phosphate is lost. Secondly, osteoporosis is a progressive condition whereas osteomalacia may occur at any age and may be due to any one of a number of causes. In the elderly osteomalacia is caused by calcium imbalance brought about either by vitamin-D deficiency or by faulty diet and hence may be regarded as only secondarily age dependent. The two conditions are often difficult to separate in the elderly, however, and in advanced age it may be more appropriate to refer to the composite syndrome as osteopenia, or bone loss.

Nordin and Exton-Smith et al. have shown that bone mass increases up to age 30–40 in both males and females. Thereafter the metacarpal index falls by about 2% per year in the case of males and 6% per year in the case of females. Hall et al.

1974) have shown that the collagen loss which accompanies bone loss is mirrored
y similar changes in soft-tissue collagen. Thus, not only is there a loss in skin
ollagen associated with the normal osteoporotic loss of bone, but where the bone
ɔss is greater than might be expected for a group of subjects of a given age, the
kin collagen is also lower than normal (*Fig.* 4.21). If the collagen content of skin is

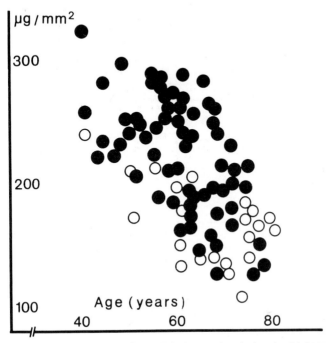

ig. 4.21. The reduction in the collagen content of the human female dermis with increasing age. The
alues are expressed in terms of µg per column of full skin thickness beneath an area of 1 mm² of skin
urface.

ɔlotted against a measurement of the degree of osteoporosis and horizontal and
ɼertical lines drawn through the mean values for each parameter, it can be seen
hat *c.*85% of subjects having below-average values for each, i.e. in the lower left
1and quadrant, are those with this abnormally high degree of osteoporosis who
ɔresent with low back pain, microfractures and collapsed end plates in the
ɼertebral bodies (*Fig.* 4.22).

Changes in articular cartilage are dependent on a variety of factors, such as age,
ɡeometry, load-bearing capacity and the dimensions of the contact zone. Gardner
1978) has stated that 'it appears certain that age-related alterations in surface
ϧtructure are not simply the result of normal or excessive joint use'. Hall (1978)
1as pointed out that the appearance of arthrotic rugosities on the femoral heads of
ϥthletes which have often been described as traumatic damage due to over-
ɪtilization of these joints cannot be solely due to this cause. Many other athletes
nistreat their joints to an equal or greater extent and do not suffer damage to their

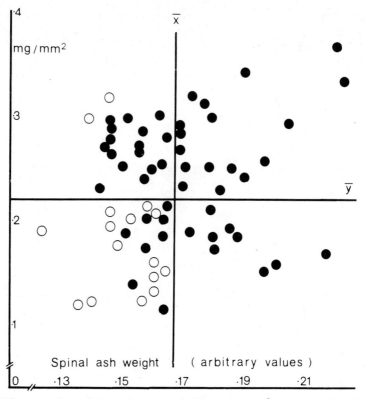

Fig. 4.22. The comparison of the total amount of collagen (mg/mm²) present in the skin of female subjects with arbitrary values (spinal ash weight) relating to the degree of osteoporosis. The horizontal ($\bar{y}$) and vertical ($\bar{x}$) lines represent the mean values for these two parameters. Closed circles represent individuals with a degree of osteoporosis typical of their age group. Open circles are for subjects presenting with low back pain, micro-fractures and collapsed end plates in the vertebral bodies and a degree of osteoporosis higher than that typical of their age groups.

cartilaginous surfaces. Damage which is almost as great can be observed on the surface of cartilages taken from the joints of subjects who, compared with the athletes, have led an almost sedentary existence. The appearance of very marked superficial irregularities on the cartilage in the case of athletes must be due to the simultaneous effect of two factors, one traumatic, one endogenous. The endogenous factor would appear to be age related and in all probability reflects the failure of the balance between catabolic and anabolic systems.

These age-related irregularities can be measured by optical means used to assess the smoothness of engineering surfaces (*Fig.* 4.23), or by the scanning electron microscope. The latter indicates the presence of perichondrocytic lacunae beneath the surface. These may 'break out' and form the early phases of more generalized surface irregularities.

Degenerative changes such as those seen in osteoarthrosis of the joints of the limbs are also frequently encountered in old age in the apophyseal and vertebral

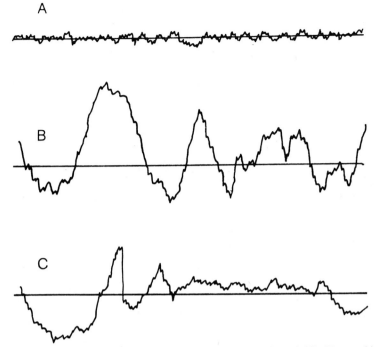

Fig. 4.23. Surface irregularities of (A) normal young, (B) arthrosic and (C) 65-year-old articular cartilages. The vertical dimensions are magnified 100 × those parallel to the surface of the tissue.

joints. In the latter, degeneration of the vertebral discs themselves complicates the picture.

De Palma and Rothman (1970) and Vernon-Roberts and Pirie (1977) have reported that all human spines from subjects aged 40 years and over show some degree of degeneration of the discs of either the lumbar or cervical regions. The major chemical changes are associated with alterations in the glycosaminoglycan content and consequent alterations in water content, especially of the nucleus pulposus. Galante (1967) and Gower and Pedrini (1969) have reported that both the nucleus pulposus and the annulus fibrosus lose water on ageing (the former by 17% between 4 and 76, the latter by 5%) (Gower and Pedrini). Hall and Reed (1973) however, although confirming the dehydration of the nucleus (26% in 90 years) report a 30% increase in the water content of the annulus until at 90 years of age the moisture content was constant throughout the whole disc at about 2 to 3 times the dry weight of the other constituents. This consolidation of the nucleus does not permit the disc to transmit vertical pressure on the end plate evenly to the peripheral collagen fibres in the annulus with the result that this portion of the disc suffers from an unequal pressure distribution. Since the change in the physical properties of the nucleus is progressive with age, it might be expected that the incidence of prolapse would also be directly age-dependent. There is, however, a peak of incidence at about age 40–50 and hence it must be assumed that changes take place in the annulus which tend to strengthen that part of the disc and that these become operative at ages above that at which the dehydration of the nucleus assumes its greatest importance. Hall and Reed (1973) showed that although the amount of collagen in the nucleus rises by only 0·075% per year throughout life the collagen in the annulus, after remaining constant throughout the early part of life, increases by nearly 1% per year during later life. This presumably strengthens the annulus and makes it possible for that portion of the disc to resist localized forces transmitted laterally through the dehydrated nucleus.

4.12.3 *Cardiovascular System*

Atherosclerotic changes in the vascular tissue and the age changes which develop alongside them are often difficult to distinguish from one another. Walton (1978) has reviewed the relationship of age and atherosclerosis and has remarked that the WHO Study Group (1958) was unable to record agreement on the sequence in which the various changes occur in the intima during the evolution of the fully developed plaque. Plaques have been noted to be especially prevalent at sites of bifurcation, in bends, and in arteries which are relatively immobilized, but can be induced in other sites by a variety of traumatic incidents involving the integrity of the endothelial lining and more especially from the point of view of connective-tissue involvement by localized disruption of the intimal membrane and/or those elastic lamellae of the media proximal to the lumen. Gerö et al. (1967) have noted small elevations of the mucoid substance in the intimal surface at those sites where atherosclerotic lesions are known to be likely to develop. However, studies on the overall distribution and synthesis of glycosaminoglycans in human arterial tissue have provided very inconsistent results. Although the sulphated glycans—chondroitin, dermatan and heparin sulphate—have been shown to increase in amount in advanced age at the expense of hyaluronic acid, and measurement of the incorporation of ^{35}S-sulphate into the sulphated glycosaminoglycans shows that increased synthesis of such compounds accompanies the onset of atherosclerosis, the metabolic activity of the enzyme systems which perform such synthetic reactions is reduced in old age (Buddecke et al., 1973). It can, however, be calculated (Hall, 1976) from Buddecke's observations (which were on cattle) if the reduction in sulphate incorporation is plotted against DNA concentration, that each cell retains its synthetic activity almost unimpaired throughout life remaining within 8% of its mean value until the eighth year of life and only falling by approximately 11% thereafter.

Gerö et al. (1960) suggested that the sulphated glycosaminoglycans (referred to as acid mucopolysaccharides at that time) form coacervates with lipid, which penetrate the vessel wall, retaining it, and modifying the physical properties of the vascular tissue. Saxl and Hall (1967) suggested that part, at least, of the reason for lipid retention in the vessel wall was its attachment to partially degraded elastin. The changes which they observed, however, might also be due to the presence of glycosaminoglycans. Injecting cholesterol-fed chickens with relatively crude prep-

rations of elastase, which might also have contained lipases, and studying
sections of the vascular wall in the electron microscope, they were able to observe
the alignment of lipid-staining particles along the incipiently degenerate elastic
fibres with the appearance of elasto-lipoprotein complexes. It appears likely that,
although the development of the aortic plaques in atherosclerosis is mainly due to
the insudation of lipid, the retention of the lipid is dependent on age-related
alterations in some component, either glycan or protein in the tissue itself.

4.12.4 *The Lungs*

Age changes which are apparent in the major bones of the skeleton can also be
observed in the rib cage—decalcification of the ribs and calcification of the costal
cartilage. When taken together with the significant degree of kyphosis which is
apparent in over 68% of subjects aged 75 and over (Edge et al., 1964), these
anatomical changes result in a marked reduction in pulmonary efficiency. The
lungs themselves become atrophied with age, the thickness of the alveolar walls
and the number of capillaries being reduced. Although there is an increase in the
total elastin content of the lung, this appears to be restricted to the pleura and
septa, there are no apparent age-related quantitative changes in the elastin or
collagen components of other areas of the lung. The functioning of the elastic
network, however, is impaired. The vital capacity falls progressively with increasing age as does the forced expired volume (Morris et al., 1971). There are also
changes in the distribution of pulmonary activity throughout the lung tissue. In
young subjects the regions furthest from the trachea are preferentially ventilated
whereas this is not the case in the elderly, especially when the subject is breathing
gently. When the breathing is forced, however, the difference between young and
old is reduced. Turner et al. (1968) have suggested that the closure of the deeper
areas of the lung in the elderly is associated with a reduction in elastic recoil of the
tissue.

Various diseases of the pulmonary organs are related to anatomical and
functional changes in lung tissue. This is especially true of emphysema where
permanent structural changes in the smaller airways, possibly due to a loss of
support for their walls, results in obstruction. The elastin content of the alveolar
tissue changes with increasing age, probably due to an increase in the level of
circulating elastase or a reduction in the plasma inhibitor.

4.12.5 *Special Organs*

In essentially cellular organs such as the liver, the kidney and the pancreas, one is
less likely to consider diseases of the connective tissues as being of major
significance, but the scaffolding which locates the various cell types in their spatial
relationships one with the other is collagenous and any changes in quantity or
nature of this scaffold will alter the rate at which metabolic intermediates, which

may be required for the overall development of a chain of metabolic processes and which are synthesized by one type of cell, are passed to another. The fibrotic changes associated with cirrhosis of the liver, for instance, in addition to reducing the cell content of the tissue, interpose new and thickened connective tissue between the remaining cells. Thus, however effective for instance, the lipid metabolism of any individual liver cell may be, the transfer of lipid to the appropriate hepatic blood vessel is impaired and the net result is the retention of lipid within the organ. Fatty livers may induce fibrosis, but once this has occurred the retention of lipid is exacerbated. Similarly, fibrotic degeneration of the kidney can impair both glomerular filtration and tubular resorption, rendering the functioning of the kidney less than optimal. The changes which take place in the eye are numerous and differ from one another in the various specialized regions of the organ. Accommodation, which is the ability to alter the focal length of the lens by contraction of the ciliary muscles, decreases twelve-fold with increasing age over the span 10–50 years. Although this may represent a failure on the part of the muscles themselves, it may indicate the progressive infiltration of the muscle by connective-tissue fibres which in youth are restricted to the sarcolemmal sheath. The lens, itself, consists of the capsule which is essentially connective tissue containing the soluble proteins of the crystalline. The lens increases in thickness from 3·7 mm to 5·1 mm between 20 and 80 years of age (Leighton and Tomlinson 1972). Deposition of fibrous protein, which is not associated with any concomitant removal, provides the material to account for this increase in thickness. This may also explain why the elderly eye becomes relatively rigidly fixed in a flattened long focus state. Kefalides (1969) and Spiro and Fukushi (1969) isolated a protein with the composition of collagen from lens capsule, but, in contrast to collagens from other sites, it contained hydroxyproline-bound glycans, consisting of glucose and galactose. Other fractions containing sialic acid, fucose and glycosaminoglycans were also observed. In the normal eye these collagen molecules are incapable of precipitation, and it may be the location of these polysaccharide-coupled-to-hydroxylysine residues which prevents registration of the α-chains in such a manner as to permit covalent cross-linkages being formed.

The vitreous, filling the region between the lens and the retina and acting as a shock absorber, is, according to Balazs (1968), similar in structure to the intervertebral disc. The outer layers of the vitreous consist of a fibrous mesh in which cells are embedded. These fibres resemble collagen in amino acid composition, but do not appear to have the typical 64 nm cross-striations which are typical of collagen from other sites in the body. They are cross-striated at 12–25 nm intervals in a fashion similar to fetal connective tissues (Schwarz, 1961). Since the 64 nm repeat is associated with the quarter-stagger lateral alignment of the tropocollagen molecules, it may well be that the high concentrations of polysaccharide in this tissue (a galactoglucan similar to that in the capsule, Dische and Zelmanes, 1955) is responsible for the inability of the tropocollagen to precipitate in the typical native 64 nm repeating form.

Cataract may be due (Sippel, 1965) to a decreased metabolic activity of the lens with increasing age. As the lens increases in size relative to surface area, the central rea, being further from the peripheral capillary bed, is starved of nutrient material nd high molecular weight components can no longer be held in solution. This ould explain nuclear sclerosis where only the central portion of the lens suffers om decreased transparency but not those situations in which the whole lens ecomes opaque. One aspect of the changing metabolism of the lens is a reduction the concentration of glutathione, a glutamic acid, cysteine, glycine tripeptide, hich because of its ability to form cystine-bound dimers on oxidation acts as a ntroller of oxidative processes in the body. Blackett and Hall (1980) have shown at another anti-oxidant α-tocopherol (vitamin E) has a role to play in the tention of a 'young' form of collagen in 'middle-aged' mice.

Ocular changes are often observed in diabetes and it has become increasingly pparent that the collagen of diabetic animals and human subjects is characterized y changes in structure and susceptibility to enzymes which are normally ssociated with individuals of greater chronological age (Kohn and Hawkin, 1978; ehera and Patnaik, 1979, 1981a, b). It may well be that some, at least, of the bserved changes in the structure and function of the eye in diabetes are related to nanges in the underlying structure and metabolism of the collagen in the various abstructures of the organ.

.12.6 *Wound Healing*

Vound healing consists of a number of separate phases, the stoppage of blood ow, the inflammatory reaction, fibrogenesis and the reabsorption of scar tissue.

When the circulating blood comes in contact with the cut surface of a wound, ne platelets carried in it come into contact with collagen and/or elastin, and ndergo a disc to sphere transformation and send out pseudopodia (Barnhart et l., 1972). After adhering to one another, either because of the interaction between latelet-carried galactosyl hydroxylsyl-glucosyl transferase and hydroxylysyl-ound galactose on the α_1 (1) CB6 peptide of collagen (Fauvel et al., 1978) or not Kivirikko and Myllylä, 1979; Menashi and Grant, 1979) the platelets release ADP hich brings about their aggregation and hence initiates the fibrin/platelet plug hich stops further loss of blood. The transformed platelets may also release imulators of fibroblast mitogenesis (Ross et al., 1974) thus potentiating the absequent synthesis of collagen fibres. Several authors have reported that the bility of collagen to induce platelet aggregation decreases with the age of the ollagen (Bankowski et al., 1967, 1969; Legrand and Pignaud, 1971). Thus, the fact nat the morphology of the platelets is not modified due to changes in the latelet–collagen interaction, may represent the first stage of an age-induced failure f wound healing. The development of an inflammatory reaction would appear to e due to the body's immunological response to partial degradation products of ne tissue and the degree to which this occurs will be dependent on the usceptibility of the connective-tissue components to attack by endogenous roteolytic enzymes—collagenase, elastase, cathepsins, etc.

As mentioned earlier, the synthesis of collagen in its native form is associated with the availability of enzymes and co-factors which permit the hydroxylation c residues in the procollagen and the absence of any one of these elements results i the production of defective collagen with inadequate mechanical properties. Thes systems are present not only in the fibroblasts, but also in the macrophages whic congregate at the site of the wound (Myllylä and Seppä, 1979). Since both ce number and cell activity are inversely related to age (Schmidt and Beneke, 1971) is immediately apparent that increasing age might be expected to reduce the degre of hydroxylation and hence the structural stability of newly-synthesized collage Uitto (1971), for instance, has demonstrated that the concentration of procollage proline hydroxylase in human skin falls by 86% over the first 60 years of life an that this is accompanied by an 80% reduction in the amount of acid-solub collagen.

The timing of the repair process varies with age. This has been demonstrate experimentally in studies of granuloma formation (Nemetschek, 1970; Heikkine et al., 1971). The chronological changes in metabolic activity of granulom tissue—which includes synthesis of collagen, oxygen consumption and activities c enzymes of the Kreb's cycle—show marked age-related differences following th implantation of a polyvinyl sponge (Heikkinen, 1973). Activity is optimal in youn animals about 3 weeks after implantation, whereas the peak in older animals is nc reached until 4 or more weeks have passed. Moreover, the activity of th granuloma is some 50% higher in the young animals and the peak is much mor acute, that of the old group rising more slowly to a lower, flatter peak. Simila results can be observed in the healing wound, but with greater difficulty becaus the newly-synthesized tissue is intermingled with that which originally formed th intact tissue before wounding, whereas the granuloma tissue is segregated from it surroundings.

4.13 Conclusions

Connective-tissue ageing is a very complex phenomenon since not only d connective tissues in various sites in the body have very different functions an hence the effect of ageing manifests itself in many different ways, but also n connective tissue consists entirely of collagen, elastin or glycosaminoglycan, an each component ages independently. Moreover, even in the case of collagen, itsel ageing manifests itself in a variety of ways; the type of collagen in a tissue ma change, Type III being replaced by Type I or vice-versa, cross-linkages may b formed and degradative changes may occur. The idea that cross-link formation i collagen can account for most of the age changes in connective tissue is now nc widely accepted, but even this is an over-simplification. Cross-link formation ma be a function of maturation and may enhance the normal functioning of one orga whilst detracting from the effective functioning of another (Table 4.7). Tissue which rely on tensile strength for their function are more likely to exhibit greate effectiveness when the number of cross-links between collagen molecules increase whereas those which require the collagen to remain in solution to provide th

Table 4.7. **The effect of increasing numbers of cross-links on the potential physiological effectiveness of individual connective tissues**

Tissue		
Dermis	Increased tone	
Vascular tissue	Enhanced compliance	Advantageous
Tendon	Greater tensile strength	
Lens	Greater opacity	
Stroma of larger organs	Reduced transport with cells	Deleterious

particular properties which are characteristic of their structure will be less effective if cross-linking increases.

Much still remains to be discovered about connective-tissue ageing and although it would not appear to occupy the prime position among age research programmes that it did some ten to fifteen years ago, enough biological and medical aspects remain unanswered to involve gerontologists for many years to come.

Recommended Reading

Connective Tissue and Ageing edited by H. G. Vogel (Excerpta Medica, 1973) and the present author's *Ageing of Connective Tissue* (Academic Press, 1976) provide a basis for further reading on connective tissue ageing. More recent material is scattered through more general books, such as Kanungo's *Biochemistry of Ageing* (Academic Press, 1980) and Viidik's *Lectures on Gerontology* (Academic Press, 1982).

References

Bailey A. J. and Robins S. P. (1973) Cross-links in collagen fibres of skin. In: Robert L. and Robert R. (ed.) *Aging of Connective Tissues: Skin.* Basel, Karger, p. 130.

Balazs E. A. (ed.) (1968) *Chemistry and Molecular Biology of the Intercellular Matrix.* Vol. 3. New York, Academic Press.

Balo J. and Banga I. (1949) The destruction of elastic fibres of vessel walls. *Schweiz. Z. Pathol. u. Bakteriol.* **12**, 350.

Banga I. (1966) *Structure and Function of Elastin and Collagen.* Budapest, Akademiai Kiado.

Banga I. and Ardelt W. (1967) Studies on the elastolytic activity of sera. *Biochim. Biophys. Acta* **146**, 284.

Bankowski E., Niewiarowski S. and Galasinski W. (1967) Platelet aggregation by human collagen in relation to its age. *Gerontologia* **13**, 219.

Bankowski E., Niewiarowski S. and Rogowski W. (1969) Decrease of platelet aggregating activity of soluble human collagen fractions during ageing. *Thromb. Diath. Haemorrh.* **21**, 441.

Barnhart M. I., Wash R. I. and Robinson J. A. (1972) A three-dimensional view of platelet responses to chemical stimuli. *Ann. NY Acad. Sci.* **201**, 360.

Beachey E. H., Chiang T. M. and Kang A. H. (1979) Collagen-platelet interaction. In: Hall D. A. and Jackson D. S. (ed.) *International Review of Connective Tissue Research.* Vol. 8. New York, Academic Press.

Behera H. N. and Patnaik B. K. (1979) *In vivo* and *in vitro* effects of alloxan on collagen characteristics of bone, skin and tendon in Swiss mice. *Gerontology* **25**, 255.

Behera H. N. and Patnaik B. K. (1981a) Increased stability of collagen following alloxan diabetes in Swiss mice. *Gerontology* **28**, 163.

Behera H. N. and Patnaik B. K. (1981b) The effect of alloxan diabetes on the characteristics of collagen of cotton pellet granuloma and dorsal skin of Swiss mice. *Gerontology* **27**, 209.

Blackett A. D. and Hall D. A. (1980) The action of vitamin E on the ageing of connective tissue. *Mech. Ageing Dev.* **14**, 305.

Buddecke E., Segeth G. and Kresse H. (1973) Age-dependent changes of ^{14}C- and ^{35}S- incorporatio
    in ox aorta glycosaminoglycans. In: Vogel H. G. (ed.) *Connective Tissues and Ageing*. Amsterdam
    Excerpta Medica, p. 62.
Buddecke E. and Sziegoleit M. (1964) Isolation, chemical concentration and age-related fractionatio
    of mucopolysaccharides from human intervertebral discs. *Hoppe Seyler Z. Physiol. Chem.* **337**, 6(
Chatterjee J. (1975) Plasma elastase levels in the elderly. *Age Ageing* **4**, 129.
Craciun E. C. (1974) Fibroblast activity related to human pure senescence versus human commo
    senescence. *Proc. 4th Eur. Symp. Basic Res. Gerontol.* p. 41.
De Palma A. F. and Rothman R. H. (1970) *The Intervertebral Disc*. Philadelphia, Saunders.
Dische Z. and Zelmanes G. (1955) Polysaccharides of the vitreous fibers. *A.M.A. Arch. Ophthal.* 5·
    528.
Edge J. R., Millard F. J. C., Reid L. et al. (1964) The radiographic appearance of the chest in persons c
    advanced age. *Br. J. Radiol.* **37**, 769.
Ejiri I. (1936) Studies on the histology of human skin, I, II and III. *Jap. J. Dermatol. Urol.* **40**, 46, 17:
    216.
Ejiri I. (1937) Studies on the histology of human skin, IV and V. *Jap. J. Dermatol. Urol.* **41**, 64, 95
Elridi S. S. and Hall D. A. (1976) Isolation of elastase from human serum. *Biochem. Soc. Trans.* **4**, 33(
Epstein E. H. (1974) α_1 (III)$_3$ Human skin collagen. *J. Biol. Chem.* **249**, 3375.
Exton-Smith A. N., Millard P. H., Payne P. R. et al. (1969) Method for measuring quantity of bon
    Lancet **2**, 1153.
Eyre D. R. (1979) Biochemistry of the intervertebral disc. In: Hall D. A. and Jackson D. S. (ed.
    International Reviews of Connective Tissue Research. Vol. 8. New York, Academic Press, p. 237.
Fauvel F., Legrand Y., Kuhn K. et al. (1978) Platelet-collagen interaction: adhesion of human bloo
    platelets to purified CB$_4$ peptide from Type III collagen. *Thromb. Res.* **12**, 273, 841.
Foster J. A., Gray W. R. and Franzblau C. (1974) Isolation and characterisation of cross-linke
    peptides from elastin. *J. Biol. Chem.* **249**, 6191.
Fujii K., Kaboki Y. and Sasaki S. (1976) Ageing of human bone and articular cartilage collager
    changes in the reducible cross-links and their precursors. *Gerontology* **22**, 363.
Galante J. O. (1967) Tensile properties of the human lumbar annulus fibrosus. *Acta Orthop. Scanc*
    Suppl. 100, 1.
Gardner D. L. (1978) Aging of articular cartilage. In: Brocklehurst J. C. (ed.) *Textbook of Geriatr*
    Medicine and Gerontology. Edinburgh, Churchill Livingstone, p. 524.
Geokas M. C., Wilding P., Rinderknecht H. et al. (1967) Determination of elastase in mammalia
    plasma and serum. *J. Clin. Invest.* **46**, 1059.
Gëro S., Gergely J., Devenji T. et al. (1960) Role of mucoid substances of the aorta in the deposition c
    lipids. *Nature* **187**, 152.
Gëro S., Virag S., Bihari-Varga M. et al. (1967) Role of mucopolysaccharides in the deposition an
    metabolism of lipids. *Prog. Biochem. Pharmacol.* **2**, 290.
Gillman T., Penn J., Bronks D. et al. (1955) Abnormal elastic fibres. *Arch. Pathol.* **59**, 733.
Gower W. E. and Pedrini V. (1969) Age-related variations in protein polysaccharides from huma
    nucleus pulposus, annulus fibrosus and costal cartilage. *J. Bone Joint Surg.* **51**, 1154.
Greiling H. and Bauman G. (1973) Age-dependent changes of non-sulphated disaccharide groups in th
    proteoglycans of knee joint cartilage. In: Vogel H. G. (ed.) *Connective Tissues and Ageing*
    Amsterdam, Excerpta Medica, p. 160.
Gryfe C. I., Exton-Smith A. N. and Stewart R. J. C. (1972) Determination of the amount of bone in th
    metacarpal. *Age Ageing* **1**, 213.
Hall D. A. (1959) Fibrous components of connective tissue with special reference to the elastic fibre. *In
    Rev. Cytol.* **8**, 211.
Hall D. A. (1965) Age changes in the levels of elastase and its inhibitor in human plasma. *Gerontolog*
    14, 97.
Hall D. A. (1966) The identification and estimation of elastase in serum and plasma. *Biochem. J.* **10**
    29.
Hall D. A. (1969) The effect of mechanical stress on the properties of reconstituted collagen. *Biochem.*
    117, 69.
Hall D. A. (1970) Co-ordinately bound calcium as a cross-linking agent in elastin and as an activatio
    of elastolysis. *Gerontologia* **16**, 325.
Hall D. A. (1971) The structure of elastic fibers. In: Elden H. R. (ed.) *Biophysical Properties of the Ski*
    New York, Wiley, Interscience, p. 187.
Hall D. A. (1976) *Ageing of Connective Tissue*. London, Academic Press.
Hall D. A. (1978) Why do joints degenerate? *Spectrum* **21**, 33.

Hall D. A. (1981) The ageing of collagenous tissues: genetic and random effects. *J. Clin. Exp. Gerontol.* 3, 201.

Hall D. A., Blackett A. D., Zajac A. R. et al. (1981) Changes in skinfold thickness with increasing age. *Age Ageing* 10, 19.

Hall D. A., Middleton R. S. W. and Zajac A. R. (1980a) Related age changes in the elastase and lipid contents of normal and hemiplegic subjects of various ages. *Mech. Ageing Dev.* 14, 293.

Hall D. A., Middleton R. S. W., Elridi S. S. et al. (1980b) Serum elastase levels following stroke in elderly subjects. *Gerontology* 26, 167.

Hall D. A. and Reed F. B. (1973) Protein/polysaccharide relationships in tissues subjected to repeated stress throughout life. II. The intervertebral disc. *Age Ageing* 2, 218.

Hall D. A., Reed F. B., Nuki G. et al. (1974) The relative effects of age and corticosteroid therapy on the collagen profiles of dermis from subjects with rheumatoid arthritis. *Age Ageing* 3, 15.

Hall D. A., Slater R. S. and Tesal S. (1973) The use of elastolytic enzymes as probes in the study of ageing in aortic tissue. *Proc. Workshop Conf. on Connective Tissue Ageing, Ulm.* Amsterdam, Excerpta Medica, p. 47.

Happey F., Naylor A., Palframan J. et al. (1974) In: Fricke R. and Hartman F. (ed.) *Connective Tissues: Biochemistry and Pathophysiology.* Berlin, Springer Verlag, p. 67.

Harkness M. L. R., Harkness R. D. and McDonald D. A. (1957) Collagen and elastin content of the arterial wall in the dog. *Proc. R. Soc. (Ser. B)* 146, 541.

Heikkinen E. (1973) Ageing of interstitial collagen. In: Robert L. and Robert B. (ed.) *Ageing of Connective Tissues—Skin.* Basel, Karger, p. 107.

Heikkinen E., Aalto M., Vihersaari T. et al. (1971) Age factor in the formation and metabolism of experimental granulation tissue. *J. Gerontol.* 26, 294.

Hilz H., Erich C. and Glaubitt D. (1963) Veränderungen von Zelldichte und Polysaccharidstoffwechsels im alternden Bindegewebe. (Alterations in cell thickness and polysaccharide metabolism in ageing connective tissues.) *Klin. Wochenschr.* 41, 332.

Jacob F. and Monod J. (1961) Genetic regulatory mechanisms in the synthesis of proteins. *J. Mol. Biol.* 3, 318.

Jacotot B., Beaumont J. L., Monnier G. et al. (1973) Role of elastic tissue in cholesterol deposition in the arterial wall. *Nutr. Metab.* 15, 46.

Jagenburg O. R. (1959) The urinary excretion of free amino acids and other amino compounds by the human. *Scand. J. Clin. Lab. Invest.* 11, Suppl. 43.

Keech M. K. (1954) The effect of collagenase and trypsin on collagen. *Anat. Rec.* 119, 139.

Kefalides N. A. (1969) The chemistry and structure of basement membranes. *Arthritis Rheum.* 12, 427.

Kissmeyer A. and With C. (1922) Chemical and histological studies on the pathological changes in the elastic tissues of the skin. *Br. J. Dermatol.* 4, 175.

Kivirikko K. I. (1970) Urinary excretion of hydroxyproline in health and disease. In: Hall D. A. and Jackson D. S. (ed.) *International Reviews of Connective Tissue Research. Vol. 5.* New York, Academic Press, p. 93.

Kivirikko K. I. and Myllylä R. (1979) Collagen glycosyltransferases. In: Hall D. A. and Jackson D. S. (ed.) *International Reviews of Connective Tissue Research. Vol. 8.* New York, Academic Press, p. 23.

Kohn R. R. and Hawkin C. R. (1978) Genetic effects on aging collagen with special reference to diabetes mellitus. *Birth Defects* 14, 387.

Koob T. J., Jeffrey J. J. and Elsen A. Z. (1974) Regulation of human skin collagenase activity by hydrocortisone and dexamethasone in organ culture. *Biochem. Biophys. Res. Commun.* 61, 1083.

Kramsch D. M., Franzblau C. and Hollander W. (1971) The protein and lipid composition of arterial elastin and its relationship to lipid accumulation in the atherosclerotic plaque. *J. Clin. Invest.* 50, 1666.

Kramsch D. M., Franzblau C. and Hollander W. (1974) Components of the protein lipid complex of arterial elastin: their role in the retention of lipid in atherosclerotic lesions. *Adv. Exp. Med. Biol.* 43, 193.

Kramsch D. M., Hollander W. and Franzblau C. (1970) The role of arterial elastin in the lipid accumulation in human atherosclerotic arteries, In: Jones R. J. (ed.) *Atherosclerosis 2nd Int. Symp.* New York, Springer-Verlag, p. 115.

Kurkinen M., Alitalo K., Hedman, K. et al. (1980) Fibronectin, precollagen and the pericellular matrix in normal and transformed fibroblast cultures. In: Viidik A. and Vuust J. (ed.) *Biology of Collagen.* London, Academic Press, p. 223.

Kurkinen M., Alitalo K., Vaheri A. et al. (1979) Fibronectin in the development of embryonic chick eye. *Dev. Biol.* 69, 589.

Labella F. S., Vivian S. and Thornhill D. P. (1966) Amino acid composition of human aortic elastin as influenced by age. *J. Gerontol.* **21**, 550.

Lansing A. I. (1955) Ageing of elastic tissue and the systemic effects of elastase. In: Wolstenholme C (ed.) *Symposium on Ageing.* London, Ciba Foundation, p. 88.

Lansing A. I., Blumenthal H. T. and Gray S. H. (1948) Ageing and calcification of the human coronary artery. *J. Gerontol.* **3**, 87.

Lansing A. I., Roberts E., Ramasarma G. B. et al. (1951) Changes with age in amino acid composition of arterial elastin. *Proc. Soc. Exp. Biol. Med.* **76**, 714.

Lansing A. I., Rosenthal T. B. and Alex M. (1950) Significance of medial changes in human pulmonary arteries. *J. Gerontol.* **5**, 386.

Layman D. L., Epstein E. H., Dodson R. F. et al. (1977) Biosynthesis of type I and type III collagen b cultured smooth muscle cells from human aorta. *Proc. Natl Acad. Sci. USA* **74**, 671.

Layman D. L. and Titus J. L. (1975) Synthesis of type I collagen by human smooth muscle cells *in vitro Lab. Invest.* **33**, 103.

Legrand Y. and Pignaud G. (1971) Some factors influencing the aggregating property of collagen. *Act Med. Scand.* Suppl. *525*, 127.

Leighton D. A. and Tomlinson A. (1972) Changes in axial length and other dimensions of the eyeba with increasing age. *Acta Opthalmol. (Copenh.)* **50**, 815.

Leutert G. and Kreutz W. (1964) Histologische Untersuchungen über die Biomorphose der mer schlichen Epiglottis. (Histological examination of age changes in human epiglottis.) *Mikr. Ana Forsch.* **72**, 96.

Linder E., Stenman S., Lehto V-P. et al. (1978) Distribution of fibronectin in human tissues an relationship to other connective tissue components. *Ann. NY Acad. Sci.* **312**, 151.

McCloskey D. I. and Cleary E. G. (1974) Chemical composition of the rabbit aorta durin development. *Circ. Res.* **34**, 828.

Matthews M. B. and Glagov S. (1966) Acid mucopolysaccharide patterns in ageing human cartilage. *J Clin. Invest.* **45**, 1103.

Medawar P. B. (1952) *An Unsolved Problem of Biology.* London, Lewis.

Menashi S. and Grant M. E. (1979) Studies on the collagen glycosyltransferase activity present i platelets and plasma. *Biochem. J.* **178**, 777.

Morris J. F., Koski A. and Johnson L. C. (1971) Spirometric standards for healthy non-smoking adults *Am. Rev. Resp. Dis.* **103**, 57.

Muir L. W., Bornstein P. and Ross R. (1976) A presumptive sub-unit of elastic fiber microfibril secreted by arterial smooth muscle cells in culture. *Eur. J. Biochem.* **64**, 105.

Myllÿla R. and Seppä H. (1979) Studies on enzymes of collagen biosynthesis and the synthesis o hydroxyproline in macrophages and mast cells. *Biochem. J.* **182**, 311.

Nemetschek T. (1970) *Altern und Entwicklung.* Stuttgart, Schattauer.

Neuberger A., Perrone J. C. and Slack H. G. B. (1951) The relative metabolic inertia of tendon collage in the rat. *Biochem. J.* **49**, 199.

Nordin B. E. C. (1971) Clinical significance and pathogenesis of osteoporosis. *Br. Med. J.* **1**, 571.

O'Brien D., Bergstedt J., Butterfield J. et al. (1960) Observations on the urinary excretion of amine acids by the premature infant. *Acta Paediat.* **49**, 258.

Reuterberg J., Allam S., Brehmer U. et al. (1977) Characterization of the collagen synthesized b cultured human smooth muscle cells from foetal and adult aorta. *Hoppe Seylers Z. Physiol. Chem* **358**, 401.

Ridge M. D. and Wright V. (1965) The rheology of skin: a bioengineering study of the mechanica properties of human skin in relation to its structure. *Br. J. Dermatol.* **77**, 639.

Ridge M. D. and Wright V. (1966) The ageing of skin. *Gerontologia* **12**, 174.

Roach M. and Burton A. C. (1959) The effect of age on the elasticity of human iliac arteries. *Can. J Biochem. Physiol.* **37**, 557.

Robert B., Hornebeck W. and Robert L. (1974) Cinetique heterogène de l'interaction élastine-élastase (Heterogenous kinetics of the interaction between elastase and elastin). *Biochimie* **56**, 239.

Robins S. P., Shimokomaki M. and Bailey A. J. (1973) The chemistry of the collagen cross-links. Ag related changes in the reducible components of intact bovine collagen fibres. *Biochem. J.* **131**, 771

Ross R., Glomset J., Kariya B. et al. (1974) A platelet dependent serum factor that stimulates th proliferation of arterial smooth muscle cells *in vitro. Proc. Natl Acad. Sci. USA* **71**, 1207.

Ruiz-Torres A. (1978) Zur frage des Umsatzes und der Polymerisation des Kollagens in Bezeihung zun Alter. (Concerning the turnover and polymerisation of collagen in relation to ageing.) *Aktue Gerontol.* **7**, 549.

axl H. and Hall D. A. (1967) Elastic tissue in relation to arterial lipids. In: Blumenthal H. T. (ed.) *Cowdrys Arteriosclerosis*. Springfield, Ill., Thomas.

chmidt W. and Beneke G. (1971) Die Proliferationskinetik von Bindegewebszellen in Beziehung zum Lebensalter. (The proliferation kinetics of connective tissue cells in relation to ageing.) In: *Molekulare und Zelluläre Aspekte des Alterns*. Stuttgart, Schaltauer.

chwarz W. (1961) Electron microscopic observations of the human vitreous body. In: Smelser G. K. (ed.) *Structure of the Eye*. New York, Academic Press, p. 283.

hoshan S. (1981) Wound healing. In: Hall D. A. and Jackson D. S. (ed.) *International Reviews of Connective Tissue Research*. New York, Academic Press, p. 1.

huster S. and Bottoms E. (1963) Senile degradation of skin collagen. *Clin. Sci.* **25**, 487.

ilberberg R. and Lesker P. A. (1973) Fine structure and enzyme activity in articular cartilage of ageing male guinea pigs. In: Vogel H. C. (ed.) *Connective Tissues and Ageing*.Amsterdam, Excerpta Medica, p. 98.

ippel T. U. (1965) Energy metabolism in the lens during ageing. *Invest. Ophthalmol.* **4**, 502.

later R. S. and Hall D. A. (1973) Actinic and ageing changes in dermal proteins. *Proc. Workshop Conf. on Connective Tissue Ageing, Ulm*. Amsterdam, Excerpta Medica, p. 241.

mith J. G. jun., Davidson E. A., Sams W. H. et al. (1962) Dermal elastin in actinic elastosis and pseudoxanthoma elasticum. *Nature* **195**, 716.

piro R. G. and Fukushi S. (1969) The lens capsule. *J. Biol. Chem.* **244**, 2049.

unbridge R. E., Astbury W. T., Tattersall R. N. et al.: (1951) The effect of ageing in elastin and collagen fibres: structural and chemical studies. *J. Gerontol.* **6**, 12.

unbridge R. E. Tattersall R. N., Hall D. A. et al. (1952) The fibrous structure of normal and abnormal skin. *Clin. Sci.* **11**, 315.

urner J. M., Mead J. and Wohl M. E. (1968) Elasticity of human lungs in relation to age. *J. Appl. Physiol.* **25**, 664.

Jitto J. (1971) Collagen biosynthesis in human skin. A review with emphasis on scleroderma. *Ann. Clin. Res.* **3**, 250.

Jnna P. G. (1896) *Histopathology of the Diseases of the Skin*. (trans. Walker N.) New York, Macmillan.

aheri A., Kurkinen M., Lehto V-P. et al. (1978) Contribution of pericellular matrix proteins in cultured fibroblasts and loss in transformation. Fibronectin and procollagen. *Proc. Natl Acad. Sci. USA* **75**, 4944.

ernon-Roberts B. and Pirie C. J. (1977) Degenerative changes in the intervertebral discs of the lumbar spine and their sequelae. *Rheumatol. Rehabil.* **16**, 13.

erzar F. (1963) *Lectures on Experimental Gerontology*. Springfield, Ill., Thomas.

iidik A. (1968) A rheological model for uncalcified parallel-fibred collagenous tissue. *J. Biomech.* **1**, 3.

Valton K. W. (1978) Atherosclerosis and ageing. In: Brocklehurst J. C. (ed.) *Textbook of Geriatric Medicine and Gerontology*. Edinburgh, Churchill Livingstone, p. 89.

Vellman W. E. and Edwards J. E. (1950) Thickness of the media of thoracic aorta in relation to age. *Arch. Pathol.* **50**, 183.

Villiams G. C. (1957) Pleiotropy, natural selection and the evolution of senescence. *Evolution* **11**, 398.

Vilson P. D. (1972) Enzyme patterns in young and old mouse livers and lungs. *Gerontologia* **18**, 36.

Volinsky R. (1970) Response of the rat aortic wall to hypertension: importance of comparing absolute amounts of wall components. *Atherosclerosis* **11**, 251.

Vood C. G. (1954) Some properties of elastic tissue. *Biochim. Biophys. Acta* **15**, 311.

Voolf L. I. and Norman A. D. (1957) Urinary excretion of amino acids and sugars in early infancy. *J. Pediatr.* **50**, 271.

Vorld Health Organization (1958) Study group on classification of atherosclerotic lesions. *W.H.O. Tech. Rep. Ser.* No. 143.

u S. Y. and Blumenthal H. T. (1960) Nature of calcium-elastin binding. *Fed. Proc.* **19**, 19.

5

Metabolism and Ageing

5.1 Introduction

The metabolic processes which determine the way in which the body maintains it function, range from the intracellular synthesis of protein to the extracellula activity of enzymes, hormones, immunoglobulins and the conductive mechanism of the nervous system. Each of these is subject to modification with advancing age This not only affects the individual metabolic processes associated with eacl particular functional element, but by the interaction of one pathway with anothe also controls the overall maintenance of bodily function.
(*Fig.* 5.1).

5.2 Intracellular Ageing

5.2.1 *Protein Synthesis*

The ultimate control of all intracellular activity resides in the genetic component o the nucleus, the DNA molecule. The complex of purines, pyrimidines, deoxyribos and phosphate which together constitute the DNA molecule, does not, however comprise the whole of the physiologically active genetic material. The chromatir strands which contain the genetic information of the cell consist, in addition t DNA, of at least two protein species, the histones and the non-histone chromo somal proteins (Kornberg, 1977; Busch, 1978). There may also be a small amoun of ribose nucleic acid (RNA) which does not, however, appear to be an essentia

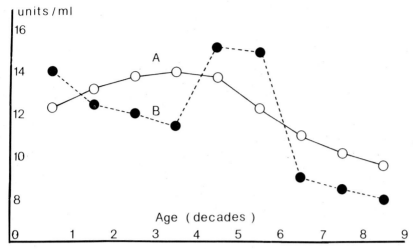

Fig. 5.1. The concentration of the enzyme elastase in the plasma of A, male, and B, female subjects (means of 5 year age groups).

structural element of the nucleoprotein. It may well be a transcriptional product of nuclear DNA retained in the nucleus to assist in protein synthesis within this particular compartment of the cell.

There are five major types of histone, H1, H2A, H2B, H3 and H4, of which the first appears to be involved in the formation of the superhelical coils of nucleosomes which are themselves constructed from the other four species of histone. The DNA in the chromatin is attached to the nucleosomes and is constrained to assume a helical structure by the H1 species of histone (*Box* 5.1).

All the histones are basic, containing appreciable amounts of lysine and arginine. H1 histone has 22 times as much lysine as arginine, whereas the ratio of these two amino acids in the other four species ranges from 2·5 : 1 to as low as 0·72 : 1. Their fundamental basicity provides the means whereby they form ionic linkages with DNA molecules, usually in a 1 : 1 ratio. This quantitative relationship between DNA and histone remains essentially unchanged throughout life.

Non-histone chromosomal proteins (NHCP) are less specifically defined components of chromatin (Elgin and Weintraub, 1975). They do, however, apparently have an equally important role to play in gene expression and repression as have the histones. Lambropoulos and Polow (1978) have isolated about 1500 different NHCPs from glial cells by iso-electric focusing techniques. Their polydispersity in the chromatin structure may indicate their importance in determining the expression of individual genes or groups of genes.

The histones and NHCPs appear to react together so as to control the availability of regions of the chromatin strand for transcription. von Hahn and Fritz (1966) and Kurtz et al. (1974) have studied the melting points of chromatin nucleoproteins and have shown that the temperature at which melting occurs rises with increasing age. O'Meara and Hertmann (1972) reported that it becomes

BOX 5.1

Chromatin strands contain histones and non-histone chromosomal proteins (NHCP) in addition t
double stranded deoxyribose nucleic acid. Four of the five different species of histone, H2A, H2B, H
and H4 are associated together to form the nucleosomes. The fifth species, H1, together with NHC
and DNA are involved in the formation of the nucleosome super helices.

NHCPs and H1 compete with one another for sites on the DNA and in this way NHCP may brin
about the dissociation of DNA and histone necessary when gene expression occurs.

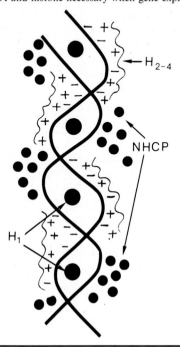

increasingly difficult to extract protein from chromatin with solutions of neutra
salt as the age of the subject from which the chromatin was derived, increased
Both these observations provide evidence for the existence of an age-dependen
increase in the number of covalent cross-linkages between DNA and protein. Th
addition of free histone to chromatin can inhibit the transcription of RNA on th
DNA template, whereas the addition of NHCP, in some instances, enhance
transcription. Since NHCP molecules have iso-electric points which vary from 3·
to 9·0 some may combine with DNA and some with histone. Such blockage of th
interactive groups in the nucleoprotein structure could result in the liberation o
DNA for transcription.

Other reactions which may control the interaction between DNA and histon
are the blockage of the ε-amino group of lysine residues by phosphorylatior
acetylation or adenylation. Steroids and calcium circulating in the plasma contrc
phosphorylation and since the presence of each of these is age modulated they ma
provide the stimulus which liberates DNA from histone prior to transcriptior

Balhorn et al. (1972) have shown that H1 histone of fetal liver is more strongly phosphorylated than that of the adult.

Cortisol controls the acetylation of chromosomal proteins (Allfrey, 1965, 1966), increasing the number of basic centres which are blocked and increasing RNA synthesis, as also does oestradiol (Libby, 1968; Hamilton et al., 1968). Hormone concentrations in the plasma decrease with age (*see* p. 147) and it is not surprising therefore that gene expression and RNA transcription are also affected by age.

Methods are being developed for the identification of the specific RNA molecules which result from the expression of individual genes, but as yet they have not been applied systematically to a variety of ageing cell lines. It is, therefore, necessary to identify the activities of individual genes by studies of the proteins, the synthesis of which they control.

.2.2 *Enzymes and Ageing*

Enzyme systems have provided the most useful tool for study in this respect. In view of their globular structure they tend to be soluble, easily extractable and easily purifiable and because of their physiological function, easily assayable. Reductions can be observed in the case of various enzymes with increasing age (Wilson, 1972, 1973; Kanungo, 1980), thus confirming that there is a decline in protein synthesis, at least in those cells in which these specific enzymes are produced.

In experimental animals, the enzymes of individual tissues can be isolated and assessed, but this is not universally possible in human subjects and much of our knowledge of changes occurring with increasing age in our own species is dependent on estimations of the amounts of enzyme present in the plasma. The level of any particular enzyme in the circulation is dependent on the rate of synthesis by the cell in which it is produced, the rate of secretion from the cell and the presence or absence of either specific or general inhibitors in the body fluids. A typical example is the enzyme elastase (*see* p. 104) where a marked peak in plasma concentration occurs in the case of female subjects (*Fig.* 5.1) at that period in their lives when the level of circulating hormones is altering most rapidly—around the time of the menopause (Tesal and Hall, 1972).

This marked elevation of the elastase level in the plasma could be due:

a. to an increased rate of synthesis by the cells of the pancreas;

b. to an increased rate of passage from the pancreas into the circulation; or

c. to a reduction in the level of the specific elastase inhibitor present alongside the enzyme in the plasma.

Elastase is synthesized by the acinar cells of the pancreas and is normally secreted in greatest amount into the pancreatic duct, in the form of a zymogen which is then converted into the active form by proteolytic enzymes also present in the pancreatic juice. Part, however, adopts an endocrine pathway and appears in the circulation. This was first assumed by Balo and Banga (1949) and has more recently been confirmed by Elridi and Hall (1976) who isolated elastase from plasma by electrofocusing techniques.

If the elevation of elastase levels in the plasma which accompanies the menopause is due to an increased rate of synthesis, it may be expected that the peak in the plasma level should coincide with a peak in the amount of the enzyme present in the pancreas itself. Loeven (1963) demonstrated that the overall level of elastase in the pancreas fell progressively with increasing age, a phenomenon which was in complete agreement with the overall reduction of the level in the plasma. He also showed, however, that in female pancreatic tissue around the time of the menopause, the content of this enzyme was so low as to be virtually immeasurable. This fact had also been observed by Hall (1964) but at that time he had ascribed the absence of this enzyme to the fact that the subject from which he attempted to obtain the enzyme, was diabetic.

The appearance of increased amounts of elastase in the plasma around the period of the menopause when the enzyme is virtually absent from the pancreas indicates that the rate of secretion from the cells of the pancreas is greater than the rate of synthesis, resulting in a depletion of the store of enzyme in the pancreatic tissue. Therefore, although there is an overall reduction in synthesis of elastase with increasing age, in both males and females, enhanced secretion in the case of the menopausal female results in the peak level observed in the plasma at this time.

The physiological activity of the enzyme in the plasma, however, is controlled by the inhibitor which accompanies it in the circulation. This is also protein in nature being in fact an α_1-globulin and hence may be subject to a reduction in synthesis as age progresses. The mean rate of reduction of the elastase content of the plasma is 15% per decade, whereas that of the inhibitor is 20% per decade. It can been seen, therefore, that the effective activity of the enzyme in the plasma is higher in the upper age groups since the inhibitor will fail to counteract the effects of the enzyme to a progressively increasing extent as the age of the subject increases (*Fig.* 5.2).

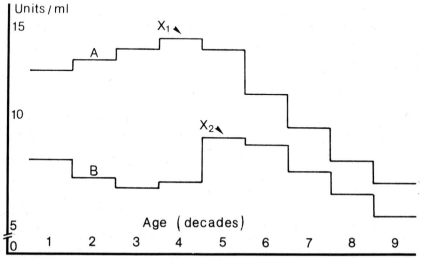

Fig. 5.2. The comparison of A, total and B, effective levels of elastase in male plasma (5 year age groups). The simultaneous presence of inhibitor moves the peak value from X_1 (35–45 years) to X_2 (45–55 years).

Balo and Banga (1949) suggested that one of the functions of the enzyme elastase might be the degradation of the elastic lamellae in the intimal and medial lamellae in the arterial walls of subjects in advanced stages of atherosclerosis. This hypothesis had in fact provided the stimulus for their original search for elastase, but the simultaneous presence of inhibitor made the acceptance of such a theory rather debatable, since in most instances the enzyme could not be assayed in plasma. The progressive reduction in inhibitor levels coupled with the peri-menopausal elevation in elastase level, however, provides a situation where the level of 'effective' enzyme assumes its highest value between 55–60 years of age, whereas the peak for males occurs some ten to fifteen years earlier. It may well be significant that this age difference is directly comparable with the age difference between the sexes in respect of the onset of clinically definable cardiovascular disease. The presence of high levels of elastase is not only associated with the preferred ages for the onset of ischaemic heart disease, but is also related to the onset of cerebrovas-cular disease. Hall et al. (1980a, b) have demonstrated that there is a marked elevation (30–40%) in the level of elastase in the plasma within 2–4 days of a cerebrovascular accident of the thrombotic type. If the patient is destined to recover from this initial stroke, the elevated level returns to the mean value for his or her age group over the ensuing three-week period. Those suffering a subsequent secondary stroke within a week to ten days demonstrate a rapid terminal increase in elastase level of between 50 and 250%. The delay occurring before peak elevation is reached, the actual percentage elevation and the rate at which the elevated level returns to normal are all age modulated (*Fig.* 5.3). It appears that the

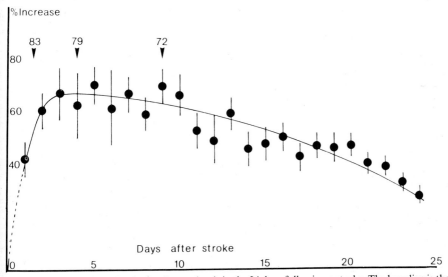

Fig. 5.3. The mean change in plasma elastase levels in the 24 days following a stroke. The base line is the mean value for normal age-matched controls. Since the first possible plasma sample could only be obtained *after* the stroke had occurred, the line joining the base value to the first mean value is dotted. The vertical lines represent the standard error of each mean. Individual peak values were attained at the arrowed points for the subject with the indicated ages.

younger the subject, the greater the elevation in elastase level which he or she can tolerate before death occurs. This may explain the changing distribution of standard error of the mean values for plasma elastase levels (*Fig.* 5.4). As age increases, those subjects with the higher elastase levels appear to die first, leaving a homogeneous group of survivors with lower plasma elastase content.

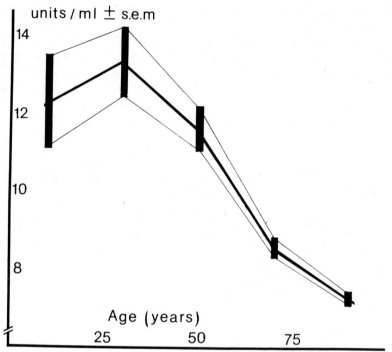

Fig. 5.4. The distribution of values for the concentration of elastase in male plasma. The vertical bars for each age group represent the standard error of each mean.

In this context, therefore, decreased protein synthesis and decreased secretion from the cells combine together to *protect* one subgroup of the population, permitting them to survive longer than their fellows.

5.3 Energy Requirements and Ageing

One of the most fundamental metabolic processes in the body is the provision of energy for normal biological function. The total energy requirement is dual in nature; first the basal metabolic requirement, and secondly that required for various forms of physical and mental activity. The basal metabolic rate of infants is relatively high compared with that of adults, a dramatic fall of about 35% occurring during the period from birth to 18 years. Thereafter the BMR does not change by more than 0·6% over the remainder of the life-span. As well as providing he basic energy for the maintenance of such bodily functions as breathing, promoting the circulation of the blood and the adequate operation of other organs of the body, the basic metabolic function of the body includes the oxidative digestion of those proteins, polysaccharides and fats, which are taken in with the diet. After a 25 g protein meal, the BMR of a 20-year-old subject rises by some 15% during the first two hours to provide an output of energy adequate for the oxidation of the protein. The level will, however, return to normal within a further three hours. A 78-year-old subject, on the other hand, requires a 26% increase in BMR to metabolize the same amount of protein. Such peak energy requirements are not attained until at least three hours after the meal and it may take as long as nine hours for the BMR to return to normal. The metabolic processes associated with digestion are, therefore, appreciably less efficient in elderly subjects and a first call on the energy content of any meal must be the enhanced energy requirement for its metabolism. The output of physical energy falls with age, partly due to an altered life-style and partly to a reduction in muscular capability. A typical group of muscles for which strength measurement can easily be obtained are those controlling the closure of the fist. Grip strength is easily assessable by means of a hand dynamometer (Shock and Norris, 1970; Shephard, 1977), and it can be seen (Fig. 5.5) that from 30 years of age onward, there is a marked decrease in grip strength. All four curves show this diminution in strength, the strongest group of muscles—in the dominant hands of male subjects—losing strength most rapidly and the least strong (female subordinate hand) diminishing least rapidly. Thus, the muscular advantage of the initially strong male is lost with ageing and a little old lady may have comparable muscular capacity as her erstwhile husky spouse.

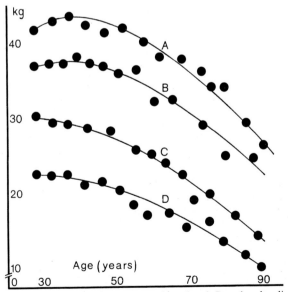

Fig. 5.5. Value for mean grip strengths of A, male dominant hand; B, male subordinate hand; C, female dominant hand, and D, female subordinate hand.

Because of the maintenance of BMR at a relatively constant level, the enhanced energy requirement for digestion and the lowered requirement for physical activity the amount whereby the caloric intake should be modified in old age is still a matter of controversy. The American *Food and Nutrition Board* of the National Academy of Sciences suggested in 1974 that intakes of 2400 kcal (10·1 megajoules and 1800 kcal (7·6 MJ) should be adequate for male and female subjects re spectively aged 51 years and over. Actual studies of daily intake in the USA suggest that, in fact, lower levels than this are normally consumed. McGandy et al. (1966 suggest that males aged 75–99 have a calorie intake of 2093 kcal/day (8·8 MJ/d whereas the survey by the US Department of Agriculture in 1965–66 gave a value of 1860 kcal/d (7·8 MJ/d) for men over 75. Since, however, McGandy et al (1966) reported a steady drop in calorie intake of 12·4 cal/d per year the value a age 51 is very close to that recommended by the National Academy of Science Lonergan et al. (1975) report slightly higher intakes for the elderly inhabitants o Edinburgh with a mean yearly decline of about 22 cal/d. These variations may be dependent on the body size of the individuals. There is not, however, any linear relationship between energy requirements and body weight for the more elderly members of the population (*Table* 5.1). As might be expected, the necessary energy intake for elderly males increases with body weight, but only up to 147 lb (74 kg) falling again at higher values. The only plausible explanation of this peak effect must be that there is a markedly reduced tendency for the more obese elderly individuals to indulge in the same degree of physical exercise as their slimmer peers.

Table 5.1. *Effect of body weight on energy requirements of males and females in the 60–90 year age group*

Body weight (kg)	Daily energy requirements (Kcal/day)	
	Males	Females
Below 50	2850	2700
50–60	2870	2830
60–70	3220	2790
70–80	2820	2810
80–90	2750	2550
90+	2200	2450

5.4 Physical Activity and Ageing

5.4.1 *Work Rate*

As mentioned earlier one of the reasons for lowered calorie intake with increasing age is a reduction in physical activity. This is a universal phenomenon over and above the reduction induced by increasing body weight mentioned in the last section. Not only is the overall strength of the muscles lowered (*Figs.* 5.5 and 5.6), but the work rate is reduced as well (*Fig.* 5·7). The reduction in work rate measured in kg.m/min is greatest when the cranking rate, using a bicycle ergometer, is lowest, falling by 37% between 30 and 80 years of age as opposed to a reduction of only 20% when the cranking rate is increased. In each case more than half of the

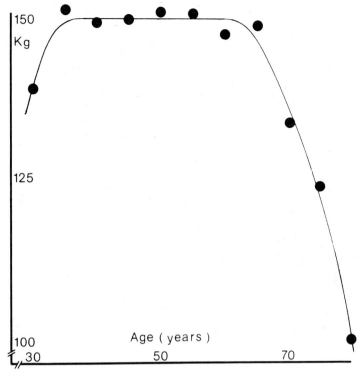

Fig. 5.6. The mean values for the strength of muscles in the arm and shoulder of male subjects aged
30–80.

reduction occurs above the age of 65. The energy expended in carrying out such
tasks is also age-dependent being, on average, 3·5% greater for elderly subjects
when an arm ergometer is used and 29% when a bicycle ergometer is employed.
(Both these tests at high cranking rates.) This difference demonstrates that the
falling away of physical activity with increasing age also varies from one muscle
system to another, and this is almost certainly the reason for a selective age-
induced failure in some sports which employ those heavily affected groups of
muscles as opposed to other sports in which 'protected' muscle groups are
operative.

5.4.2 *Neuromuscular Performance*

Age changes in muscular activity are dependent on alterations in muscle mass
(Larsson et al., 1979), neuromuscular co-ordination (Skinner et al., 1982),
muscular endurance (Frolkis et al., 1976), joint and soft-tissue flexibility (Howald
et al., 1975) and muscle metabolism.

    Changes in muscle mass are often assessed by measurements of the circum-
ference of the limbs. Thus measurements of the circumference of the upper arm

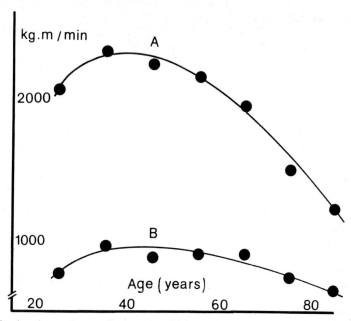

Fig. 5.7. The changing work rate of leg muscles with increasing age using a bicycle ergometer. Curve A represents the values obtained when the cranking rate was lowest; B when the cranking rate was highest.

and the thigh are taken as an indication of the muscle status of the body. However this 'mass' is dependent not only on the number of muscle fibres present in the bundle, but also on the size of the individual fibres. The atrophy which occurs in old age is due not only to a loss in the size of the muscle fibres, but also to a reduction in their number. Fibres disappear (Rowe, 1969). The strength of a muscle can be enhanced at any age by training, but this does not result in the formation or the re-formation of any loss due to ageing, but solely to an increase in size of those fibres which are present at the commencement of the training programme. Therefore, although training can repair some of the changes associated with age, it cannot reverse the ageing effect totally.

Anabolic steroids have been shown to increase muscle size by activating the appropriate cells to produce more actin and myosin. This effect is, however, dependent on the existence of an adequate number of viable cells, and if cell loss in age-atrophied muscle is considerable, the administration of steroids will not be effective in promoting the synthesis of new muscle protein.

The neuromuscular complex suffers equally with other regions of the central nervous system from changes in conduction and alterations in synaptic transmission (*see* Chapter 8). The number of neurons and their size is also reduced and their excitability threshold is raised. The nett result of these changes is an overall reduction in the efficiency of the neuromuscular network with raised reaction time and the utilization of a larger number of motor units for a given work load.

5.5 Carbohydrate Metabolism and Ageing

5.5.1 *Oxidation*

The major source of energy in the body is the oxidation of carbohydrate, fat and protein, each being degraded first into two carbon atom molecules. Then, in the form of pyruvate, they are converted into carbon dioxide and water with the liberation of energy by the operation of the enzymes of the Krebs cycle. All such oxidative processes are initially dependent on the presence and the uptake of molecular oxygen.

The uptake of oxygen from the atmosphere is dependent on fully effective lungs. Adequate inspiration is conditional on easy lung movement, a process which is restricted in the elderly by kyphosis, present in 68% of those over 75 years of age (Edge et al., 1964) and by calcification of the costal cartilage (Saltzman et al., 1963). Both these factors prevent the lungs from filling properly and reduce the volume of inhaled air. The lung tissue itself also alters with age. The elastic fibres in the elastic tissue surrounding the ducts and the mouths of individual alveoli are reduced both in number and in size, resulting in a failure to maintain the potency of the minor airways. These changes in anatomical structure coupled with a reduction in the strength of the musculature of the rib cage result in a decreased vital capacity and expired volume. Both of these fall progressively throughout life, the latter being reduced at a greater rate than the former (37% as opposed to 24·5%). Hence the replacement of oxygen-depleted air by fresh oxygen-rich air is appreciably lower in an elderly subject (aged 70+) than in a young adult. The effective uptake of oxygen across the alveolar surfaces is dependent on the percentage of the available airways which are opened with each inhalation and this is affected by posture in the elderly to a greater extent than in the young. Lower airways are preferentially closed in the seated elderly subject and conscious effort is required for the optimum utilization of this portion of the lung tissue. The difference between the oxygen levels in the alveoli and in the pulmonary arteries increases with age but this difference can be almost completely overcome by deep breathing, which can, even in the elderly, bring into play the major portion of the alveolar surface.

Oxygen is carried in the blood in combination with the haemoglobin component of the erythrocytes. Age changes in the oxygen capacity of the blood are dependent on two factors:

 a. the ageing of the individual erythrocytes; and
 b. the fact that subtle differences exist between the red cells of young and old subjects.

Red cells are synthesized in bone marrow and as this tissue is gradually converted into fatty (yellow) marrow with increasing age, its haematopoietic activity declines. In the iliac crest, for instance, the cellularity of the red marrow falls from 79% during the first decade of life to less than 38% at ages above 70. The cellular activity of even yellow marrow can, however, be stimulated by a variety of factors such as erythropoietin, hormones, anoxia, bleeding and haemolysis with the result that normal elderly subjects can respond to appreciable blood loss by initiating the synthesis of new cells at a rate which is comparable to that demonstrated by their younger counterparts (Van Dyke and Auger, 1965).

The normal erythrocyte exists in the circulation for 100–120 days passing rapidly through its own personal ageing process during the later portion of this period. Under normal circumstances dying erythrocytes are replaced quantitatively, hence any changes in function due to the ageing of individual cells has little effect on the functioning of the whole red cell mass. However, if for any reason the synthesis of erythrocytes is impaired the proportion of ageing cells in the total cell mass will be increased and its oxygen-carrying capacity reduced.

A reduction in the quantity or quality of circulating erythrocytes is accepted as a suitable definition of anaemia (Britton, 1969). Although anaemia is not an inevitable concomitant of ageing, it does occur in an appreciable proportion of individuals over 60 years of age. Hyams (1978) gathered together the results of 21 community surveys carried out during the previous two decades. Although the incidence was less than 10% in 70% of the surveys in the case of males, it was more than 20% in 35% of the groups of females. In these surveys definitions of anaemia varied slightly. Usually the erythrocyte count is towards the lower limits of the normal range of between 4·7 and 6·5 million/mm^3. A more effective definition, however, is that of the World Health Organization (1959) which recommended that a haemoglobin level of 13 g/dl should be taken as the critical criterion for anaemia. This definition permits both defective quantity and defective quality to be considered simultaneously—in both cases the net effect being a reduction in the oxygen-carrying capacity of the blood. Iron deficiency, whether it leads to anaemia or not, is very common in the elderly. Failure to assimilate iron from the gut is associated with a deficiency in the hydrochloric acid content of the stomach. Achlorhydria is increasingly prevalent in the elderly (*Table* 5.2) (Bloomfield and Pollaud, 1933) leading to iron deficiency in many subjects.

Table 5.2. *Incidence of achlorhydria at various ages (Adapted from Bloomfield and Pollaud, 1933)*

Age (years)	Incidence (rate per 1000)
20–24	53
30–39	95
40–49	167
50–59	240
60 +	354

Effective haematopoeisis is dependent on the presence in the diet and absorption from the gut of vitamin B_{12}—cobalamin. This absorption is accomplished by an intrinsic factor in the gastric mucosa. In its absence pernicious anaemia develops. Low levels of haemoglobin result in a reduction in the amount of oxygen carried to the peripheral tissues and hence in a reduction in the oxidative processes which provide the necessary energy for muscular and other activity.

The first stage in the liberation of energy in the tissues of the body takes the form of anaerobic glycolysis; the conversion of glucose (derived from glycogen stored in he cells) to pyruvate (*Fig.* 5.8). This is then followed by the decarboxylation of pyruvate by the sequence of processes which combine to form the Krebs citric acid cycle (*Fig.* 5.9) For these reactions to take place, nicotine adenine dinucleotide (NAD), adenosine diphosphate (ADP), co-enzyme A (CoA), flavine adenine dinucleotide (FAD) and numerous enzymes are required. NAD, CoA and FAD levels are dependent on the availability of nicotinic acid, pantothenic acid and riboflavin, all of which are present as vitamins in meat and vegetables. There is convincing evidence that elderly subjects may have reduced levels of nicotinic acid (Kirk, 1962), pantothenic acid (Schmidt, 1951) and riboflavin (Dymock and Brocklehurst, 1973) but only in the first and last of these is there definite evidence of frank deficiency, the blood levels being lower than those accepted as necessary for fully effective metabolism.

Of the enzymes concerned in glycolysis and in the tricarboxylic acid cycle (*Fig.* 5.9) many have been shown to be defective in old age (*Tables* 5.3, 5.4 and 5.5), a major proportion have been shown to decrease with increasing age in a variety of tissues. In some instances: phosphofructokinase, pyruvate kinase, succinate dehydrogenase, malate dehydrogenase and glucose-6-phosphatase, the amounts of enzyme in the tissue may either rise or fall with increasing age depending on the species, sex or tissue under consideration. With these marked age variations in the enzymes of glucose metabolism, it is hardly surprising that the energy production of the body becomes decreasingly efficient with increasing age.

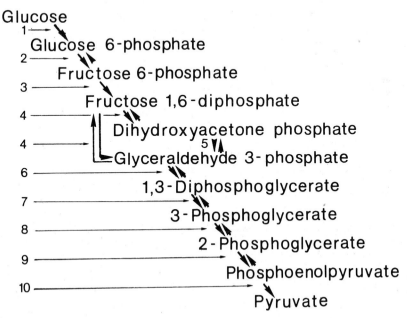

Fig. 5.8. The intermediate pathway in the conversion of glucose to pyruvate. The numbers to the left refer to the enzymes involved, as listed in *Table* 5.3.

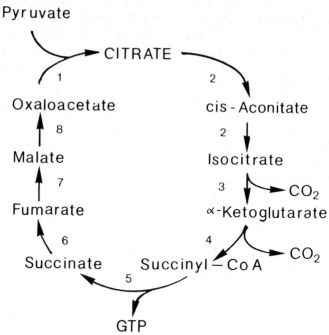

Fig. 5.9. The Krebs citric acid cycle. The numbers refer to the enzymes involved, as listed in *Table* 5.4.

Table 5.3. Reported age changes in the enzymes of the glycolysis pathway. Those systems marked with an asterisk either fail to change or are actually raised with increasing age in other tissues or animal sources. No observations are available in the case of enzymes for which the later columns are empty. The numbers preceding each entry in the Table refer to appropriate points in the scheme outlined in Fig. 5.9.

No.	Name	E. C. code	Tissue	Animal	Effect of ageing	Reference
1	Hexokinase	2.7.1.1	Aorta	Man	No change	Kirk (1957)
2	Phosphoglucose isomerase	5.3.1.9				
3	Phosphofructo-kinase	2.7.1.11	Aorta	Man	Raised	Ritz and Kirk (1967)
4	Aldolase	4.1.2.12	Sleletal muscle	Man	Reduced	Steinhagen-Thiessen and Hilz (1976)
5	Triosephosphate isomerase	5.3.1.1				
6	Glyceraldehyde-3-phosphate dehydrogenase	1.2.1.13				
7	Phosphoglycerate kinase	1.1.1.95				
8	Phosphoglycero-mutase	2.7.5.3				
9	Enolase	4.2.1.11	Aorta	Man	No change	Wang and Kirk (1959)
10*	Pyruvate kinase	2.7.1.40	Heart	Rat	Reduced	Chainy and Kanungo (1978)

*Table 5.4. **Reported age changes in the enzymes of the citric acid cycle (details as in Table 5.3)***

No.	Name	E. C. code	Tissue	Animal	Effect of ageing	References
1	Citrate synthetase	4.1.3.7				
2	Aconitase	4.2.1.2	Aorta	Man	No change	Kirk (1961)
3	Isocitrate dehydrogenase	1.1.1.42	Prostate	Mouse	Raised	Mainwaring (1968)
4	α-ketoglutarate dehydrogenase	1.2.4.2				
5	Succinyl CoA synthetase	6.2.1.4				
6*	Succinate dehydrogenase	1.3.99.1	Aorta	Man	Reduced	Kirk (1959a)
7	Fumarase	4.2.1.2	Aorta	Man	Reduced	Kirk (1959b)
8*	Malate dehydrogenase	1.1.1.37	Kidney	Rat	Reduced	Schmuckler and Burrows (1967)

*Table 5.5. **Reported changes with age in those enzyme systems involved in the mobilization of glucose from glycogen stores; glucogenesis and the pentose pathway (details in Table 5.3)***

No.	Name	E. C. code	Tissue	Animal	Change with age	Reference
1	Phosphorylase	2.4.1.1	Aorta	Man	Reduced	Kirk (1962)
2	Glycogen branching enzyme	2.4.1.18				
3	1,6,Glucoxidase	3.2.1.33				
4*	Phosphoglucomutase	2.7.5.1	Liver	Mouse	Raised	Wilson (1972
5*	Glucose-6-phosphatase	3.1.3.9	Kidney	Mouse	No change	Wilson (1972)
6	Glucose-6-phosphate dehydrogenase	1.1.1.49	Aorta	Man	Reduced	Kirk et al. (1959)
7	Phosphatase	3.1.3.1	Liver	Rat	Reduced	Barrows et al. (1962)
8	6-Phosphogluconate dehydrogenase	1.1.1.43	Prostate	Mouse	Raised	Mainwaring (1968)

5.6 Conclusions

The maintenance of all forms of bodily activity is dependent on the retention of an adequate cellular metabolism. Since cellular metabolism is progressively impaired as ageing proceeds, the functioning of organs and tissues is rendered less efficient. The changes observed may appear to be due to alterations in enzyme levels, but in effect modifications at this level of organization are not the fundamental basis of any particular ageing process but are part way along an ageing pathway that starts with the cellular DNA and may finish in some distant target organ (*see Fig.* 10.1).

Recommended Reading

The Biochemistry of Ageing, Kanungo M. S. (1980) London, Academic Press. Professor Kanungo provides two very useful chapters, relevant to the topics considered here, on nucleic acid metabolism and enzyme changes respectively.

References

Allfrey V. G. (1965) In: San Pietra A., Lamborg M. R. and Kenney F. T. (ed.) *Regulatory Mechanisms for Protein Synthesis in Mammalian Cells*. Vol. II. New York, Academic Press, p. 65.

Allfrey V. G. (1966) Structural modifications of histones and their possible role in the regulation of ribonucleic acid synthesis. *Canad. Canc. Conf.* **6**, 313.

Balhorn R., Chalkey R. and Granner D. (1972) Lysine-rich histone phosphorylation, a positive correlation with cell replication. *Biochemistry* **11**, 1094.

Balo J. and Banga I. (1949) The destruction of the elastic fibres of vessel walls. *Schweiz. Z. Pathol. u. Bakteriol.* **12**, 350.

Barrows C. and Chow B. (1959) Studies on enzymes in arterial tissue. In: Lansing A. I. (ed.) *Arterial Wall*. Baltimore, Williams & Wilkins. p. 192.

Bloomfield A. L. and Pollaud W. S. (1933) *Gastric Anacidity: its Relation to Disease*, New York, Macmillan.

Britton C. J. C. (1969) *Disorders of the Blood*, 10th ed. London, Churchill.

Busch H. (ed.) (1978) *The Cell Nucleus Chromatin Parts A & B*, Vol. IV. New York, Academic Press.

Chainy G. B. N. and Kanungo M. S. (1978) Effects of testosterone and estradiol on the activity of pyruvate kinase of the cardiac and skeletal muscles of rats as a function of age. *Biochem. Biophys. Acta* **540**, 65.

Dymock S. M. and Brocklehurst J. C. (1973) Clinical effects of water soluble vitamin supplementation in geriatric patients. *Age Ageing* **2**, 172.

Edge J. R., Millard F. J. C., Reid L. et al. (1964) The radiographic appearance of the chest in persons of advanced age. *Br. J. Radiol.* **37**, 769.

Elgin S. C. R. and Weintraub H. (1975) Chromosomal proteins and chromatin structure. *Ann. Rev. Biochem.* **44**, 725.

Elridi S. S. and Hall D. A. (1976) Isolation of elastase from human serum. *Biochem. Soc. Trans.* **4**, 336.

Frolkis V. V., Martynenko O. A. and Zamostyan V. P. (1976) Aging of the neuromuscular apparatus. *Gerontologia* **22**, 244.

von Hahn H. and Fritz E. (1966) Age related alterations in the structure of DNA. *Gerontologia* **12**, 237.

Hall D. A. (1964) *Elastolysis and Ageing*. Springfield, Ill., Thomas.

Hall D. A., Middleton R. S. W., Elridi S. S. et al. (1980a) Serum elastase levels following a stroke in elderly subjects. *Gerontology* **26**, 167.

Hall D. A., Middleton R. S. W. and Zajac A. R. (1980b) Related age changes in the elastase and lipid contents of normal and hemiplegic subjects of various ages. *Mech. Ageing Dev.* **14**, 293.

Hamilton T. H., Widnell C. C. and Tata J. R. (1968) Synthesis of ribonucleic acid during early estrogen action. *J. Biol. Chem.* **243**, 408.

Howald J., Ehrsam R., Rüegger B. et al. (1975) Conception and evaluation of a simple fitness test. *Schweiz. Z. Sportmed.* **23**, 57.

Hyams D. E. (1978) The blood. In: Brocklehurst J. C. (ed.) *Textbook of Geriatrics and Gerontology*. 2nd ed. Edinburgh, Churchill Livingstone, p. 560.

Kanungo M. S. (1980) *Biochemistry of Ageing*. London, Academic Press.

Kirk J. E. (1957) Enzyme activities and co-enzyme concentration of human arterial tissue and their relation to age. In: *4th Congr. Internat. Assoc. Gerontol.* Fidenza, Tito Mattioli, p. 288.

Kirk J. E. (1959a) Enzyme activities of human arterial tissue. *Ann. N.Y. Acad. Sci.* **72**, 1006.

Kirk J. E. (1959b) The 5-nucleotidase activity of human arterial tissue in individuals of varying ages. *J. Gerontol* **14**, 288.

Kirk J. E. (1961) The aconitase activity of arterial tissue in individuals of various ages. *J. Gerontol.* **16**, 25.

Kirk J. E. (1962) Variations with age in the tissue content of vitamins and hormones. *Vitam. Horm.* **20**, 67.

Kirk J. E. (1962) The glycogen phosphorylase activity of arterial tissue in individuals of various ages. *J. Gerontol.* **17**, 154.

Kirk J. E., Wang K. and Brandstrupp N. (1959) The glucose-6-phosphate and 6-phosphogluconate dehydrogenase activities of arterial tissue in individuals of various ages. *J. Gerontol.* **14**, 25.

Kornberg R. D. (1977) Structure of chromatin. *Ann. Rev. Biochem.* **46**, 931.

Kurtz D. I., Russell A. R. and Sinex F. M. (1974) Multiple peaks in the derivative melting curve of chromatin from animals of varying age. *Mech. Ageing Dev.* **3**, 37.

Larsson L., Frimby G. and Karlsson J. (1979) Muscle strength and speed of movement in relation to age and muscle morphology. *J. Appl. Physiol.* **46**, 451.

Libby P. R. (1968) Histone acetylation by cell-free preparations from rat uterus. *Biochem. Biophys. Res. Commun.* **31**, 59.

Loeven W. A. (1963) The enzymes of the elastase complex. In: Hall D. A. (ed.) *International Reviews of Connective Tissue Research, Vol. 1.* New York, Academic Press.

Lonergan M. E., Milne J. S., Maule M. M. et al. (1975) A dietary survey of older people in Edinburgh. *Br. J. Nutr.* **34**, 517.

McGandy R. B., Burrows C. H. and Spanias A. et al. (1966) Nutrient intakes and energy expenditures in men of different ages. *J. Gerontol.* **21**, 581.

Mainwaring W. I. P. (1968) The effect of testosterone on the age associated changes in the ventral prostate gland of the mouse. *Gerontologia*, **14**, 133.

O'Meara A. and Hertmann R. (1972) A modified mouse liver chromatin preparation displaying age-related differences in salt dissociation and template ability. *Biochem. Biophys. Acta* **269**, 419.

Ritz F. and Kirk, T. E. (1967) Phosphofructokinase and sorbital dehydrogenase activities of arterial tissue in individuals of various ages *J. Gerontol.* **22**, 433.

Rowe R. W. D. (1969) The effect of senility on skeletal muscles in the mouse. *Exp. Gerontol.* **4**, 119.

Saltzman H. A., Sieker H. D. and Green J. (1963) Hexosamine and hydroxyproline content in human bronchial cartilage from aged and diseased lungs. *J. Lab. Clin. Med.* **62**, 78.

Schmidt V. (1951) Excretion of pantothenic acid in young and old individuals. *J. Gerontol.* **6**, 132.

Schmuckler M. and Barrows C. H. jun. (1967) The effect of age on dehydrogenase heterogeneity in the rat. *J. Gerontol.* **22**, 8.

Shephard R. J. (1977) *Physical Activity and Aging.* London, Croom Helm.

Shock N. W. and Norris A. H. (1970) Neuromuscular coordination as a factor in muscular exercise. In: Brunner D. and Joke E. (ed.) *Physical Activity and Ageing* Baltimore, University Park Press.

Skinner J. S., Tipton C. M. and Vailas A. C. (1982) Exercise, Physical Training and the Ageing Process. In: Viidik A. (ed.) *Lectures on Gerontology.* London, Academic Press, p. 407.

Steinhagen-Thiessen E. and Hilz H. (1976) Age dependent decrease in creatine kinase and aldolase activity in human striated muscle. *Mech. Ageing Dev.* **5**, 447.

Tesal I. S. and Hall D. A. (1972) The hormonal control of enzymes involved in the age-mediated degradation of connective tissue. *Proc. Internat. Cong. Gerontol. Kiev* **2**, p. 58.

Van Dyke D. and Auger H. O. (1965) Patterns of marrow hypertrophy and atrophy in man. *J. Nucl. Med.* **6**, 109.

Wang K. and Kirk J. E. (1959) The enolase activity of arterial tissue in inviduals of varying age. *J. Gerontol.* **14**, 444.

Wilson P. D. (1972) Enzyme patterns in young and old mouse livers and lungs. *Gerontologia* **18**, 36.

Wilson P. D. (1973) Enzyme changes in ageing mammals. *Gerontologia* **19**, 79.

World Health Organization (1959) Iron deficiency anaemia. Report of a study group. *WHO Tech. Rep. Ser.* No. **182**, p. 4.

6

The Endocrine System and Ageing

6.1 Introduction

Nearly a century ago Brown-Séquard (1889) suggested that structural and functional changes in certain tissues and organs which were consequent on the ageing process could be reversed or prevented by the administration of extracts or cell suspensions from hormone-producing organs. This concept has since been supported by various workers (Steinach, 1920; Voronoff, 1920, 1929; and Niehans 1954), all of whom have subscribed to relatively controversial rejuvenation procedures based on hormone replacement therapy. They believed it was not sufficient merely to supply the individual hormones themselves, but that the cells which synthesized them must also be administered. There is little evidence for the successful treatment or prevention of ageing in this fashion, but on the other hand increasing evidence has been amassed over the years which indicates that deficiencies in hormone or hormone receptors may be of importance in initiating the ageing process.

Pitman (1962), for instance, claimed that age effects were induced by a slowly developing hypofunction of the thyroid, but even the thyroid glands of elderly subjects can respond normally when subjected to stimulation by the thyroid stimulating hormone (TSH) (see below). It appears likely, therefore, that age effects may originate further up the hypophyseal–pituitary–thyroid axis. Before considering the possibility of a single site for the origins of the ageing process, it is appropriate to consider the control of synthesis of various endocrine factors by substances emanating from the pituitary (Box 6.1).

142

BOX 6.1

The control of the hypothalamic–pituitary–adrenal–reproductive axis. Releasing hormones are evolved by the hypothalamus to control the function of the pituitary. Corticotrophin releasing hormone (CRH) and luteinizing hormone releasing hormone (LHRH) stimulate the production of adrenocorticotrophic hormone (ACTH) and follicle stimulating hormone (FSH) and luteinizing hormone (LH) respectively. ACTH stimulates the adrenal cortex to produce cortisol (C). LH stimulates testosterone (T) secretion by the Leydig cells of the gonads. Feedback control (dotted lines) of hypothalamic activity originates in the gonads, the adrenal cortex and the pituitary; T, C and ACTH inhibiting hypothalamic function. 1, CRH; 2, LHRH; 3, FSH; 4, ACTH; 5, LH; 6, T; 7, Oestradiol; 8, C.

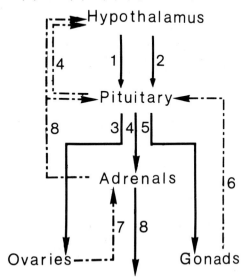

6.2 The Pituitary–Adrenal Axis

6.2.1 Synthesis of Hormones under the Control of the Anterior Pituitary

The anterior pituitary, stimulated by polypeptide-releasing factors originating in the hypothalamus, produces a variety of trophic hormones which stimulate various endocrine organs throughout the body. Somatotrophin (growth hormone) affects the size and shape of the body by direct action on the fibroblasts. As mentioned above, TSH stimulates the thyroid to synthesize thyroxine, whilst the adrenocorticotrophic hormone (ACTH) stimulates the adrenal cortex to synthesize the corticosteroid hormones. The gonadotrophic hormones effect the synthesis of various sex hormones by the gonads and control particular stages of the reproductive process. The presence in the circulation of hormones which are the products of adrenocortical activity, controls either the activity of the appropriate trophic hormone or its synthesis by the pituitary under the influence of releasing factors originating in the hypothalamus.

Hess and Reigle (1970) have demonstrated that the corticosterone concentration in rat plasma does not rise to a similar extent in old animals as in young ones following stimulation of the arenal cortex by the inhalation of ether vapour or by the injection of ACTH and this has also been observed in cattle (Riegle and Nellor 1967), goats (Riegle et al., 1972) and mice (Grad and Khalid, 1968). The secretion of somatotrophin (growth hormone, GH) by the pituitary is increased in stressful situations and during sleep. After exercise GH output can be seen to increase by comparable amounts in young and old (over 70 years of age) subjects (Laron et al. 1970), but there does not appear to be a significant difference between the effect of sleep on the output of GH by old and young, the pituitaries of the former group secreting appreciably lower quantities. M. R. P. Hall (1978) suggested that this might be due to a failure of the 'sleep test', since elderly subjects may not remain fully asleep during the testing procedure. D. A. Hall (1981) has drawn attention to the fact that the changing synthesis of different types of collagen by fibroblasts and smooth muscle cells may be due to the intervention of a hormone in the expression of those genes which are specific for the synthesis of Type I and Type III collagen. The suggestion had been made previously (Comfort, 1979) that changing *function* of the ageing animal might be under the control of a variety of adrenal, thyroid and gonadal hormones. It seems likely, however, that *structural* changes may also be directly under the control of the pituitary by the intervention of growth hormone (*Figs.* 6.1 and 6.2). The level of GH in the plasma remains relatively constant in adults after two major fluctuations in early life. This correlates directly with the

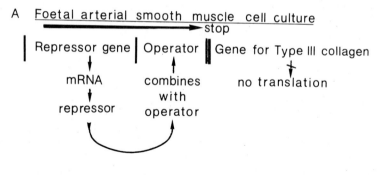

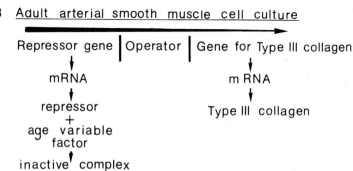

Fig. 6.1. Suggested role of the Jacob–Monod operon concept in the differential control of the synthesis of Type III collagen by cultured smooth muscle cells from A, fetal and B, adult human aorta.

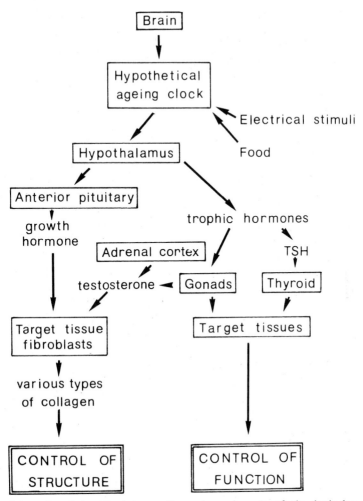

Fig. 6.2. Schematic relationship between the various elements of the brain–hypothalamus–pituitary–adrenal axis, showing the way both the *structure* and *function* of target tissues throughout the body may be controlled through the hypothetical ageing clock.

alterations which are apparent in collagen type which are most pronounced during the transition from fetal to adult status.

Some gonadotrophic hormone levels start to change in certain individuals during the immediately premenopausal years. Plasma follicle stimulating hormone (FSH) rises over the period 34 to 39 years (Reyes et al., 1977), but no changes occur during this period in the levels of luteinizing hormone (LH). Immediately after the menopause, however, both FSH and LH levels rise dramatically, although a slight fall may occur above the age of 70 (*Fig.* 6.3). In the premenopausal situation, secretion of FSH and LH is repressed by feedback inhibition of the pituitary by circulating oestradiol. When ovarian synthesis of this hormone ceases at the

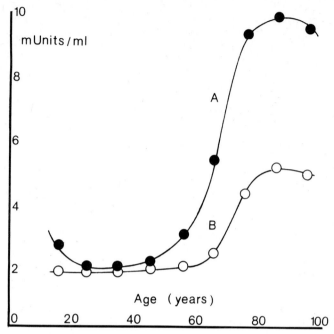

Fig. 6.3. Age-related changes in the plasma levels of A, follicle stimulating hormone and B, luteinizing hormone.

menopause this negative feedback is no longer effective and the pituitary synthesis of gonadotrophins proceeds unabated.

6.2.2 *Ageing and Adrenal Activity*

The adrenal cortex produces two major groups of steroid hormones: the gluco-corticoids and the androgens. Of the former group, cortisol circulates in the plasma in combination with a specific protein (transcortin) to the extent of about 99% of its total concentration. The 1% free cortisol is rapidly metabolized in the liver and the kidney to be replaced by more steroid which is released from combination with transcortin. Changing levels of cortisol in the plasma control ACTH production by the pituitary and the effect of this trophic agent on the adrenal cortex remains constant throughout life. The rate at which cortisol is metabolized by the liver and the kidney, however, does decrease with increasing age and this results in a progressive decrease in 24 h excretion of the total 17-hydroxycorticosteroids which include all the metabolites of cortisol, namely: tetrahydrocortisol, tetrahydrocortisone, allotetrahydro-cortisol and cortolone (*Fig.* 6.4). If these excretion rates are expressed in terms of creatinine excretion, however, it can be seen that the relationship between 17-OH corticosteroid and creatinine excretion remains within 5% of a mean value of 40 mg/g over the whole age range from 20 to 80 (Romanoff et al., 1970). These observations were in

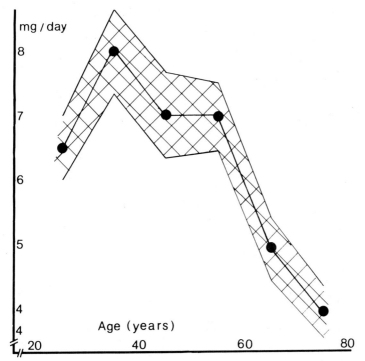

Fig. 6.4. Age-related changes in 17-HO steroids in human plasma. The cross-hatched area defines 1 standard deviation on either side of mean values for each ten year age group.

agreement with those of West et al. (1961) who reported a reduction in the rate of removal of cortisol from the circulation, following the administration of 1 mg/kg to men over 60, associated with a significant decrease in the renal clearance of creatinine and sulphobromphthalein.

Glycocorticosteroid hormones bind to specific receptors on cells in the liver, skeletal muscle, adipose tissue, the central nervous system and the reticulo-endothelial system. Roth (1974) observed that cortisol-binding sites in rat kidney were twice as numerous in the liver cells of 12-month-old rats (Sprague-Dawley and Wister) as in similar cells of 2-month-old animals, but Latham and Finch (1976) only found a 20% increase in binding sites in cells from fully senescent C57BL/6J rats. In human subjects, Singer et al. (1973) observed a 70% reduction between 30–40 and 66–80 years of age. Receptors in the muscle tissue (Roth, 1974), epididymal fat pads (Roth, 1976) and splenic leucocytes (Roth, 1975 a and b) of rats have also been reported to be reduced by between 40 and 60% with increasing age. In all these instances the glucocorticosteroids combine with DNA and nuclear non-histone protein within the cells, regulating the transcription of specific messenger RNA. This phenomenon, therefore, decreases with advancing age.

The production of adrenal androgens in females amounts to only 75% of the total level of circulating androgens, the rest originating in the ovaries. There are, therefore, marked changes in androgen levels in the blood after the menopause (*se* p. 149). In males the synthesis of androgens by the *zona reticularis* of the adrena cortex is markedly affected by age in contrast to the production of corticosteroid by the *zona fasciculata* (Migeon et al., 1963). Both dehydroepiandrosteron (DHEA) and androsterone decrease by upwards of 80% between 20 and 70 year of age.

The changing function of these androgens with increasing age in males and females respectively is dealt with in detail on pp. 155 and 149.

6.2.3 *Age Changes in Sex Hormones—the Menopause*

Female sex hormones, the oestrogens, are derived from androgen precursors testosterone in the case of oestradiol and androstendione in the case of oestrone Both these precursors are interconvertible or can be derived individually from dehydroepiandrosterone (DHEA) (*Fig.* 6.5). In the premenopausal woman oestro gens and their precursors are derived partly from the ovaries and partly from the

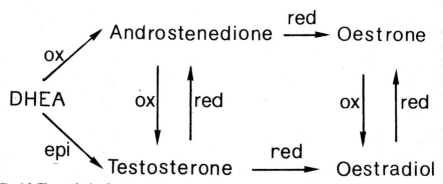

Fig. 6.5. The synthesis of oestrogens from dehydroepiandrosterone (DHEA). DHEA is epimerized to produce testosterone. Oxidation and reduction pathways are labelled 'ox' and 'red'. In premenopausa women, 99% of the testosterone is derived from DHEA, 1% from androstenedione. 75% of the latter is synthesized by the adrenals, 25% by the ovaries, which also produce 60% of the oestrone and virtually all the oestradiol. 35% of the oestrone is produced by reduction of androstenedione and 5% by reduction of oestradiol. At the menopause, all ovarian synthesis ceases throwing the onus for oestroger synthesis on the adrenal gland.

adrenals. At the menopause ovarian activity ceases abruptly and the ovarian supply of oestradiol ceases completely. Since a small amount may be synthesized by the reduction of oestrone, however, the supply of oestradiol to the system is maintained at a low level (about 5% of that during the premenopausal period). Contrary to these generally held views as to the postmenopausal fate of the oestrogens, Chakravati et al. (1976) have claimed that although both oestrone and oestradiol levels fall to about 20% of the premenopausal level, the latter continues to be synthesized at about 20% of the premenopausal level for the next thirty years, whereas the level of oestrone falls steadily. These different views have not yet been

econciled. Siiteri (1975) has observed that obesity may be of importance in the
ontrol of oestrogen levels. Many authors have suggested that oestrone production
•y obese elderly women is greatly in excess of leaner age-matched controls, which
:self may increase by 100%. This may explain the higher degree of osteoporosis
/hich may be associated with obesity in postmenopausal women. Crilly et al.
1981) have, however, failed to demonstrate any correlation between the oestrone
r the androstendione levels and the excess weight of obese elderly subjects.

After the menopause the levels of the androgens, androstendione and testosterone,
ither increase in the plasma or at least remain unchanged, as is also true of the
najor adrenal precursor—DHEA. Since oestradiol is some 4 times more potent an
•estrogen than oestrone, the 95% loss of the former, even allowing for a doubling
•f the oestrone level, results in a postmenopausal shift in oestrogen/androgen
•alance in favour of a more male-oriented metabolism. This, coupled with the
•rogressive decrease in the remaining oestrogen (oestrone) accounts for the
ncreasing masculinization of elderly females, resulting in the onset of male
econdary sex characteristics, such as a redistribution of active hair follicles on the
ace and an increased incidence of male type baldness.

Other symptoms are apparent in the female who has reached the 45–55 age
,roup. The two terms: *climacteric* and *menopause* are often used loosely to define
he same stage in the life of the female. The former may be defined, however, as
hat phase in the ageing process of the female which is marked by a total loss of
eproductive capacity. The menopause on the other hand is a much more
electively defined stage in the ageing process when the final menstrual cycle has
•ccurred. This takes place *during* the climacteric and is accompanied by other
ymptoms and complaints. The reduction in ovarian activity which ultimately
loses down menstrual activity also results in hot flushes, sweating, atrophic
aginitis and various psychological factors.

.3 Hormones and the Skeleton

.3.1 *The Effect of Sex Hormones*

n man the total bone mass of the skeleton attains its optimum level at the
essation of growth towards the second half of the third decade. Thereafter,
•rogressive bone loss (osteoporosis) may result in up to 15% of the skeletal mass
.isappearing during the ensuing six decades (Nordin, 1976). Various methods have
•een employed to measure bone loss, including direct assessment of the densities of
tandardized spinal radiographs, photon absorption (Cameron and Sorenson,
963) and hand X-ray (Garn et al., 1964; Exton-Smith et al., 1969; Nordin, 1971;
iryfe et al., 1972). Those methods which are based on hand X-rays rely for
juantification solely on linear measurements and hence permit standardization
nd the elimination of differences between results obtained by different groups of
vorkers. The measurements required are the inner and outer diameters (d and D)
•f the cortex at the mid-point of the second metacarpal. Various combinations of
hese two measurements and in some instances also the length of the metacarpal

(L) have been employed to provide indicators of osteoporosis known as *metacarp.*
indices (MI). These have been defined variously by the terms: $D - d/I$
$D^2 - d^2/D^2$, and $D^2 - d^2/DL$. In all cases a reasonable degree of correlation h;
been observed between the calculated value for MI and the ash content (
incinerated samples of bone. The present author has applied the equatio
$MI = (D^2 - d^2)/D^2 \times 100$ (Nordin, 1971) and the values for MI in *Figs.* 6.7 and 6.
were obtained in this way.

Newton-John and Morgan (1968) suggested that the age-related increase in th
incidence of fractures of the neck of the femur and Colles fractures of the distal en
of the radius is a function of that fraction of the population whose bone statu
expressed in terms of MI values, is lower than the value typical of their age grou;
They plotted values for MI against age and showed that by the end of the nint
decade about 40% of all males and 70% of all females had a bone status which wε
below the lower limits of normal in young individuals, i.e. the mean value for ag(
20–40 minus 2 standard deviations. Gallagher et al. (1973) demonstrated that thes
hyperosteoporotics, who might be of any age over forty, usually presented wit
back pain and could be shown on X-ray to have collapsed end plates in a numbε
of their vertebral bodies and microfractures of the spinous processes. Because (
this X-ray appearance they refer to these individuals as having crush fracture
(*Box* 6.2).

BOX 6.2

Hyperosteoporosis (or crush fracture syndrome, Gallagher et al., 1973) shows itself especially in tŀ
vertebral column by malformation of the vertebral bodies. The end plates which are normally straig.
and at right angles to the spinal axis collapse and each vertebra assumes a biconcave appearance. Th
results in the anterior and posterior extremities of pairs of vertebrae approaching closer to one anoth
since a given volume of intervertebral disc has now to fill the more extensive central gap. The spino
processes may actually touch one another and microfractures of these regions are often observed
X-rays. These changes in the vertebral bodies result in the development of inflammatory response
and the patients present with pain in the lumbar region of the spine.

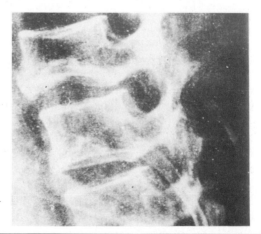

Osteoporosis can be defined as a condition in which the whole of the bone mass lost (organic matrix as well as calcium phosphate) in contrast to osteomalacia here the effect is purely one of decalcification, with areas of uncalcified organic matrix revealed in sections of affected bone. Hyperosteoporosis such as that mentioned by Newton-John and Morgan (1968) appears to be an enhancement of the normal forms of osteoporosis typical of comparable age groups. The reduction in skeletal mass which is typical of all forms of osteoporosis may be attributed to any one of a variety of types of reaction affecting bone metabolism.

It may be due to:

a. Decalcification resulting in the liberation of a form of organic matrix which differs from that present in normal or osteomalacic tissue in that it can suffer subsequent degradation by normal proteolytic enzymes.

b. The activation of enzyme systems which are absent from normal or osteomalacic bone and which are capable of degrading the matrix after decalcification.

c. An impaired balance between osteoblastic and osteoclastic processes resulting in a failure to replace bone lost through normal remodelling.

It is still not fully clear which of these possibilities is the correct one. Some evidence can be obtained, however, from a consideration of the nature of the organic matrix itself and a comparison of the changes which apparently occur in the tissue component during ageing and the development of osteoporosis and comparable changes occurring in similar material elsewhere in the body. Over 90% of the matrix consists of Type I collagen, a type which also occurs in a number of other sites in the body. The most readily available site is the dermis. It is well known that the thickness of the dermis decreases with increasing age (Meema et al., 1964; Hall et al., 1981). The concentration of collagen also decreases with age (Reed and Hall, 1974) and if the amount of collagen present in a column of full skin thickness (Shuster and Bottoms, 1963) is plotted against age, it can be seen that not only is there a progressive loss of collagen from the dermis with increasing age, but values for subjects with evidence of hyperosteoporosis are on average lower than those for age-matched controls (Hall, 1976) (see Fig. 4.21).

The majority of these individuals have passed their menopause, but although age is an important factor, it cannot be the only one which determines that excessive bone loss shall occur. The total amount of collagen present in the skin is not, for instance, the only parameter which changes with increasing age. The nature of the collagen also changes. The proportion of the collagen which is soluble in 2 M NaCl falls with advancing age, but the solubility of the collagen in the skin of the hyperosteoporotic group is greater than that of the skin of age-matched controls (Fig. 6.6). Since neutral salt-soluble collagen usually represents that fraction which has most recently been synthesized and hence is not cross-linked, it might be inferred that the dermal fibroblasts of the hyperosteoporotic subjects are themselves hyperactive. Newly-synthesized collagen is, however, not the only form of the protein to demonstrate excessive solubility. Some forms of partially degraded collagen are also highly soluble. In normally ageing subjects the residue, after exhaustive extraction of dermis with 2 M NaCl, is decreasingly

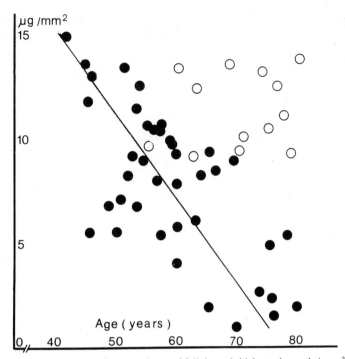

Fig. 6.6. The collagen extractable from a column of full dermal thickness beneath 1 mm² surface with 2 M neutral sodium chloride. Filled circles represent normal individuals, open circles those with a higher degree of osteoporosis than age-matched controls. The regression line, although not highly significant in view of the scatter, does show that all the hyperosteoporotic subjects have a higher level of neutral-salt-soluble collagen than normal individuals of similar age.

susceptible to collagenase, but this enzyme is capable of dissolving increasing quantities of the neutral-salt extracted residue of hyperosteoporotics of increasing age. It appears, therefore, that the collagen present in the skin of hyperosteoporotics becomes increasingly degraded with increasing age. The deficiency in oestradiol secretion at the menopause, or possibly the associated alteration in the androgen/oestrogen balance may, therefore, provoke bone loss by activation of collagenolytic enzyme systems.

Crilly et al. (1981) have suggested that hyperosteoporosis may be due to the malabsorption of calcium, possibly due to low plasma concentrations of 1,25 dihydroxy D_3 and 25-hydroxy D_3 (Gallagher et al., 1973; Bishop et al., 1980). They reported a significantly reduced uptake of radiocalcium (0·5 units/h as against 0·76 units/h; $P<0·01$) in a group of hyperosteoporotic individuals when compared with age-matched controls. However, in their paper these observations are accompanied by figures for the ratio of urinary hydroxyproline to urinary creatinine which rises as the calcium uptake falls (0·02 molar as against 0·01 molar; $P<0·005$) indicating that faulty calcification cannot be the only factor involved. Enhanced collagenolysis must also have a role to play in the loss of bone

.3.2 *Age and Steroid Osteoporosis*

t has been appreciated for some time that the administration of steroid drugs may
esult in some degree of osteoporosis. The synthetic corticosteroid, prednisolone,
or instance, reduced the MI value (*Fig.* 6.7). This is apparent over a wide range of

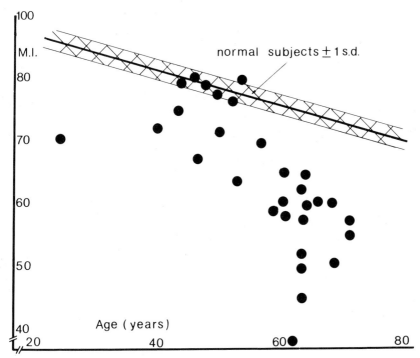

ig. 6.7. Individual points represent values for the metacarpal indices (MI) of subjects receiving
rednisolone as a therapeutic agent in the alleviation of rheumatoid arthritis. The regression line
±1 s.d.) is for an age-matched group of normal subjects.

ge groups, the MI for prednisolone-treated subjects being in the main lower than
hat of age-matched controls receiving no drug. Once again, this effect in the bone
:an be compared with a comparable effect in the dermis (Hall et al., 1974)
Fig. 6.8). Low collagen content in the dermis is directly correlated with low values
or MI in exactly the same fashion as with the hyperosteoporotics (*Fig.* 6.9).
There is, moreover, an observable relationship between the effect of the steroid and
he age of the subject. Both the total collagen and the neutral salt-soluble fraction
ire affected by steroid therapy in the same way as in the hyperosteoporotic group
see above) and the effects are significantly greater in the older age group (*Table* 6.1).
A direct comparison of the results obtained for the osteoporotic indices and dermal
:ollagen contents of the idiopathic hyperosteoporotic and steroid hyperosteo-
)orotic groups (*see Figs.* 4.22 and 6.9) shows that the effects are very similar. It
nay be, therefore, that the aetiology of the osteoporosis which is the cause of crush

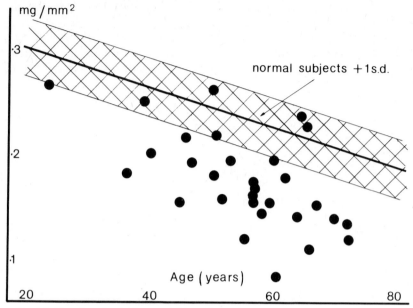

Fig. 6.8. The alteration with age of skin collagen for the subject described in *Fig.* 6.7.

Table 6.1. **The effect of age and prednisolone treatment on the levels of collagen and the fraction soluble in 2 M NaCl in the full skin thickness of human subjects**

Treatment	Age group (years)	Total collagen ($\mu g/mm^2$ skin surface)	Soluble collagen ($\mu g/mm^2$ skin surface)
1. Controls	20–56	(a) 242 ± 49	(c) $1\cdot0 + 1\cdot1$
	57–78	(b) 225 ± 69	(d) $0\cdot8 \pm 0\cdot7$
2. Prednisolone	20–56	(a) 196 ± 48	(c) $1\cdot6 \pm 0\cdot6$
	57–78	(b) 177 ± 42	(d) $2\cdot2 \pm 0\cdot8$

There are significant differences ($P<0\cdot05$) between the following groups: 1(a) and 2(a); 1(b) and 2(b); 1(c) and 2(c); 1(d) and 2(d) and 2(c) and 2(d).

fractures could be due to the secretion by the adrenal cortex of excessive amounts of corticosteroid which will have the same effect on the skeleton as synthetic steroids administered for therapeutic reasons.

In the study of the effect of prednisolone, dermal biopsies were obtained from a limited number of individuals before and after a year's treatment. *Fig.* 6.10 records the amount of collagen lost from a column of dermis beneath 1 mm² of skin surface during the year. The loss is directly proportional to the age of the subject and ranges from about 10% of the amount present at the commencement of treatment in a 40-year-old subject to over 30% in subjects in the eighth or ninth decades of life. If it can be assumed that changes of a comparable magnitude occur in the skeleton, the administration of steroids is contraindicated to an even greater extent in elderly subjects than in young or middle-aged patients.

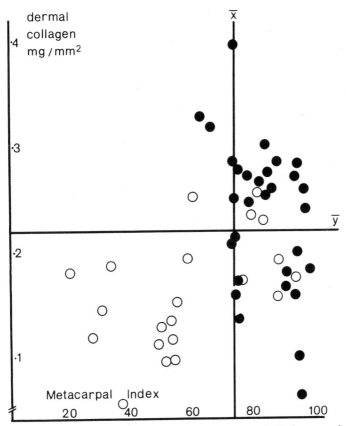

Fig. 6.9. Comparison of osteoporosis and skin collagen (cf. *Fig.* 4.22) for normal and steroid-osteoporotic subjects.

5.4 Male Sex Hormones

5.4.1 *The Male Reproductive Function*

Because there is no dramatic functional event, comparable with the menopause, at any stage in the ageing of the normal male, it has been erroneously assumed that sexual activity in the male continues unabated well into the senium. The male clearly differs from the female in retaining some degree of reproductive capacity long after the failure of the ovary. Martin (1977) has suggested, however, that arousal, erectile function of the penis and ejaculation, whether coupled with coitus or not, decreases in a roughly linear fashion from a peak value at 30 years of age to about 65. A falling off in the rate at which sexual activity decreases, apparent above 65 years of age, cannot necessarily be taken as indicating a resurgence of sexuality at this age. It is more likely that, as in most cross-sectional studies, it represents the survival of a sub-population who are characterized by having an above normal sexual appetite. Whether this can be taken as confirmation of the

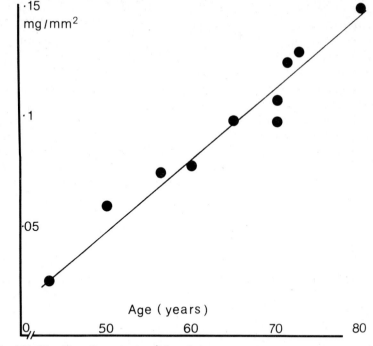

Fig. 6.10. The skin collagen ($\mu g/mm^2$) lost during one year's treatment with prednisolone.

belief, widely held in the middle ages, that the longevity of the king could b
assured by the provision of nubile bed mates (Comfort, 1964) still remains to b
seen.

6.4.2 *Spermatogenesis*

It is appropriate at this point to examine the changes in testicular activit
associated with ageing in the male. Testosterone is the major androgen secreted b
the testis and its level in testicular venous blood first increases by 75% (from *c*.4 t
c.7 mg/ml) over the first twenty years following puberty and then falls back to it
immediately postpubertal value over the ensuing 6 decades (Baker et al., 1976)
Therefore, over the major portion of the life-span changing but adequate amount
of testosterone are available to maintain male secondary sex characteristics (bear
growth and pubic hair) and masculine mental attitudes such as libido an
aggression. The anabolic function of the hormone is effected by the interaction o
its major metabolite 5-α-dihydrotestosterone (DHT) with specific cytosol receptor
in target cells. The DHT-cytosol complex is transferred to the nucleus where it
association with the DNA molecule brings about the expression of genes essentia
for the synthesis of tissue proteins.

The lowered levels of testosterone may be due to a reduction in the number o

eydig cells in the testis (Sarjent and McDonald, 1948) or to a reduction in the
sponse of the cells to gonadotrophins (Longcope, 1973; Mazzi et al., 1974). Both
H and FSH levels in the circulation increase with increasing age (Baker et al.,
)76) (see Fig. 6.3). LH exerts its main effect on the Leydig cells and in view of the
crease which occurs from age 40–90, the reduced secretion of testosterone must
dicate a falling response of the testis to gonadotrophic action. It is not, however,
ossible to ascertain whether the lowered response is due to cell loss or cell
embrane modification. FSH stimulates spermatogenesis, probably by activating
e synthesis of the appropriate enzyme systems to provide those polyunsaturated
tty acids which are required for the development of sperm head phospholipids
ee Chapter 7).

Once again the apparent reduction in these enzymes with increasing age must
dicate a reduction in receptor response since the levels of FSH increase.

4.3 *The Prostate*

enign or malignant hypertrophy of the prostate with its accompanying symptoms
f obstruction of the bladder outlet are apparent in the majority of males over the
ge of 60 (Flocks, 1964; Franks, 1976). Such changes are non-existent in castrates
nd subjects with lowered pituitary function (Moore, 1944), indicating that the
ypertrophy of the structure is induced by either circulating hormones or their
tracellular metabolic products. Various enzyme systems in the prostate tissue
ppear to be increased with age, leading to enhanced metabolism of testosterone to
χ-dihydrotestosterone and it may be an increase in this metabolite which activates
e anatomical changes leading to hypertrophy.

.5 **Thyroid Function and Ageing**

.5.1 *The Synthesis of Thyroxine and Tri-iodothyronine*

1 the thyroid gland, molecules of tyrosine are iodinated to produce active thyroid
ormones. The first one or two iodine atoms are introduced into the benzene
ucleus of the tyrosine molecule at carbon atoms 3 or 3 and 5. If the thyroid fails to
inction correctly, this initial iodination reaction is inhibited. Pairs of molecules
re then conjugated with one another through the hydroxyl groups on carbon
tom 4 to provide the complex thyronine molecule in which a pair of benzene
uclei are linked through an oxygen atom (*Fig.* 6.11). The conjugation of
iolecules of mono- or di-iodotyrosine produces the active hormones tri- or tetra-
)dinated thyronine (thyroxine, T_4). The latter is symmetrically iodinated whereas
ie active form of the former molecule, tri-iodothyronine (T_3), is di-iodinated in
ie benzene ring which contains the $-CH_2-CH(NH_2)COOH$ substituent. Di-
)dination in the other ring results in the formation of an inactive form of T_3 —
everse T_3.

There is little evidence for a failure of iodination in elderly human subjects, who

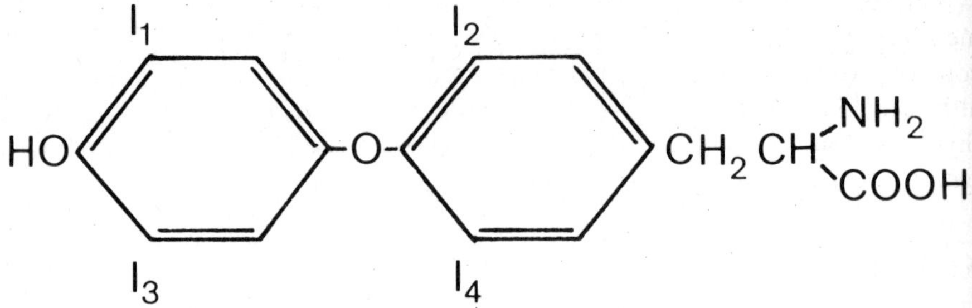

Fig. 6.11. Thyroxine (tetraiodothyronine, T_4) synthesized from tyrosine by iodination and oxidativ condensation of two molecules. Deiodination can occur in either of the two ways by the removal of I or I_2 to give tri-iodothyronine (T_3) or reverse T_3 respectively.

are capable of responding to thyrotrophin which stimulates the release of th hormone from the thyroid gland, and to severe illness which also acts as a stimulant of secretion (Gregerman and Solomon, 1967) by releasing enhance levels of active hormone into the circulation. This is not due to an increase in TSH or to the thyrotrophin-releasing hormone (TRH) both of which, under thes conditions, remain unchanged thus indicating that age-related primary failure o the thyroid does not occur in the elderly (Snyder and Utiger, 1972).

Of the active hormone present in the gland 90% is bound to protein thyroglobulin, and before it is secreted from the gland it has to be liberated from this carrier. TSH promotes this liberation. The amount of hormone secreted by the pituitary is not affected by age, but there does appear to be evidence for a reductio in the effect of the releasing hormone which originates in the hypophysis.

6.5.2 *Thyroid Function in the Elderly*

Defining a normal range of thyroxine (T_4) and tri-iodothyronine (T_3) in the sera o elderly individuals is difficult. There are a number of contradictory observations One group of authors suggest that T_4 levels do not change with age (Rubinstein e al., 1973; Westgren et al., 1976), whereas others report a decrease (Hermann et al. 1974) or an increase (Britton et al., 1975). Most of the reported studies have bee carried out on groups of hospitalized elderly subjects and the existence of variou pathological conditions superimposed on ageing pheonomena may invoke a varie response. Chronic liver disease (Green et al., 1977), diabetic keto-acidosis (Naeij et al., 1978) and nephrosis (Gavin et al., 1978) reduce the formation of T_3 from T by the deiodination of the hydroxyl-bearing benzene ring, but increase th formation of the inactive form of T_3 (reverse T_3) resulting from the deiodina tion of the other benzene ring. Alterations in the levels of thyroxine-bindin protein (TBP) also occur in many euthyroid subjects with non-thyroid disease and could appear to be one of the major causes of excessively low levels of serun thyroxine in elderly subjects.

Normal functioning of the thyroid is essential for survival since there are few metabolic processes in the body which are not directly or indirectly under thyroid control. However, from the observations reported above, it is apparent that although changes in thyroid function comparable with the two extremes of thyrotoxicosis and myxoedema may occur in the elderly, they are due to glandular pathologies rather than to ageing itself.

5.6 Insulin

5.6.1 The Effects of Faulty Carbohydrate Metabolism

The presence of enhanced levels of glucose in the plasma of elderly subjects following the ingestion of a test meal consisting of glucose has long been appreciated (Spence, 1921; Marshall, 1931; Andres, 1971). The reasons for such an apparent diabetic response are, however, numerous. In some individuals this condition represents a direct continuation of the acute, potentially lethal keto-acidotic, insulin-sensitive form of diabetes which often occurs in early youth and which has been labelled 'juvenile onset diabetes', although it can occur at any age. This form of diabetes is associated with a marked reduction in the synthesis of insulin by the β-cells of the islets of Langerhans in the pancreas, or by enhanced levels of the enzyme insulinase which is present in the liver and destroys circulating insulin (Czerkawski and Bingle, 1963). Insulin promotes the entry of glucose into peripheral cells. They do this by combining with receptor sites on the cell membrane. It is possible to extract the receptor structure from cell membranes by treatment with neutral detergents when it can be shown to consist of a glycoprotein of molecular weight 135 000 daltons. The receptor only represents about 1/25 000 of the cell surface, but the rate of association with insulin is very high $(c.10^7 \text{ M}^{-1}/\text{sec}^{-1})$ so that virtually every insulin molecule which approaches the cell becomes attached to the cell. The glycoprotein may either not be synthesized to the same extent in old tissues, or its structure may be faulty so that it is incapable of attracting and binding the circulating insulin. Another possible explanation for a lowered response to administered insulin with increasing age is that as the lean body mass is reduced, the number of receptors is also lowered quantitatively (Rosenbloom et al., 1976). This may, however, not be the whole story. Insulin not only combines with cells in the lean body mass to promote the uptake of glucose, but is also involved in the metabolic reactions of adipocytes. Hence in obese subjects the proportion of insulin available for carbohydrate metabolism may well be markedly reduced as reaction with receptors on the adipocytes will decrease the level of insulin available for interaction with the receptors on the peripheral muscle cells.

6.6.2 Insulin Response

Andres and Tobin (1975), using the 'hyperglycaemic clamp' method in which the plasma glucose level is maintained at a fixed but elevated level by continuous monitoring and adjustment of the intravenous glucose infusion, showed tha elderly subjects did not respond as rapidly to increased glucose levels as did norma younger subjects. The level of plasma insulin rose more slowly in elderly subjects i the glucose level was maintained at relatively low levels, but when the glucos content was raised to over 300 mg/dl, the rise in insulin content in the plasma wa comparable in both young and old. The amount of insulin synthesized by the β-cells of the islets of Langerhans in the pancreas would appear to be adequat even in advanced age and the low insulin response cannot account for the age related decline in glucose tolerance.

6.7 Miscellaneous Non-steroid Endocrine Factors

6.7.1 *Epinephrine and Norepinephrine* (*see* Chapter 8)

6.7.2 *Serotonin* (*see* Chapter 8)

6.7.3 *Acetylcholine* (*see* Chapter 8)

6.7.4 *Dihydroxyphenylalanine (L-DOPA)* (*see* Chapter 8)

6.7.5 *Glucagon*

There is little evidence for a decrease in the secretion of this peptide hormone. It: effect on blood glucose levels is directly opposite to that of insulin, promoting the mobilization of glucose from glycogen stores in the body. It stimulates the formation of cyclic CMP in the membranes of the target cells.

6.7.6 *Gastrin*

This substance which is found in the pyloric antrum of the stomach stimulates the secretion of acid by the parietal cells of the gastric mucosa and at highe concentrations stimulates pepsin secretion by the chief cells. Indirect evidence fo either decreasing secretion or increasingly defective reaction with receptors can be deduced from figures for the increasing incidence of achlorhydria with advancing age (*see Table* 5.2).

6.7.7 *Pressor Substances and Hypertension*

Hypertension is increasingly apparent in elderly subjects; nearly 30% of those over 65 have high blood pressure. Mean systolic pressure rises by 20–40 mmHg between 60 and 90 and the levels for women are invariably higher than for men. Diastolic pressure does not appear to be affected to a significant degree by either age or sex. Increasing pressure is a significant risk factor for stroke, congestive heart failure and coronary artery disease (Shurtlett, 1974; Kannel, 1975, 1976; Kannel et al., 1970, 1971). The biochemical changes which precipitate hypertension originate in the kidneys. These organs release renin in response to low blood volume and alterations in sodium ion concentration. Renin acts enzymatically on a circulating α_2-globulin to form a decapeptide, angiotensin I. This peptide is not physiologically active but the removal of two amino acids causes the production of angiotensin II which acts to return blood volume deficits and blood pressure to normal by activating the adrenal release of aldosterone. Excessive production of angiotensin II results in a displacement of the blood pressure towards higher levels. Angiotensin II also opens the intercellular spaces in the endothelial lining of the larger blood vessels (Constantinides and Robinson, 1969) thus permitting the penetration of lipoproteins and platelets to the intimal membrane where they may result in the formation of plaques and mural thrombi.

6.8 Conclusions

The age changes which are apparent in the levels of circulating hormones do not in general result from faulty synthesis by the adrenals, gonads, ovaries, pancreas, etc. Nor in most instances does synthesis of the stimulating factors alter markedly with increasing age. The main faults in the endocrine axis appear to be related either to the effect of the various hierarchies of hormone on their respective end-organs or to the activity of the hypophysis.

It has been suggested that the whole endocrine control of metabolism may in fact derive from a hypothetical 'ageing clock' situated 'above' the hypophysis (Comfort, 1979) (*see Fig.* 6.2). This clock might be expected to receive stimuli from the brain, from the external environment via the central nervous system, or from elements of the diet, processing them in response to the passage of time and passing them on to the hypophysis. In this way, the 'clock' could ensure that changes in metabolic activity would occur at precise chronological points in the life-span or could advance or retard this specific response. Moreover the 'clock' could also control age-related changes in the structural components of the body (*see Fig.* 6.2).

Recommended Reading

Two recent books provide important contributions to our knowledge of the effect of ageing on the endocrine system: Green M. (ed.) (1981) *Clinics in Endocrinology and Metabolism. Endocrinology and Ageing.* Saunders; and Korenman S. G. (ed.) (1982) *Endocrine Aspects of Ageing.* Elsevier Biomedical.

References

Andres R. (1971) Aging and diabetes. *Med. Clin. North Am.* **55**, 835.
Andres R. and Tobin J. D. (1975) Aging and the disposition of glucose in explorations in aging. *Adv. Exp. Med. Biol.* **61**, 239.
Baker H. W. G., Burger H. G., de Kretser D. M. et al. (1976) Endocrinology of aging: pituitary testicular axis. *Proc. 5th Int. Congr. Endocrinol.* p. 479.
Bishop J. E., Norman A. W., Coburn J. W. et al. (1980) Studies in the metabolism of calciferol XVI. *Min. Electrol. Mec.* **3**, 181.
Britton K. E., Ellis M., Miralles J. M. et al. (1975) Is T_4 toxicosis normal biochemical finding in elderly women? *Lancet* **2**, 141.

Brown-Séquard, C. (1889) Des effets produit chez l'homme pas l'injection sous-cutané d'un liquid retiré des testicules fraise de chien. (Effects produced in man by the subcutaneous injection of a liqui obtained from fresh dog testicles) *Compte Rendu Soc. Biol.* **41**, 415.

Cameron J. R. and Sorenson J. (1963) Measurement of bone mineral *in vivo*: an improved method *Science* **152**, 230.

Chakravarti S., Collins W. P., Foreast J. D. et al. (1976) Hormone profiles after the menopause *Br. Med. J.* **2**, 784.

Comfort A. (1964) *Ageing: the Biology of Senescence.* Edinburgh, Churchill Livingstone.

Comfort A. (1979) *The Biology of Senescence.* Edinburgh, Churchill Livingstone.

Constantinides P. and Robinson M. (1969) Ultrastructural injury of arterial endothelium. *Arch. Pathol* **88**, 99.

Crilly R. G., Francis R. M. and Nordin B. E. C. (1981) Steroid hormones, ageing and bone. In: Green M. (ed.) *Clinics in Endocrinology and Metabolism.* London, Saunders, p. 115.

Czerkawski J. W. and Bingle J. P. (1963) The interaction of a basic protein extract of pancreas and insulin. *Biochem. J.* **87**, 34.

Exton-Smith A. N., Millard P. H., Payne P. R. et al. (1969) Method for measuring quantity of bone *Lancet* **2**, 1153.

Flocks R. H. (1964) Benign prostatic hypertrophy: Its diagnosis and management. *Med. Times* **92**, 519.

Franks L. M. (1976) The natural history of prostatic cancer. In: Marberger H. (ed.) *Prostatic Disease.* Vol. 6. New York, Liss, p. 103.

Gallagher J. C., Aaron J., Horsman A. et al. (1973) The crush fracture syndrome in post menopausal women. *Clin. Endocrinol. Metab.* **2**, 293.

Garn S. M., Rohmann C. A., Behar M. et al. (1964) Compact bone deficiency in protein-calorie malnutrition. *Science* **145**, 1444.

Gavin L. A., McMahon F. A., Castle J. N. et al. (1978) Alterations in serum thyroid hormones and thyroxine-binding globulins in patients with nephrosis. *J. Clin. Endocrinol. Metab.* **46**, 125.

Grad B. and Khalid R. (1968) Circulating corticosterone levels in young and old, male and female C57BL/6J mice. *J. Gerontol.* **23**, 522.

Green J. R. B., Snitcher E. J., Mowat N. A. G. et al. (1977) Thyroid function and thyroid regulation in euthyroid men with chronic liver disease: evidence of multiple abnormalities. *Clinical Endocrinol.* **7**, 453.

Gregerman R. I. and Solomon N. (1967), The acceleration of thyroxine and triiodothyronine turnover during bacterial pulmonary infection and fever. *J. Clin. Endocrinol.* **27**, 93.

Gryfe C. I., Exton-Smith A. N. and Stewart R. J. C. (1972) Determination of the amount of bone in the metacarpal. *Age Ageing* **1**, 213.

Hall D. A. (1976) *Ageing of Connective Tissue.* London, Academic Press.

Hall D. A. (1981) The ageing of collagenous tissues: genetic and random effects. *J. Clin. Exp. Gerontol.* **3**, 201.

Hall D. A., Blackett A. D., Zajac A. R. et al. (1981) Changes in skinfold thickness with increasing age. *Age Ageing* **10**, 19.

Hall D. A., Reed F. B., Nuki G. et al. (1974) The relative effects of age and corticosteroid therapy on the collagen profiles of dermis from subjects with rheumatoid arthritis. *Age Ageing* **3**, 15.

Hall M. R. P. (1978) The endocrine system: hypophysoadrenal axis. In: Brocklehurst J. C. (ed.) *Textbook of Geriatric Medicine and Gerontology.* Edinburgh, Churchill Livingstone, p. 452.

Hermann J., Rusche H. J., Kroll H. J. et al. (1974) Free triiodothyronine and thyroxine levels in old age. *Horm. Metab. Res.* **6**, 239.

Hess G. D. and Reigle G. D. (1970) Adrenocortical responsiveness to stress and ACTH in aging rats. *J. Gerontol.* **25**, 354.

Kannel W. B. (1975) The role of blood pressure in cardiovascular disease—the Framingham Study. *Angiology* **26**, 1.

Kannel W. B. (1976) The Framingham study. *Br. Med. J.* **2**, 1255.

Kannel W. B., Wolf P. A., Verter J. et al. (1970) Epidemiologic assessment of the role of blood pressure in stroke—the Framingham Study. *JAMA* **214**, 301.

Kannel W. B., Gordon T. and Schwartz M. J. (1971) Systolic diastolic blood pressure and risk of coronary heart disease: the Framingham Study. *Am. J. Cardiol.* **77**, 325.

Laron Z., Doron M. and Amikan B. (1970) Plasma growth hormone in men and women over 70 years of age. In: Bruner D. and Jokl E. (ed.) *Medicine and Sport.* Vol. 4. Basel, Karger, p. 126.

Latham K. R. and Finch C. E. (1976) Hepatic glucocorticoid binders in mature and senescent C57BL/6J male mice. *Endocrinology* **98**, 1480.

Longcope C. (1973) The effect of human chorionic gonadotropin on plasma steroid levels in young and old men. *Steroids* **21**, 583.

Marshall F. W. (1931) The sugar control of the blood in elderly people. *Q. J. Med.* **24**, 257.

Martin C. E. (1977) Sexual activity in the aging male. In: Money J. and Monstafi E. (ed.) *Handbook of Sexology.* Amsterdam, ASP. Biol. Med. Press, p. 813.

Mazzi C., Riva L. R. and Bernasconi D. (1974) Gonadotrophins and plasma testosterone in senescence. In: James V. H. T., Serie M. and Martini L. (ed.) *The Endocrine Function of the Human Testis,* Vol. 2. New York, Academic Press.

Meema H. E., Sheppard R. H. and Rappaport H. (1964) Roentgenographic visualization and measurement of skin thickness and its diagnostic application in acromegaly. *Radiology* **82**, 411.

Migeon C. J., Green O. P. and Eckert J. P. (1963) Study of adrenocortical function in obesity. *Metabolism* **12**, 718.

Moore R. A. (1944) Benign hypertrophy and carcinoma of the prostate. Occurrence and experimental production in animals. *Surgery* **16**, 152.

Naeije R., Golstein J., Clumeck N. et al. (1978) A low T_3 syndrome in diabetic ketoacidosis. *Chem. Endocrinol.* **42**, 1769.

Newton-John H. F. and Morgan D. B. (1968) Osteoporosis: disease or senescence? *Lancet* **1**, 232.

Niehans P. (1954) *Cellular Therapy.* Munich, Urban & Schwarzenberg.

Nordin B. E. C. (1971) Clinical significance and pathogenesis of osteoporosis. *Br. Med. J.* **1**, 571.

Nordin B. E. C. (1976) *Calcium, Phosphate and Magnesium Metabolism.* London, Churchill Livingstone.

Pitman J. A. (1962) The thyroid and aging. *J. Am. Geriatr. Soc.* **10**, 10.

Reed F. B. and Hall D. A. (1974) Changes in skin collagen in osteoporosis. In: Fricke R. and Hartmann F. (ed.) *Connective Tissues: Biochemistry and Pathophysiology.* Berlin, Springer-Verlag, p. 290.

Reyes F. J., Winter J. S. D. and Faiman C. (1977) Pituitary-ovarian relationships preceding the menopause. *Am. J. Obstet. Gynecol.* **129**, 557.

Riegle G. D. and Nellor J. E. (1967) Changes in adrenocortical function during aging in cattle. *J. Gerontol.* **22**, 83.

Riegle G. D., Przekop F. and Nellor J. E. (1972) Changes in adrenocortical responsiveness to ACTH infusion in aging goats. In: Robertson O. H. (ed.) *Endocrines and Aging.* MSS Information Corp., New York, p. 33.

Romanoff L. P., Thomas A. W. and Baxter M. N. (1970) Effect of age on pregnanediol excretion in man. *J. Gerontol.* **25**, 98.

Rosenbloom A. L., Goldstein S. and Yip C. C. (1976) Insulin binding to cultured human fibroblasts increases with normal and precocious aging. *Science* **193**, 412.

Roth G. S. (1974) Age-related changes in specific glucocorticoid binding by steroid-responsive tissues of rats. *Endocrinology* **94**, 82.

Roth G. S. (1975a) Age-related changes in glucocorticoid bindings in rat splenic leucocytes: Possible cause of altered adaptive responsiveness. *Fed. Proc.* **34**, 183.

Roth G. S. (1975b) Reduced glucocorticoid responsiveness and receptor concentration in splenic leucocytes of senescent rats. *Biochim. Biophys. Acta* **399**, 145.

Roth G. S. (1976) Reduced glucocorticoid binding site concentration in cortical neuronal perikarya from senescent rats. *Brain Res.* **107**, 345.

Rubinstein H. A., Butler V. P., jun. and Werner S. C. (1973) Progressive decrease in serum triiodothyroxine concentrations with human aging: radioimmunoassay following extraction of serum. *J. Clin. Endocrinol. Met.* **37**, 247.

Sarjent J. W. and McDonald J. R. (1948) A method for the quantitative estimate of Leydig cells in the human testis. *Mayo Clin. Proc.* **23**, 249.

Shurtlett D. (1974) Some characteristics related to the incidence of cardiovascular disease and death. Framingham study. 18 year follow up. *US Dept Health Educ. & Welfare. Pub. NIH.* **74–599.**

Shuster S. and Bottoms E. (1963) Senile degradation of skin collagen. *Clin. Sci.* **25**, 487.

Siiteri P. K. (1975) Post-menopausal oestrogen production. *Front. Horm. Res.* **3**, 40.

Singer S., Ito H. and Litwa G. (1973) ³H-cortisol binding by young and old human liver cytosol proteins *in vitro. Int. J. Biochem.* **4**, 569.

Snyder P. J. and Utiger R. D. (1972) Inhibition of thyrotropin response to thyrotropin-releasing hormone by small quantities of thyroid hormones. *J. Clin. Invest.* **51**, 2077.

Spence J. C. (1921) Some observations on sugar tolerance with special reference to variations found at different ages. *Q. J. Med.* **14**, 314.

Steinach E. (1920) *Rejuvenation through Experimental Restoration of Pubertal Glands.* Berlin, Springer-Verlag.

Voronoff S. (1920) *Studies on Methods for increasing Vital Energy and Prolongation of Life.* Paris Gosset.
Voronoff S. (1929) *Testicular Grafting from Ape to Man.* London, Bretans.
West C. D., Brown H., Simons E. L. et al. (1961) Adrenocortical function and cortisol metabolism in old age. *J. Clin. Endocrinol. Met.* **21**, 1197.
Westgren U., Burger A., Ingemansson S. et al. (1976) Blood levels of 3,5,3-triiodothyronine and thyroxine. *Acta Med. Scand.* **200**, 493.

7

Lipids, Atherosclerosis and Age

7.1 Introduction

Numerous theories have been developed to account for the age changes which take place in the artery wall and to determine which of the various pathological phenomena provide the fundamental stimuli for atherogenesis. As long ago as 1856, Virchow suggested that injury to various sites in the intima of the vessel wall predisposed it to an inflammatory response, ultimately resulting in the proliferation of smooth muscle cells deeper in the vascular tissue. Rokitansky (1852) and later Duguid (1946) suggested that the raised plaque which developed at such sites of intimal trauma, consisted, at least in part, of an organized mural thrombus. Platelets adhered to the connective tissue which was revealed when the layer of endothelial cells lining the vessel was ruptured, liberating plasma clotting factors which precipitated a red 'tail' of fibrin and erythrocytes, superimposed on the white 'head' of the thrombus, which mainly consisted of platelets. This organized thrombus on the wall surface has a structure which is distinct from the amorphous, unorganized clot which clotting factors could induce in the body of the plasma. French (1966), Mustard and Packham (1975) and Ross and Glomset (1973, 1976) have more recently modified this concept to take into account the other major theories of atherogenesis, namely those which ascribe importance to haemodynamic factors and to the infiltration of lipids carried on specific lipoproteins in the circulation. This 'response to injury' hypothesis suggests that plaques, intimal lesions, and ultimately medial degeneration and calcification, result from a disruption of the endothelial cell layer. This may be due to physical trauma, or may result from the action of angiotensin, which it has been shown is capable of opening up the inter-endothelial cell junctions and enhancing the penetration of plasma constituents into the internal elastic lamina (Constantinides and Robinson, 1969). Once the smooth endothelial surface is interfered with, the lining of the vessel becomes susceptible to shearing stresses which result from turbulent plasma flow within the lumen of the vessel. Such turbulence is most likely to occur close to arterial bifurcations and this may explain why areas of massive plaque formation appear to be preferentially located immediately downstream of the points where major vessels leave the aorta. Disruption of the elastic lamellae is followed by fibrotic repair which results in the deposition of new connective tissue, particularly collagen, in the region of the lesion. Once precipitated, this fibrous material acts as a substrate for enzymes carried by the circulating platelets, causing the latter to adhere to the tissue and to aggregate one with another (Beachey et al., 1979) and initiating thrombus formation as mentioned above. Among the plasma components which penetrate into the intima are lipoproteins which become bound to structures within the vascular tissue underlying the original lesion. In this way plaques consisting of collagen, fibrin and lipid develop. They may ultimately either partially obstruct the lumen of the vessel concerned or possibly become detached, when they may be carried by the circulation to some other site in the body, where they can completely occlude a vessel of smaller bore.

The disruption of the endothelial surface and the penetration of lipid can occur at any age. In young subjects, however, lipid perfused experimentally into vascular tissue from lipid-rich plasma can be readily eluted again by subsequent perfusion with lipid-poor plasma or by plasma containing appreciable concentrations of high-density lipoprotein (Gresham, 1976). The retention of lipid within the vascular tissue which occurs in elderly subjects with atheromatous tendencies must, therefore, be due to one of the following age-modulated factors:

a. Age changes in the vascular tissue itself, or
b. Age changes in the constitution of the plasma lipoproteins.

7.2 Age Changes in Vascular Tissue

7.2.1 General Changes

One of the major difficulties associated with attempts at the elucidation of the aetiology of atheromatous lesions in man is the impossibility of drawing up a definitive timetable of events leading to the occurrence of the more complex forms of arterial lesion. Under normal circumstances arterial tissue can only be obtained for examination and analysis at autopsy and there is no way of ascertaining whether lipid or fibrous components precede one another in the plaque or again whether these two precede intimal and subintimal degradation, or are dependent on such changes. Frank calcification such as is observed in Monckeberg's degeneration always appears to develop late in the sequence of events, but as will be mentioned below less massive but highly important depositions of calcium may precede this extensive calcification. With the exception of this, there is no way of determining whether all the pathological phenomena observed at autopsy, in the aorta of a 35-year-old subject, for instance, precede or follow the different types of lesion observed in a 45-year-old. Moreover, although lesions similar to those occurring in man can be induced by a variety of techniques in experimental animals and some types of lesion may develop spontaneously in other animals, there is no way one can ascertain whether the metabolic pathways which bring about the formation of these similar, but not identical lesions in animals are identical to those which are operative in man. Nor is it possible to perform epidemiological studies in man to examine the incidence of vascular disease in general. It is necessary to assess the changing function of some end organ such as the heart or the brain, or the failure of peripheral circulation leading to claudication or Raynaud's disease before the existence of vascular disease can be deduced with any degree of certainty.

Allowing for these uncertainties, however, post-mortem examination of the vascular wall can demonstrate the sorts of change which do occur with age.

7.2.2 Elastic Lamellae

The media of the aortic wall consists of circumluminar elastic lamellae lying roughly parallel to the internal elastic lamina. The spaces between adjacent lamellae are crossed by fine elastic fibres which anastomose with one another and lie in between bundles of collagen fibres and smooth muscle cells. As the organism ages, there are marked changes in the amounts of these various constituents (Table 7.1). This is especially true if the vessel is atheromatous. An apparently early stage in the development of arterial disease is the fragmentation and subsequent replication of the internal elastic lamina. Following the initiation of a lesion and the development of a plaque, the internal elastic membrane and the adjacent two or three medial elastic lamellae may become degraded, losing their circumluminar integrity and their typical staining properties. It was disappearance of this elastic tissue which originally led Balo and Banga (1949) to search for an elastolytic enzyme. Subsequently Saxl and Hall (1967) showed that the degradation of elastic tissue in vivo in a chicken which had been previously fed a diet rich in cholesterol resulted in the combination of the globular elastin, resulting from the action of the

Table 7.1. **The changing composition of human arterial wall with age**

Tissue component	Age changes
Total collagen	Increase
Type I collagen	Decrease
Type III collagen	Increase
Elastin	Decrease
Partial degraded collagen (pdc)	Increase
Glycosamino, glycans	Decrease
Cholesterol esters	Increase

injected elastase, with the lipid which had infiltrated into the vascular wall to form
particles of lipid/protein complex—elastolipoprotein (*Fig.* 7.1). As an organism
ages, the two major protein species, collagen and elastin are joined by a third, pdc
which has a number of physical and chemical properties characteristic of elastin
(Hall, 1976). This material may represent some of the sub-plaque elastin which
Kramsch et al. (1970) have shown to be more susceptible to elastase than intact
elastin; material which is also rich in lipid. It would appear likely, therefore, that
the elastin and collagen degradation products which are present in the arterial wall
of elderly subjects provide suitable sites for lipid deposition and retention.

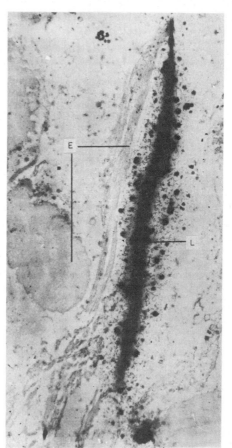

Fig. 7.1. Complexes formed between elastin (E) and lipid (L) in the aorta of a chicken to which cholesterol
had been administered to the diet and pancreatic elastase intravenously (Saxl and Hall, 1967).

7.2.3 *Calcium Content of Aorta*

The similarity between this form of pdc and that identified in the dermis (p. 99)
can be seen when the calcium content of the tissue is examined. Lansing et al.
(1948) showed that the amino acid analysis of aortic elastin, partially purified by

extraction with cold alkali, altered as the age of the subject increased. The differences were those which would be expected if pdc were associated with the semi-purified elastin. The nature of pdc in ageing aorta can be deduced from a study of the effect of elastase on it. Hall (1976) has shown that pancreatic elastase exists in two forms. One, which is calcium-rich, attacks those areas in elastin which have free carboxyl and hydroxyl groups appropriately located. The enzyme/substrate complex is formed through a calcium atom co-ordinately bound through carboxyl and hydroxyl groups located on both enzyme and substrate (Hall, 1970).

The other form of enzyme, which is calcium-poor, attacks those regions of the substrate which are cross-linked by co-ordinately-bound calcium (*see Fig.* 4.18). This form of the enzyme breaks the co-ordinate cross-link in the substrate and forms a similar enzyme/substrate complex to that created by the calcium-rich form of the enzyme. A study of the activities of the two forms of enzyme permits the amount of co-ordinately bound calcium present in a sample of substrate to be determined. In this way Hall (1973) demonstrated that the amount of calcium in the media increased with age (*Table* 7.2). Yu and Blumenthal (1960) have also reported that part of the calcium in the aortic elastin from elderly subjects is not susceptible to extraction even with chelating agents such as ethylene diamine tetra-acetic acid (EDTA). Hall (1970) showed that the co-ordination constant for the calcium–elastin complex was greater than that for calcium EDTA and hence the calcium remaining in elastic tissue after EDTA extraction is in the co-ordinately bound form. The increasing amount of elastin-bound calcium (*Table* 7.2) may act as a seed for the formation of hydroxyapatite, the form of the calcium salt in the highly calcified Monckeberg's aorta.

Table 7.2. *The ratios of the susceptibilities of various sections of human aorta at different ages to digestion by two forms of elastase, E and ECa. The enzyme E attacks those regions of the elastin structure which are rich in calcium whereas ECa attacks the calcium-poor regions. High values for the ratio therefore indicate regions rich in co-ordinately bound calcium*

Tissue	Age (years) 21	47	75
Intima	0·67	0·92	1·05
Inner layers of media	0·92	1·00	1·09
Centre of media	1·50	1·46	1·14
Adventitial border of media	0·78	0·82	0·87

The pdc may be derived from preformed collagen or may be a product of smooth muscle cell activity. Stemerman and Ross (1972) demonstrated that 5–7 days after the disruption of the endothelial surfaces by the passage of a balloon catheter through a monkey's internal iliac artery and aorta, smooth muscle cells could be seen migrating through the fenestrations in the circumluminar elastic lamellae towards the intima, where they accumulated in considerable number.

Within a month 20–30 layers of newly proliferated smooth muscle cells surrounded
by newly formed connective tissue were apparent in the region of the intimal
membrane. Six months later the lesions had regressed fully, unless the experiment
were conducted in hypercholesterolaemic animals when the lesions were permanent (Ross and Harker, 1974). The lipid which penetrated the wall from the lipid
rich plasma was retained and was taken up by both the smooth muscle cells and by
the surrounding newly-formed connective tissue.

7.3 Lipid Infiltration

7.3.1 *Insudation Theory*

Age variations in the metabolism of lipid in the vascular system have long been
associated with the onset of atherosclerosis (Virchow, 1856; Aschoff, 1924;
Anitschkow, 1933), but the mechanisms whereby individual species of lipid either
ingested with the diet or synthesized within the body, are transformed into
beneficial or dangerous forms are similar in a variety of tissues and organs. Hence
it is possible to predict the type of metabolic modification which may affect the
lipids of the cardiovascular system by studies of changes taking place elsewhere in
the body (*see* p. 185).

Lipids as a whole represent a very varied group of bodily constituents which can
be fractionated by a number of different physical and chemical techniques. There
are four major classes of lipid: free fatty acids, neutral glycerides, steroids and
phospholipids, which occur in different proportions in tissues and in the circulation in complexes of greater or less degree of intricacy. The first three species
are hydrophobic and hence have to be carried in the circulation by attachment to
hydrophilic molecules. In tissues, however, their hydrophobic nature permits them
to associate with other non-polar substances such as elastin (*see above*) to which
they become attached by the formation of van de Waal's forces between the long
chain acyl groups in the lipid and the long chain mono-amino-mono-carboxylic
acid residues—leucine, isoleucine and valine—in the elastin molecules. Phospholipids on the other hand are capable of interaction with both hydrophobic and
hydrophilic molecules because of the phosphoryl residues and the basic components which substitute one of the hydroxyl groups of the central glycerol molecule.
They can, therefore, solubilize hydrophobic substances such as triglycerides and
cholesterol esters since they are capable of straddling the interface between lipid
and aqueous phase, in the same fashion as polar detergents.

7.3.2 *Lipoproteins*

In the fasting circulation, lipid complexes containing varying amounts of the
individual species of lipid are carried on and solubilized by protein. These
lipoproteins can be fractionated by ultracentrifugation, electrophoresis or precipitation into various classes with differing physical properties. On the basis of

heir flotational properties they are classified as individual species of lipoprotein anging from very low (VLDL) to high density (HDL) (*Box* 7.1). Their chemical :omposition may vary considerably, however, and the values given for cholesterol, riglyceride, phospholipid and protein content represent mean values for each :lass. In post-prandial plasma lipid droplets, the chylomicrons also occur. These :ontain only sufficient protein (1–1·5%) to maintain their spherical structure and he triglyceride which constitutes the major portion of their mass varies in chemical :omposition with variations in the diet.

Frederickson et al. (1965) have shown that the appearance of excessive amounts)f the various forms of lipoprotein in the plasma can be associated with varying

---

BOX 7.1

The lipoproteins in plasma can be separated into groups by a variety of physical processes— ultracentrifugation, electrophoresis and precipitation. The accepted nomenclature for these lipoprotein groups—very low-density lipoprotein (VLDL), low-density lipoprotein (LDL) and high-density lipoprotein (HDL) based on ultracentrifugal properties does not define individual molecular species, but groups with similar physical properties. Each group is characterized by mean values for triglyceride, cholesterol, phospholipid and protein content, as indicated in each bar diagram. In lipaemic plasma, triglyceride-rich micelles, the chylomicrons, are suspended in the plasma.

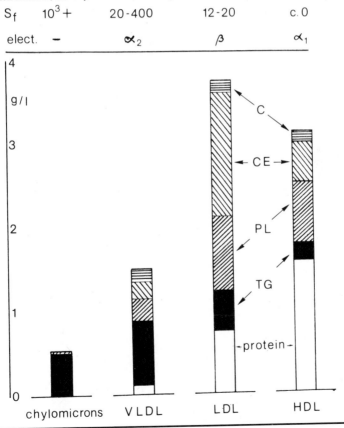

levels of risk of developing cardiovascular disease (*Table* 7.3). Lipoprotein levels in the plasma change with age (*Fig.* 7.2), rising rapidly in early adulthood in males and more slowly in females. The rise in the level in the female plasma continues up to about 75 years of age, whereas the high level attained by age 30 in males falls slightly after 60 years of age.

Table 7.3. **The effect of increasing concentrations of sf 0–20 and 20–400 lipoproteins on the mortality risk ratio for human subjects aged 50+**

	Plasma lipoprotein concentration (mg/dl)	Mortality risk ratio
sf 0–20		
	300	<50
	350	70
	400	95
	450	105
	500	150
	550+	>150
sf 20–400		
	100	<55
	130	93
	160	95
	190	105
	220	135
	250	135
	280+	>146

7.3.3 Cholesterol

Since the observations by Anitschkow (1913, 1933) that lesions in the vascular wall, similar in many respects to those present in human atherosclerosis, can be induced in experimental animals by the administration of cholesterol in the diet (*Fig.* 7.3), studies on the association of cholesterol with atherosclerosis and age have become very common. The measurement of cholesterol by various methods related to the original one devised by Liebermann–Burkhardt has proved to be accurate and repeatable and hence attempts have been made to make use of such assays for the assessment of the risk developing CHD. The total cholesterol content of plasma rises with increasing age (*Fig.* 7.4) in both males and females, peaking at between 65 and 80. Recent epidemiological studies (Kannel, 1971) have shown that the correlation between the total cholesterol level and the risk of developing CHD is relatively low (*Table* 7.4) and that a closer correlation can be obtained with the LDL-cholesterol level. Total and HDL-cholesterol are, however, easier parameters to measure than LDL-cholesterol, since HDL-cholesterol can be assayed after the LDL and VLDL fractions have been precipitated with magnesium sulphate and heparin (Lopez-Virella et al., 1977).

The level of HDL-cholesterol which rises with age (*Fig.* 7.5) is in itself a good indicator of CHD risk, being negatively related to the onset of the disease. In fact.

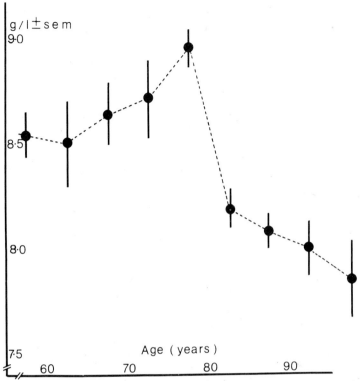

Fig. 7.2. Changing levels of lipoprotein in females aged 50 + to 90. Each point represents the mean of a five year age group ± s.e.m.

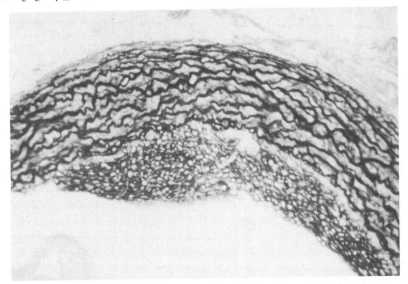

Fig. 7.3. An internal plaque in the aorta of a rabbit which had been fed for two months a diet containing 5% butter and 0·5% cholesterol.

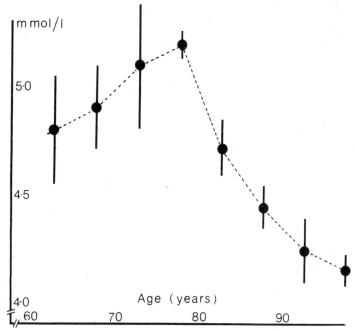

Fig. 7.4. Age-related changes in total plasma cholesterol levels in female subjects (cf. *Fig.* 7.2).

Table 7.4. **The importance of different lipid parameters as predictors of CHD in human subjects aged 50+**

Lipid	Men	Women
Total cholesterol in plasma (TC)	1·98	2·26
HDL cholesterol (HDL-C)	14·03	21·21
LDL cholesterol (LDL-C)	4·39	4·53
Triglyceride (TG)	0·51	9·52
TC/HDL-C	17·11	20·41

however, the best indicator calculable from total and fractional cholesterol levels is the ratio of total cholesterol to HDL-cholesterol. A value of between 4 and 5 for the ratio is consonant with an average degree of risk (*Table* 7.5). A five-fold increase in the ratio in the case of males, results in a three-fold increase in risk, whereas a similar increase in risk is brought about by a 2·5-fold increase in the ratio in the case of females. The fact that it is the ratio which provides the best indicator of risk explains why some individuals with relatively low total cholesterol levels develop CHD, whereas others with high levels do not. In the first instance, they will not be protected by high HDL-cholesterol levels, whereas in the second high HDL-cholesterol levels will temper the effect of cholesterol carried on the other lipoprotein fractions.

The value of this ratio rises in a statistically significant fashion ($P<0.05$) with increasing age up to 75–80 (*Fig.* 7.6). From the graph and from the data in

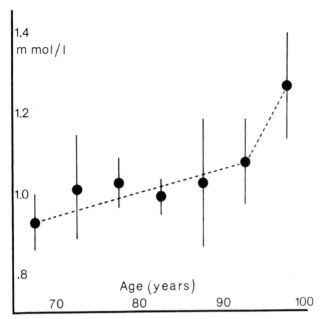

Fig. 7.5. Age-related changes in high-density lipoprotein cholesterol (cf. *Fig.* 7.2).

Table 7.5. **The levels for the ratio total cholesterol/HDL-cholesterol typical for average and above and below average risk of developing CHD**

Sex	Risk	TC/HDL-C
Male	0·5 × average	3·43
	average	4·97
	2 × average	9·55
	3 × average	23·99
Female	0·5 × average	3·27
	average	4·44
	2 × average	7·05
	3 × average	11·04

From these figures it can be seen that males are about twice as tolerant of high values for the ratio as females.

Table 7.5, it can be deduced that the risk of an elderly female subject developing CHD over the age range 55–90 will increase from 0·83 to 1·25 attaining an average value for risk (1·0) at age 70–75. Above 80, the risk decreases.

7.3.4 *Lipoproteins and Lipid Infiltration*

The various lipoproteins do not contain only cholesterol and it may, therefore, be insufficient merely to determine the ratios between the cholesterol contents of

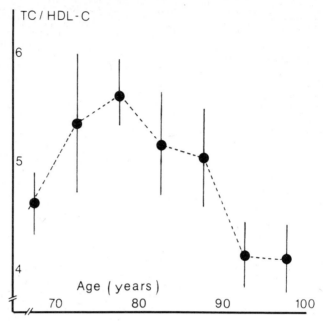

Fig. 7.6. Age changes in the ratio of total plasma cholesterol to HDL-cholesterol (females as in *Fig* 7.2).

various species of lipoproteins. It is possible to calculate the relative amounts of individual lipoproteins by the quantification of electropherograms and recordings of ultracentrifugal separations. Neither of these methods, however, provides results which demonstrate a comparable degree of accuracy to that associated with chemical determinations, and hence methods have been devised to permit the relative masses of the individual lipoproteins to be calculated from triglyceride and cholesterol assays (*Box* 7.2).

The LDL content of female plasma rises from 55 to 80 and then falls dramatically (*Fig.* 7.7). The difference between the mean values for a group aged 75–80 (300 mg/dl) and a second group aged 80–85 (280 mg/dl) is significant at the 99·5% level. The HDL content does not change appreciably over the age range 55–95. The rise demonstrated by the small number in the age group 95–100 is significant even though the scatter of these values is considerable. The ratio of LDL:HDL (*Fig.* 7.8) shows a more significant peaking than the ratio of total cholesterol to HDL-cholesterol, but the age group in which the peak occurs is the same, 75–80.

7.3.5 *Postprandial Lipid*

After the ingestion of a lipid-rich meal the total lipid content of the plasma increases rapidly, reaching a peak level between 3 and 5 hours after the meal (*Fig.* 7.9). Part of this increase occurs in the VLDL fraction, but the major increase

OX 7.2

ince lipid deposition in vascular tissue is associated with high levels of low-density lipoprotein (LDL)
nd inversely proportional to the concentration of high-density lipoprotein (HDL), the ratio of these
vo provides a useful measure of cardiovascular lipid pathology. Although LDL and HDL can be
:parated by electrophoresis, it is not particularly easy to quantify the amounts of the two lipoproteins.
ecause of this, the ratio of total cholesterol to HDL cholesterol has been used more frequently. This
atio, however, does not take into account the triglyceride and protein contents of the lipoproteins,
omponents which differ markedly in LDL and HDL.

Mr Frank Bowers of Enzypharm Biochemicals has suggested to the author that a third
neasurement—the total triglyceride content of the plasma—permits three equations to be derived using
:ccepted mean values for the triglyceride and cholesterol content of very low-density, low-density and
igh-density lipoproteins, namely:

$$HDL = (HDL\text{-}C) \times 5.9$$
$$0.5\ VLDL + 0.1\ LDL = TC - 0.235\ (HDL\text{-}C)$$
$$0.19\ VLDL + 0.45\ LDL = TC\text{-}HDL\text{-}C$$

he solution of these simultaneous equations provides figures for the levels of the three lipoproteins.
uch calculations are only applicable to fasting plasma, since non-fasting plasma may contain
riglyceride-rich chylomicrons in addition to the three lipoproteins.

It can be seen that the relationships of TC/HDL-C to age (A) and LDL/HDL (B) (calculated in this
ashion) to age differ from one another. Above 75 years of age, although both ratios fall in a similar
ashion, the LDL/HDL ratio decreases steadily from age 55 whereas the TC/HDL-C ratio is still rising
ver the age range 55–75. The LDL/HDL ratio appears to be more closely related to the lowered
usceptibility of very elderly subjects to cardiovascular disease over the whole range 55–95.

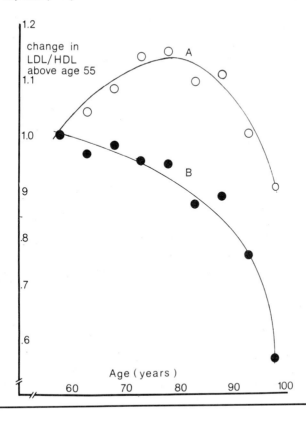

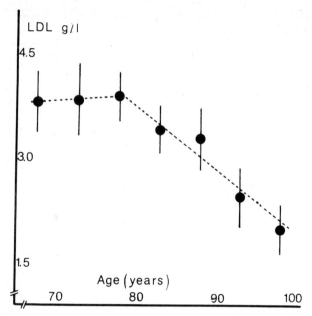

Fig. 7.7. Mean LDL content of female plasma (5 year age groups). Calculated by the method described in Boxes 7.3 and 7.4.

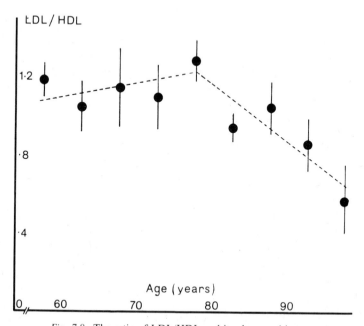

Fig. 7.8. The ratio of LDL/HDL and its change with age.

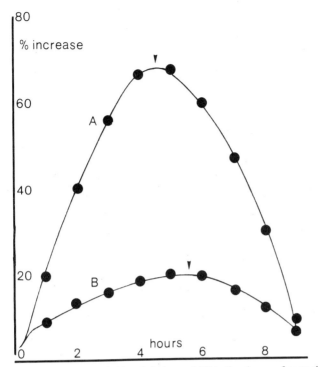

Fig. 7.9. The appearance of total lipid (A) and cholesterol (B) in the plasma of normal human subjects after the ingestion of a fat-rich meal.

occurs in the particulate chylomicron fraction and measurements of the opacity of the plasma can be used to assess the appearance and disappearance of lipid from the circulation. The removal of lipid from the plasma is dependent on the presence of the enzyme lipoprotein lipase (LPL) which is released from sites on the vascular wall and activated by heparin (*Fig.* 7.10). LPL levels fall with increasing age (Boberg et al., 1972) and this results in the retention of lipaemia for longer periods following the ingestion of lipid by an elderly subject.

If this were the only factor operative under these circumstances, it might be difficult for any elderly subject to maintain their plasma lipid levels low enough to prevent massive infiltration into the vascular tissue merely on the basis of a transendothelial gradient. Fortunately this is prevented to a certain extent by alterations in the rate of appearance of lipid in the circulation, probably due to a reduction in the rate of absorption from the gut. The total cholesterol (TC) and triglyceride levels in the plasma 3 hours after a lipid-rich meal fall to between one-half and one-third over the age range to 60–95. Moreover, the mean value for the increase in HDL-cholesterol 3 hours after the lipid-rich meal rises about six-fold (*Fig.* 7.11). Together these factors protect elderly subjects against potentially deleterious effects of lipid ingestion and consequently hold in check the potential risks of atherogenesis associated with faulty diet.

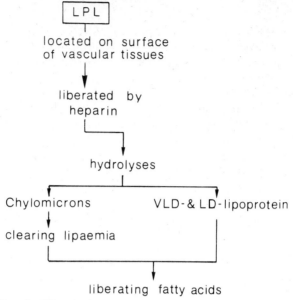

Fig. 7.10. The role of lipoprotein lipase in the removal of neutral lipid from the plasma.

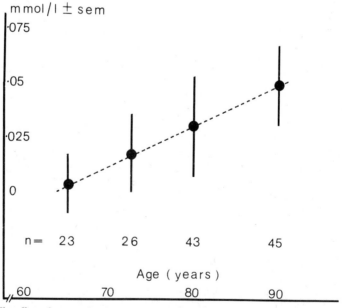

Fig. 7.11. The effect of age on the appearance of HDL-cholesterol in the plasma three hours after the ingestion of a fat-rich meal.

.3.6 *Phospholipid/cholesterol Ester Ratios in the Vascular Wall*

The cholesterol which is present in the aortic wall, whether it is a component of the cytoplasm of the mural cells or attached to protein in the extracellular matrix is mostly in the form of esters. The amount of cholesterol ester in the vascular tissue increases progressively with increasing age (*Fig.* 7.12) (Boberg et al., 1972) but this is not the only form of lipid to increase. The phospholipid content of the vascular wall also increases, but whereas between 10 and 90 years the cholesterol ester content increases 2·5-fold, the phospholipid level only increases by 60%. Hence the ratio of cholesterol ester to phospholipid increases four-fold over this period. The mean ratio in normal non-atherosclerotic tissue is 1·44, whereas that in athero-sclerotic plaques is 2·44. Further evidence for a positive attraction of lipid into the atherosclerotic tissue can be observed when these values for the cholesterol ester: phospholipid ratio are compared with those for LDL—1·68 and HDL—·44. If the penetration of lipid into the atherosclerotic tissue were merely due to a lipid gradient across the endothelial interface, the level could not rise above that in the plasma. The rise in cholesterol ester : phospholipid must be due to

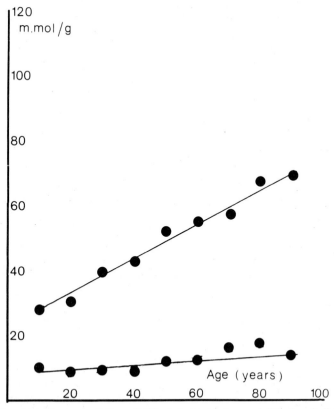

Fig. 7.12.   The changing concentration of (A) cholesterol esters and (B) phospholipid in human vascular tissue with increasing age.

a preferential uptake of cholesterol ester. Nevertheless the lower level in the HDL fraction must indicate that subjects with high levels of this lipoprotein species are less likely to provide the high ratio of cholesterol ester to phospholipid which is typical of the arterial lesion.

The ratio of these two species of lipid is dependent on the presence of the enzyme, lecithin cholesterol acyl transferase, which catalyses the transfer of acyl groups (fatty acid residues) from phospholipid to cholesterol. The types of phospholipid and cholesterol ester which are in equilibrium with one another is dependent on the availability of the various fatty acids. Both species take up increasing amounts of the linoleic acid series of fatty acids (essential fatty acids) as age increases (*Tables* 7.6 and 7.7). However, if the intake of essential fatty acids in the diet is defective, the mammalian organism changes over to the utilization of those fatty acids which can be synthesized within the body, the non-essential fatty acids of the oleic acid series.

Table 7.6. **Fatty acid composition of the phospholipid fractions in low and high density lipoproteins. Polyunsaturated acids are more prevalent in HDL phospholipid**

Fatty acid	LDL (%)	HDL (%)	LDL/HDL
16:0	32·1	30·2	1·06
16:1	1·6	1·4	1·14
18:0	15·9	16·0	0·99
18:1	12·0	12·4	0·97
18:2	20·0	20·3	0·97
20:4	6·7	8·5	0·79

Table 7.7. **Fatty acid composition of the cholesterol ester content of low and high density lipoproteins. Polyunsaturated acids are most prevalent in HDL cholesterol ester, but not to as marked an extent as in the phospholipid** (see Table 7.6)

Fatty acid	LDL (%)	HDL (%)	LDL/HDL
16:0	10·8	10·7	1·01
16:1	3·3	3·2	1·03
18:0	1·3	1·2	1·08
18:1	19·3	18·9	1·02
18:2	51·9	52·2	0·99
20:4	5·8	6·3	0·92

If a rat is fed an essential fatty acid-deficient diet for 2 months (Burdett et al., 1974), the level of the fatty acids of the linoleic ($\omega6$) series of say the liver are reduced and their place taken by members of the oleic ($\omega9$) series (*Fig.* 7.13). If the rat is only 2·5 months old, the fall in linoleic acid (18:2 $\omega6$) and arachidonic acid

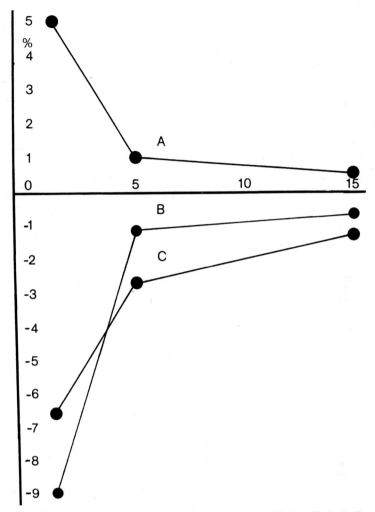

Fig. 7.13. The effect of age on the levels of essential and non-essential fatty acids in the livers of mice maintained for periods of two months on essential fatty acid-deficient diets (A) 20 : 3 ω9, eicosotrienoic acid; (B) 20 : 4 ω6, arachidonic acid, (C) 18 : 2 ω6, linoleic acid.

(20 : 4 ω6) and the rise in eicosotrienoic acid (20 : 3 ω9) can be seen quite clearly. At 7·5 months, the negative difference between the levels of the 18 : 2 ω6 and 20 : 4 ω6 acid at the beginning and end of the two months restricted diet is smaller as also is the positive difference between the before and after levels of 20 : 3 ω9. By 17·5 months the differences have fallen even further. The rates of change over in the 17·5 month animals is only 25% of that in the 2·5-month-old group of animals. Thus it appears that as the rats age their capability of replacing the members of the essential fatty acid series by those which can be synthesized is reduced to a quarter

of its original value. This implies that the animals are less suited to overcome insults to their metabolism consequent on changes in an external factor—their diet

7.4 Metabolism of Polyunsaturated Fatty Acids (PUFA)

7.4.1 PUFA Content of Ageing Tissues

In the rat liver, the two major constituents of the linoleic acid series are linoleic acid itself and arachidonic acid. Between 9 and 90 weeks there is a significant rise in the level of linoleic acid (9–33 weeks) followed by a slight fall thereafter. Arachidonic acid on the other hand falls and then rises, although neither change is significant (Burdett, 1974). If the liver lipids are fractionated into triglyceride, phospholipid and cholesterol ester, it can be shown that the major systematic changes in linoleic acid occur in the phospholipid fraction which peaks at 11 weeks and the cholesterol ester in which the linoleic acid content rises steadily from 9 to 76 weeks. The fall in linoleic acid content in the phospholipid fraction of the liver lipid is mirrored by a similar change in the plasma phospholipid ($24 \cdot 12 \pm 2 \cdot 16$ to $17 \cdot 50 \pm 2 \cdot 67$: a fall which is significant at the $99 \cdot 5\%$ level). The total content of $\omega 6$ fatty acids is maintained at a roughly constant level throughout this portion of the life-span of the rat by a significant rise in the level of circulating arachidonic acid ($15 \cdot 16 \pm 1 \cdot 56$ to $22 \cdot 07 \pm 2 \cdot 50$: $P < 0 \cdot 005$).

The linoleic acid component of the cholesterol ester fraction of the liver lipid rises significantly between 11 and 76 weeks ($23 \cdot 03 \pm 2 \cdot 22$ to $28 \cdot 07 \pm 2 \cdot 42$: $P < 0 \cdot 05$) and this is accompanied by a comparable but rather variable rise in arachidonic acid level ($14 \cdot 12 \pm 2 \cdot 34$ to $19 \cdot 92 \pm 6 \cdot 60$). The changes in plasma cholesterol ester fatty acids do not, however, mirror the liver changes, there being a significant fall in linoleic acid ($28 \cdot 57 \pm 7 \cdot 53$ to $21 \cdot 49 \pm 2 \cdot 24$: $P < 0 \cdot 0005$), and a significant rise in arachidonic acid ($42 \cdot 45 \pm 3 \cdot 60$ to $49 \cdot 44 \pm 5 \cdot 03$: $P < 0 \cdot 005$).

One of the difficulties associated with attempts to correlate changes in liver and plasma lipids with age is the fact that both these lipid pools are greatly affected by dietary changes. The variation in lipid in the vascular tissue and in encapsulated organs such as the testes is far more likely to be buffered against diurnal variation following lipid ingestion. There is a significant fall in the overall phospholipid content of the testes between 9 and 33 weeks from 13·5 to 11·5 mg/g wet weight and since this represents the major lipid component of the organ (triglycerides and cholesterol esters together amount to less than 1·5 mg/g), any changes in phospholipid fatty acids represent overall changes in the organ as a whole. The modification of the $\omega 6$ linoleic acid series progresses farther than arachidonic acid in the testes, individual fatty acids with as many as twenty-four carbon atoms and five double bonds being present (see Box 7.3). Because of the greater constancy of the lipid composition in organs such as the testes, in which there is less than 1% change in lipid composition in one testis when a fatty acid is injected into the other (a count of only 6500 cpm was observed in one testis 24 hours after the injection of 7·9 million cpm $1-{}^{14}C$ linoleic acid albumin complex into the other), it is possible to observe true age changes in this organ. The linoleic acid content of the testes hospholipid falls significantly over the period 11 to 90 weeks (5.56 ± 0.26 to $28 \pm 0.09 : P < 0.005$) the $\omega6$ eicosotrienoic acid concentration rises (0.92 ± 0.36 to $50 \pm 0.20 : P < 0.005$) as do the levels of $22:4 \omega6$; $22:5 \omega6$; $24:4 \omega6$ and $24:5 \omega6$. he arachidonic acid ($20:4 \omega6$) level oscillates more than the others, but there is a neasurable overall fall with age.

The transformation of linoleic acid to longer chain, more highly unsaturated pecies takes place by the alternate desaturation and chain elongation (*Box* 7.3) Marcel et al., 1968). The enzyme responsible for the introduction of the third ouble bond into linoleic acid, $18:2 \omega6$, known as 6-olefinase (Brenner, 1971) can lso desaturate members of the oleic ($\omega9$) and α-linolenic acid ($\omega3$) series. Competitive inhibition of its action on oleic acid occurs when linoleic acid itself is lso present. This explains why the metabolism of ingested essential fatty acids ormally takes precedence over that of non-essential fatty acids (p. 182). End roduct inhibition also occurs and this could explain why the concentration of rachidonic acid falls with increasing age, if the enzyme which is capable of esaturating the initially present $18:2 \omega6$ is progressively inhibited by the products f the reaction.

OX 7.3

he conversion of linoleic acid to longer chain more highly unsaturated acids. It is possible for linoleic $18:2 \omega6$) acid to be converted to higher homologues by chain elongation followed by desaturation or y desaturation followed by chain elongation. The preferred pathway from linoleic acid ($18:2 \omega6$) to rachidonic acid ($20:4 \omega6$) (heavy arrows) consists initially of desaturation to γ-linolenic acid ($18:3$ o6) followed by chain elongation to the eicosotrienoic acid ($20:3 \omega6$: homo-γ-linolenic acid) and a urther desaturation to arachidonic acid ($20:4 \omega6$).

Young rats augment this pathway by the alternative route in which chain elongation to produce nomo-γ-linolenic acid is followed by desaturation (Hall and Burdett, 1975).

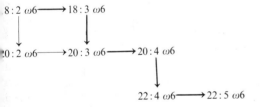

The administration of linoleic and γ-linolenic ($20:3 \omega6$) acids to the testes of living rats of varying age, however, presents an alternative explanation. Radioactive linoleic and γ-linolenic acids were administered as their albumin complexes by direct injection into one testis each of groups of rats of age 7·5, 47 and 73 weeks; 24 hours later the rat was killed, the testis removed and the lipid extracted. The phospholipid fraction was then separated on the basis of its degree of unsaturation by argentation thin-layer chromatography (Hall and Burdett, 1975). The mean amounts of $18:2 \omega6$ converted into trienes and higher polyunsaturates, into tetraenes and higher polyunsaturates and into pentaenes were then recorded for each age group (*Table* 7.8). The same procedure was carried

out following the administration of radioactive 18:3 ω6 except that the series of
derived polyunsaturates commenced in this instance with the tetraenes since the
administered fatty acid was itself a triene. It can be seen that the pattern of
metabolism differs according to age and to the degree of unsaturation of the

Table 7.8. *The effect of the administration of (a) linoleic
and (b) γ-linolenic acids by injection in the testes of
rats of various ages on the proportion of the fatty acids
appearing as phospholipid with more highly unsaturated
constituents. The figures for trienes, for instance, include
that portion of the total which has passed through the
triene stage on its way to tetraene and pentaene. The points
at which the distribution patterns for different degrees of
unsaturation change are indicated by vertical dotted lines*

a, Linoleic acid administered			
Dienes	—	—	—
Trienes	21·6	15·3	14·7
Tetraenes	12·5	8·7	7·7
Pentaenes	1·6	0·8	0·7
b, γ-linolenic acid administered			
Trienes	—	—	—
Tetraenes	26·7	28·4	19·1
Pentaenes	2·9	2·4	1·3

administered fatty acid. Thus in the case of 18:2 ω6, in the youngest age group
21·6% of the original diene is converted to triene or above, of which 12·6% is
further converted to tetraene or above and of this 1·6% is finally converted to
pentaene. The pattern of metabolism in the upper two age groups is completely
different, a smaller amount is converted from diene to more highly unsaturated
homologues and smaller amounts are subsequently converted to tetraenes and to
pentaenes. There is, however, little difference between the patterns of metabolism
in either of the two older groups. Conversely in the case of the administration of
18:3 ω6 the age split occurs between 47 and 73 weeks and not as in the case of
18:2 ω6 between 7·5 and 47. A possible explanation of this might be that the
enzyme system which introduces the third double bond may become defective as
age progresses. Although the preferred pathway from 18:2 ω6 to 20:4 ω6 would
appear to be 18:2 ω6→18:3 ω6→20:3 ω6→20:4 ω6 there are other possibilities.
During the early life of the rat when its reproductive capacity is being developed
its requirements for spermatogenesis will be considerable. It may be, therefore,
that to provide adequate amounts of polyunsaturated material for incorporation
into the phospholipid-rich head of the spermatozoa, the rat calls into play one of
the other possible pathways such as 18:2 ω6→20:2 ω6→20:3 ω6, etc. As
maturity is reached, the maintenance of a sperm bank appropriate to the rat's
requirements by the Sertoli cells may not require the amount of linoleic acid
metabolism essential in youth and maturation and hence this latter pathway is
switched off leaving the preferred pathway, identified by Marcel et al., 1968. As the
animal ages and its reproductive capacity is reduced, even this pathway becomes
partially redundant and this as well becomes less effective. Such a timetable of

vents could account for the different metabolic patterns observed following the administration of linoleic and γ-linolenic acids.

In the arterial wall, the presence of polyunsaturated fatty acid-rich phospholipids assists in the mobilization of cholesterol, preventing it from being deposited. If enzyme systems for the desaturation of the linoleic acid become steadily deficient as age progresses, it would be expected that the cholesterol would accumulate since there would be fewer polyunsaturated acyl groups available for transfer under the action of lecithin cholesterol acyl transferase.

If this suggestion is accepted there would appear to be no rational reason to attempt to reduce the accumulation of cholesterol within vascular tissue of elderly subjects by feeding diets rich in linoleic acid. It would be more appropriate to consider the possibility of bypassing that part of the pathway which was defective and administering one or other of the polyunsaturated fatty acids which result from the desaturation and chain elongation of linoleic acid.

Arachidonic acid would appear to be the most suitable since this particular fatty acid accumulates in tissues forming an appreciable component of cell membrane structures. There are, however, two factors which militate against the administration of preparations rich in arachidonic acid: first, arachidonic acid is readily peroxidized and its retention in an unoxidized state would necessitate the simultaneous administration of antioxidants which might themselves have unwanted effects on the organism. Secondly, arachidonic acid provides the substrate for the synthesis of prostaglandin E, a powerful metabolite required in physiologically well-defined concentrations in various tissue throughout the body. The provision of arachidonic acid in excessive amounts in the liver and/or the circulation might result in the uncontrolled synthesis of prostaglandin with marked non-physiological effects.

It is, therefore desirable to consider whether one or other of the intermediates between linoleic acid and arachidonic acid is suitable for replacement therapy. Of these two—γ-linolenic acid and homo-γ-linolenic acid—the latter is exceptionally ephemeral, only appearing in exceptionally small concentrations in most mammalian tissues. γ-linolenic acid, however, which is the first product of the desaturation pathway from linoleic to arachidonic acid is present in appreciable amounts in the oil of the seeds of the evening primrose (*Oenethara*). The major portion of this unsaturated fatty acid present in the triglycerides of this oil is linoleic acid, but 10% is γ-linolenic acid (Riley, 1949). The administration of γ-linolenic acid to rats rendered hypercholesterolaemic with a cholesterol-rich or saturated fatty acid-rich diet results in a significant reduction in the level of circulating cholesterol (the late T. Davies, private communication), and its administration to human subjects with xanthelasma also reduced the associated hypercholesterolaemia.

7.5 Conclusions

The development of atheroma in the vascular tissue is a multifactorial process, one element of which is age. The lipid which is present in the circulation varies in composition as the subject ages, and this alteration determines to some degree the ease with which it penetrates the vessel wall and once within the tissue remains there. Age-modulated changes in vascular tissue itself, however, predispose the protein content of the latter to combine with the lipid and to retain it. These changes may be present without any overt physiological symptoms, and it is no until the degree of alteration or the type of lesion, be it at the original site or elsewhere in the vasculature, is sufficient to markedly reduce the blood supply to an important end organ that the cumulative effects of altered lipid metabolism modified vascular tissue and age produce a phenomenon which is of clinical significance.

Recommended Reading

There are numerous publications on atherosclerosis but few dealing with the general topic of lipid changes in old age. For a good survey of the fundamental biochemistry of the lipids one of the best recent publications is *Lipid Biochemistry* by M. I. Gurr and A. T. James (1980). Chapman & Hall 3rd ed.

References

Anitschkow N. (1913) Über die Veranderungen der Kaninchenaorta bei experimentaller cholesterin steatose. (The alterations occurring in rabbit aorta as the result of cholesterol feeding.) *Beitrag Pathol. Anat.* **56**, 379.

Anitschkow N. (1933) Experimental arteriosclerosis in animals. In: Cowdry E. V. (ed.) *Arteriosclerosis* New York, Macmillan. p. 271.

Aschoff L. (1924) *Lectures in Pathology*. New York, Hoeber, p. 131.

Balo J. and Banga I. (1949) The destruction of the elastic fibres of vessel walls. *Schweiz. Z. Pathol. n Bakteriol.* **12**, 350.

Beachey E. H., Chiang T. M. and Kang A. H. (1979) Collagen-platelet interaction. *Int. Rev. Connect Tissue Res.* **8**, 1.

Boberg J., Carlson L. A. and Fröberg S. (1972) Serum and tissue lipids in relation to age. In: Carlson L. A. (ed.) *Nutrition in Old Age*. Stockholm, Almquist & Wiksell, p. 61.

Brenner R. R. (1971) The desaturation step in the animal biosynthesis of polyunsaturated fatty acid *Lipids* **6**, 567.

Burdett P. E. (1974) Fatty Acids and Ageing. *Ph.D. Thesis, University of Leeds.*

Constantinides P. and Robinson M. (1969) Ultrastructural injury of arterial endothelium. *Arch. Pathol* **88**, 99.

Duguid J. B. (1946) Thrombosis as a factor in the pathogenesis of coronary atherosclerosis. *J. Pathol Bact.* **58**, 207.

Fredrickson D. S., Lees R. S., Hatch F. T. et al. (1965) A system of phenotyping hyperlipidaemias using L and H electrophoretic method. *Circulation* **31**, 321.

French J. E. (1966) Atherosclerosis in relation to the structure and function of the arterial intima, with special reference to the endothelium. *Int. Rev. Exp. Pathol.* **5**, 253.

Gresham G. A. (1976) Atherosclerosis: its causes and potential reversibility. *Triangle* **15**, 39.

Hall D. A. (1970) Co-ordinately bound calcium as a cross-linking agent in elastin and as an activator o elastolysis. *Gerontologia*, **16**, 325.

Hall D. A. (1973) Collagène et élastine: modifications dues a l'âge. (Collagen and elastin; age modifications.) *Méd. Hyg* **31**, 1.

Hall D. A. (1976) *Ageing of Connective Tissue*. London, Academic Press.

Hall D. A. and Burdett P. E. (1975) Age changes in the metabolism of essential fatty acids. *Biochem Soc. Trans.* **3**, 42.

Kannel W. B. (1971) Current status of the epidemiology of brain infarction associated with occlusive arterial disease. *Stroke* **2**, 295.

Kramsch D. M., Hollander W. and Franzblau C. (1970) The role of arterial elastin in the lipid accumulation in human atherosclerotic arteries. In: Jones R. J. (ed.) *Atherosclerosis 2nd Int. Symp.* New York, Springer-Verlag, p. 115.

Lansing A. I., Blumenthal A. T. and Gray S. H. (1948) Aging and calcification of the human coronary artery. *J. Gerontol.* **3**, 7.

Lopez-Virella M. F., Stone P., Ellis S. et al. (1977) Cholesterol determination in HDLs separated by three methods. *Clin. Chem.* **23**, 882.

Marcel Y. L., Christiansen K. and Holman T. (1968) The preferred metabolic pathway from linoleic acid to arachidonic acid. *Biochim. Biophys. Acta* **164**, 25.

Mustard J. F. and Packham M. A. (1975) The role of blood and platelets in atherosclerosis and the complication of atherosclerosis. *Thromb. Diath. Haemorrh.* **33**, 444.

Riley J. P. (1949) Seed fat of *Oenothera bienis L. J. Chem. Soc.* 2728.

Rokitansky C. von (1852) *A Manual of Pathological Anatomy.* Vol. 4. Trans. Day G. E. London, Sydenham Society, p. 261.

Ross R. and Glomset J. A. (1973) Atherosclerosis and the arterial smooth muscle cell. *Science* **180**, 1332.

Ross R. and Glomset J. A. (1976) The pathogenesis of atherosclerosis. *N. Engl. J. Med.* **295**, 369, 420.

Ross R. and Harker L. (1974) Hyperlipidaemia and atherosclerosis. *Science* **193**, 1094.

Saxl H. and Hall D. A. (1967) Elastic tissue in relation to arterial lipids. In: Blumenthal H. T. (ed.) *Cowdry's Arteriosclerosis.* 2nd ed. Springfield, Ill., Thomas.

Stermerman M. B. and Ross R. (1972) Experimental atherosclerosis. I. Fibrous plaque formation in primates: an electron microscopic study. *J. Exp. Med.* **136**, 768.

Virchow, R. von (1856) *Plogose und Thrombose im Gefassystem, gesammette Abhandlungen zur wissenschaftlichen Medizin.* Frankfurt am Main, Meidinger Sohn, p. 458.

Yu S. and Blumenthal H. T. (1960) Nature of calcium-elastin binding. *Fed. Proc.* **19**, 19.

8

The Ageing of the Nervous System

8.1 Introduction

A full understanding of age changes in the central nervous system calls for a study of its anatomy, its function and the behavioural effects resulting from variations in its physiology. A broader spectrum of techniques has been employed in such studies than in most other aspects of age research. These include computerized tomography, xenon-133 clearance, angiography, electroencephalography and electromyography for studies of the intact organism; a variety of electrophysiological and biochemical techniques for the examination of excised tissues and psychological quantification of the behavioural aspects of brain function.

Because of the diversity of methodologies available for studies of the ageing process as it affects the nervous system, and the catholic nature of the information which can arise from them, it might be expected that this particular aspect of age research could offer the greatest hope for the solution of at least one of the major facets of ageing. The effect of improvements in sanitation, other aspects of public health and the chemotherapy of infectious diseases over the past century has been to ensure that an increasing proportion of the population survives to ages at which the diseases of senility are prevalent. One such condition is organic brain disease which results in so many elderly subjects sitting cabbage-like in old persons' homes with little appreciation of their surroundings. A full explanation of the physiological changes which bring about dementias of this type and of the senile loss of memory could pave the way for an alleviation of one of the most pathetic sequelae of ageing, one which incapacitates the elderly subject to a far greater extent than most physical changes. Psychogeriatricians can provide a certain degree of help for

190

ome elderly demented subjects, and this will be referred to in passing below, but his chapter deals more specifically with the underlying factors which determine the vay in which age affects the nervous system rather than their alleviation.

3.2 Macro-structural Changes of the Nervous System

3.2.1 *The Brain*

The cerebrum is divided into two hemispheres by the longitudinal fissure but the wo halves are united by the corpus callosum. In young subjects the cerebrum occupies over 90% of the total cranial space and in the case of European males a mean value for this volume may be taken as about 1450 cm^3. Other non-European peoples, such as Eskimos, appear to have mean values which are greater than this, whereas Australian aborigines have among the lowest mean value of below 1300 cm^3. Among Europeans, however, there is a wide variation amounting to nearly $\pm 30\%$. Hence, although cerebral atrophy often occurs in elderly subjects, the volume of some highly atrophic elderly brains may still be well within one standard deviation of the mean value for young subjects. Thus, if mental performance could be correlated with cerebral volume, the changes observed in old age would not necessarily be significant. Moreover, individual differences in this measurement are also partly a function of general body size.

Therefore, just as it seems highly unlikely that differences between the cranial capacities of different racial groups of human subjects can be correlated with differing mental ability, it is equally unlikely that the degree of cerebral atrophy can be correlated directly with the onset of impaired mental function in the elderly.

8.2.2 *The Extracerebral Nervous System*

Although neurones separated by synaptic clefts are present within the brain, the complex branching and anastomosis of nerve fibres apparent in the white tissue makes it very difficult to identify age changes in the individual transmission pathways in most regions of the brain. The structure of afferent and efferent extracerebral neurones can be identified more easily. Each nerve cell consists of a body containing the nucleus, surrounded by cytoplasm which branches into a series of fine dendritic processes. The main portion of the neurone consists of the axon, sheathed down the greater part of its length by phospholipid-rich myelin. However, every 1–2 mm along the length of the axon the sheath is interrupted by constrictions—the nodes of Ranvier—where channels for the transport of sodium and potassium ions are grouped closely together. The distal end of the axons are distended to form synaptic termini from which impulses are transmitted across the interneural gap to receptors located in the dendrites of adjacent cells. These synaptic clefts between one neurone and the next are of the order of 20 mm in width. The sequential transport of first sodium ions and then potassium ions, through the channels located in the nodes of Ranvier, acts as a booster for the

transmission of the action potential down the axon at velocities of between 1 an
100 m/sec, by neutralizing the negative charge inside the neurone and depolarizin
the membrane. The energy for the final stage of the transmission, across th
synaptic cleft, is provided by mitochondria located in the synaptic bulb (*Fig. 8.1*

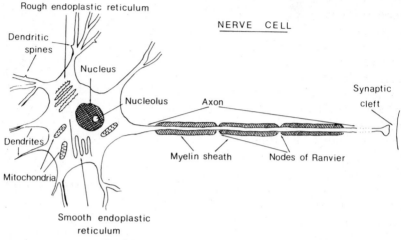

Fig. 8.1. The structure of a typical neurone.

There is little evidence for complete demyelinization of the senile neurone, but a
mild degree of myelin loss does occur in association with reduced nerve conduction. The dimensions of the synapses do not apparently increase with
increasing age. Decreased synaptic transmission appears, therefore, to be o:
functional rather than anatomical origin (*see below*).

8.2.3 Cellular changes

Initial claims that massive cell loss might account for impaired brain function in
elderly subjects (Andrew, 1952) has been challenged by Königsmark and Murphy
(1972) and by Hanley (1974). Hanley suggested that faulty sampling techniques
might account for the reported losses. He cited results published over the previous
100 years and claimed that the ratio of cell counts in old and young animals moved
closer to unity as methods for the preparation of brain tissue were improved. More
recently, Tomlinson and Henderson (1976) and Henderson et al. (1980) have
confirmed the observations of Brody (1955, 1970) and Shefer (1972) that nerve cell
loss is considerable in certain regions of the brain, but not in others. Brody (1955)
reported a 30% loss of cells in all layers of the superior temporal gyrus. In 1970 he
observed heavy losses from the superior frontal gyrus. Tomlinson and Henderson,
and Henderson et al. using a computerized particle analyser to study eleven
different regions of the brain reported a significant ($P<0.001$) loss of neurons
(3300 entities larger than 19 µm/100 mm^2 falling to 1500 over the period 20 to 90
years). Hall T. C. et al. (1975) have shown that there is a marked reduction in the

number of cerebellar Purkinje cells in normal elderly subjects. Motor neurones in the human lumbosacral spinal cord do not change in number during the first six decades of life, but fall by 27% over the next three to four decades (Tomlinson and Irving, 1977). The locus coeruleus (Vijayashankar and Brody, 1979 and Tomlinson et al., 1970), the splanchnic (Low et al., 1977) and the putamen (Bugiani et al., 1978) all show moderate to severe loss of neurones in normal ageing. Other brain tissues, such as the ventral cochlear nucleus (Königsmark, 1969; Königsmark and Murphy, 1970 and 1972), the abducens and the trochlear nuclei (Vijayashankar and Brody, 1977), the mammillary bodies (Wilkinson and Davis, 1978) and the inferior olive (Monagle and Brody, 1974) all retain an unchanged neuronal population well into the ninth decade.

These observations have all been made on brain tissues from supposedly normal ageing subjects, but there is not much evidence for appreciably greater losses in cases of senile dementia. Alterations in the morphology of the cells rather than in their number characterize the changes attributable to dementia.

The dendritic processes of neurones provide the linkage areas between adjacent axons. Silver impregnation of brain sections by one of the modifications of Golgi's original method, shows that many neurones demonstrate marked losses not only of the terminal dendrites but also of the dendritic spines as well. Feldman and Dowd (1974) and Feldman (1976) have reported that the pyrimidal neurones of the rat's visual cortex lose up to 40% of their dendritic spines between 3 and 29 months. Scheibel (1978) reported losses in dendrites in the human pre-frontal and temporal cortices leading to irregularly thickened and distorted cellular bodies and ultimately to neuronal death (Schiebel and Schiebel, 1976). Although such changes appear in some areas of the normal ageing brain (Buell and Coleman, 1979) this sort of change is more characteristic of Alzheimer's disease, Jacob–Creutzfeld disease, Pick's disease and Huntingdon's chorea. A further change in the micro-anatomy of the neurones in senile dementia of the Alzheimer type is the development of neurofibrillary tangle (*Fig.* 8.2). In this form of degeneration silver-staining helically-wound filamentous bodies are apparent in the cytoplasm of many of the neurones. Each one of the pair of fibrils is about 10 mm thick and they are twisted around one another with a helical pitch of about 160 nm. They are completely dissimilar to the normal neurotubules and neurofilaments which can be observed in those parts of the neuronal soma which are not occupied by the tangle.

In a proportion of elderly subjects, senile plaques develop. These bodies, silver-staining like the neufibrillary tangles, can vary in diameter from 15–200 μm. The central region of each plaque consists of material with all the staining properties of amyloid and this is surrounded by tangled dendritic material and there is also evidence for the presence of neurofibrillary material.

8.3 The Lipids of the Central Nervous System

8.3.1 *Myelin*

The total myelin content of human brain white matter decreases by 30% with increasing age (Berlet and Volk, 1980). Since 78% of this substance is lipid it is

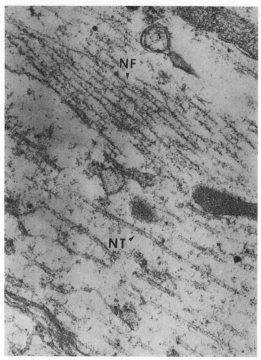

Fig. 8.2. Neurofibrillary tangles in a case of Alzheimer's disease, (NT); normal fibrils, (NF). (Reproduced with the permission of Plenum Press and the authors, Wisnieski, Sinatra, Iqbal and Grundke-Iqbal, from *Aging a Cell Structure*, Johnson J. E. jun. Ed. 1981.)

not surprising that some of the major changes are associated with quantitative changes in lipid synthesis. There are about 1500 different lipids in the myelin sheath. Some 30% of these are present in appreciable amounts. Of the phospholipids, phosphatidyl ethanolamine is present in the young adult in the largest concentration (11·7%) followed by phosphatidyl choline (lecithin) and phosphatidyl serine which are present in similar amounts (7·5% and 7·1% respectively). Phosphatidyl inositol is only present in trace amounts (0·6%). Sphingosine-based lipids, such as sphingomyelin (6·4%) and the cerebrosides (22%), are also present. Sun and Sun (1979) have suggested that ageing is associated with a qualitative rather than a quantitative change in the lipid constituents of myelin. However, phosphatidyl ethanolamine and plasmalogen levels do change in a quantitative fashion. Of even greater importance, however, is a significant decrease in the polyunsaturated acyl groups of various individual phosphoglycerides.

8.3.2 *Fatty Acids*

Gangliosides are characterized by the presence of fatty acids with C_{20} or longer chains, whereas cerebrosides do not contain acids with chains shorter than C_{24}.

Rouser and Yamamato (1969) demonstrated that the ethanolamine-containing phosphoglycerides contain increasing amounts of C18:1 and C20:1 as age progresses, whereas arachidonic acid, C20:4, and the longer and more highly unsaturated acids C22:4 and C22:6 decrease with age. The fatty acid composition of the cerebroside and sulphatide components of the sphingolipids of the human brain does not change with age, but the saturated fatty acids such as 18:0 increase at the expense of the mono-unsaturated fatty acid 24:1 in the myelin of the extracerebral nerves (Samorajski and Rolsten, 1973; Heipetz et al., 1977).

8.3.3 Cerebrovascular Disease and Lipids

In Chapter 7, evidence is presented which indicates that variations in the lipid composition of the plasma result in the development of atheromatous changes in the arterial wall leading to alterations in vascular function. This is not only true of the central vascular system but also of the peripheral vessels of which those in the brain may be regarded as the most important.

Hall D. A. et al. (1980a, b) have shown that the level of circulating elastase which increases when a subject experiences a cerebrovascular accident (see Chapter 5) is associated with marked changes in the level of cholesterol or more specifically with the ratio of total to HDL-cholesterol. Enhanced levels of circulating lipid do increase the levels of elastase in the plasma which it has been suggested originates in the pancreas, but Hall and Wilkinson (1962) have also shown that elastase can be liberated following the mechanical disruption of platelets. If these blood components are involved in the formation of an intracerebral thrombosis, their integrity will be impaired once they have adhered to collagen in the vessel wall and this metamorphosis could result in the release of elastase. Hence the high lipid levels in the plasma and the elevated elastase levels may represent associated but not directly sequential effects.

8.3.4 Lipofuscin

The presence of pigmented bodies in the cytoplasm of post-mitotic cells has been appreciated since the end of the first decade of the present century (Stübel, 1911). This material, variously known as age-pigment and lipofuscin, has a typical fluorescence, activated at 365 nm with an emission wavelength of 340 nm in tissues from young animals, moving to the higher wavelength of 380 nm in older animals. It is apparent from this that, despite its name, age-pigment is present even in young tissues. Strehler et al. (1959), however, have demonstrated that the lipofuscin content of human myocardium increases linearly from 0·5% by volume in the first decade of life to 6% in the tenth decade. Treff (1974) similarly reported a progressive increase in the human cerebellar nucleus dentatus. In this instance, however, the rate of increase of the lipofuscin content of the nerve cells rose with age (Fig. 8.3). In rats there were significant increases in the lipofuscin content of

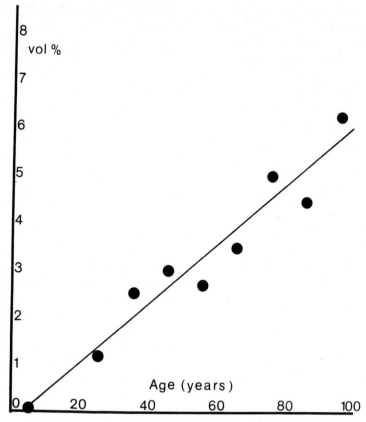

Fig. 8.3. The accumulation of lipofuscin in human cardiac tissue.

the hippocampus, the cerebral cortex, and the Purkinje and granular cell layers o
the cerebellum between 9–11 months and 26–29 months of age (Strehler, 1977). In
many instances level was unmeasurable in the younger age group, but where a
finite value was recordable, the mean increase, during the 13·5 months, which
represents a period when the animals were truly ageing, was over 6-fold.

Hendley et al. (1963), Strehler (1964) and Siakotis and Koppang (1973) have
analysed lipofuscin and have demonstrated that this pigment results from the
accumulation of autoxidation products of the lysosomal lipids and lipid constitu
ents of other cell organelles. The involvement of autoxidation in the developmen
of lipofuscin would appear to indicate that a deficiency in anti-oxidant function
might represent the basic biochemical lesion. In fact, a deficiency in the naturally
occuring anti-oxidant, vitamin E, does increase the rate of lipofuscin deposition
Although Strehler (1977) claims that supplementation of this natural anti-oxidan
does not appear to protect against pigment accumulation, Blackett and Hall (1981
have reported a marked reduction in lipofuscin accumulation and an improve
ment in neuromuscular coordination in mice fed diets to which vitamin E has been

added (Blackett and Hall, 1981a; Airey and Hall, 1983). They agree with Strehler 1977) however, in failing to observe any overall extension of life-span (Blackett and Hall 1981b; Airey, 1983). The vitamin does, however, appear to have a significant effect on survival during the first half of the life-span, during which period it also affects other parameters known to alter with age, such as the physical and chemical properties of connective-tissue components (Blackett and Hall, 1980).

8.4 Cerebral Blood Flow

Normal elderly subjects, without any signs of psychological disease, were shown by Dastur et al. (1963) to have identical cerebral blood flow (CBF) to a comparable group of young individuals, although a group with minimal physical abnormalities, but with intact cerebral structures had significantly lowered CBF. Wang et al. (1970), on the other hand, reported a significant difference between values for CBF in young and old healthy individuals. Tomlinson et al. (1970) and Roth (1971) identified regions of cerebral softening which appeared to be secondary to cerebral ischaemia. Studies of these lesions enabled them to differentiate a specific group of senile dements from those exhibiting the changes typical of Alzheimer's disease—those with senile plaques. O'Brien and Mallett (1970) suggested that the functional changes indicated that, rather than an overall decrease in CBF, this form of cerebral disease was most likely to be due to a mosaic of normal and pathologically ischaemic tissues. These observations are in agreement with the findings of computerized tomography which indicate the presence of foci of involvement rather than a global reduction in cerebral mass.

8.5 Transmitters and the Ageing Nervous System

8.5.1 The Function of Transmitters

Birren and Schaie (1976) have reported that the age-induced loss of speed and accuracy of various behavioural patterns increases as the complexity of the pattern increases. Moreover, Shock (1974) has shown that if any reaction requires the co-ordinated activity of more than one organ system, it regresses more rapidly with age than when a single organ is involved. From these observations it may be deduced that the interaction of cell on cell and organ on organ represents the site at which the ageing process exerts its deleterious effects. In the nervous system the point of such interaction is the synapse. The electrical impulse, the action potential, is transmitted down the axon but cannot cross the synapse. In the synaptic terminus the action potential has to be replaced by a chemical transmitter which can cross the gap and which after interaction with specific postsynaptic receptors can initiate further action potentials. Other substances may also cross the synapse and inhibit the onward transmission of an action potential. The first chemical

substances to be identified as activators were acetylcholine and norepinephrine
and a study of these two substances and their absence or presence in a variety of
synapses has demonstrated the importance of six factors in synaptic activity
namely:

a. synthesis in the presynaptic terminals;
b. storage of the transmitter in pre-synaptic granules;
c. release of the transmitters;
d. response of receptors in the post-synaptic dendrite;
e. inactivation of excess transmitter;
f. reabsorption of intermediates in presynaptic terminals (*Fig.* 8.4).

On the basis of studies of these factors, the transmitters listed in *Table* 8.1 have
been identified. The sites of activity of some of these various transmitters have been

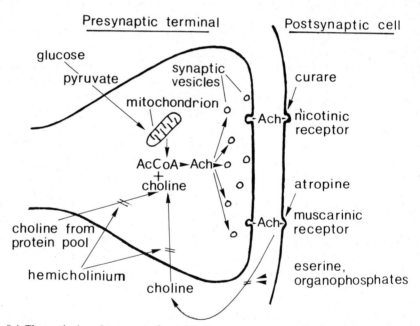

Fig. 8.4. The synthesis and transport of acetylcholine across a synapse. Similar effects are apparent at
non-cholinergic synapses where other transmitters are involved. The muscarinic and nicotinic receptors
are distributed unevenly throughout various regions of the brain.

Table 8.1. **Transmitters in**
synaptic transport

Acetylcholine
Epinephrine
Dopamine
Serotonin
γ-butyric acid
Glutamic acid
Glycine

identified and they have been shown to act conjointly or antagonistically in various regions of the brain.

8.5.2 Acetylcholine (AcCh)

Choline, partly derived from protein by the methylation of glycine and partly reabsorbed across the synaptic cleft, accumulates in the presynaptic terminus prior to acetylation. The acyl group is derived from acetyl co-enzyme A (Ac-CoA) and is transported to the choline molecule under the control of the enzyme choline acetyltransferase. (ChAc). Over the period from 10 to 60 years, there is a 50% reduction in the level of this enzyme (0·38 nmol/g/h to 0·2 nmol/g/h) in the thalamus, and a 66% reduction in the cerebral cortex. The degradative enzyme acetylcholine esterase (AChE), present in the region of the receptor on the postsynaptic side of the cleft, however, also falls with age in the thalamus (66%) but doubles in the cerebral cortex (Ordy and Brizzee, 1975). Since the onward transmission of the action potential is dependent on the amount of the transmitter which reacts with the receptor and is subsequently metabolized, it might be deduced that thalamic response will be reduced with increasing age, whereas the greater rate at which the lower concentration of AcCh available in the cortical synapse is metabolized, might be expected to permit this particular neuronal linkage to retain its activity virtually unabated throughout life. In the cerebral cortex of the chicken, an initial rise in both enzymes between hatching and three months is followed by a progressive drop in the level of ChAc activity (3·0–1·0 μmoles/min/g over the next 33 months). The hydrolytic enzyme AChE, however, decreases at a comparable rate for the first 17 months of this ageing period, but thereafter rises again by 350%. The ratio of the activities of the two enzymes (AChE/ChAc) thus rises from 0·7 to 140 between 20 and 36 months. It is not possible to determine from these observations, however, whether there is a reduction in synaptic transfer since sites of AChE activity may not be identical with the receptor sites, and a proportion of the acetylcholine in the synaptic cleft may be hydrolysed without activation of the receptor and hence without achieving the onward transmission of the impulse.

8.5.3 Dopamine and Norepinephrine (Noradrenaline)

The oxidation of tyrosine by the enzyme tyrosine hydroxylase, followed by the decarboxylation of the 3:4 dihydroxy amino acid (dopa), yields the amine, dopamine (Fig. 8.5). Further oxidation, catalysed by the enzyme dopamine-β-oxidase, (of the side chain methylene group in this instance), results in the formation of norepinephrine (noradrenaline). These two catecholamines act as synaptic transmitters in the caudate nucleus, globus pallidus, putamen, basal ganglia, the hindbrain and the hypothalamus. Dopamine is present to the extent of 2·45–3·75 μg/g in the caudate nucleus in the adult human, and the level remains approximately the same throughout the rest of life. Norepinephrine, on the other hand, originally present at a level of 0·35 µg/g in the adult hypothalamus falls to about half this concentration by the ninth decade (Ordy, 1982).

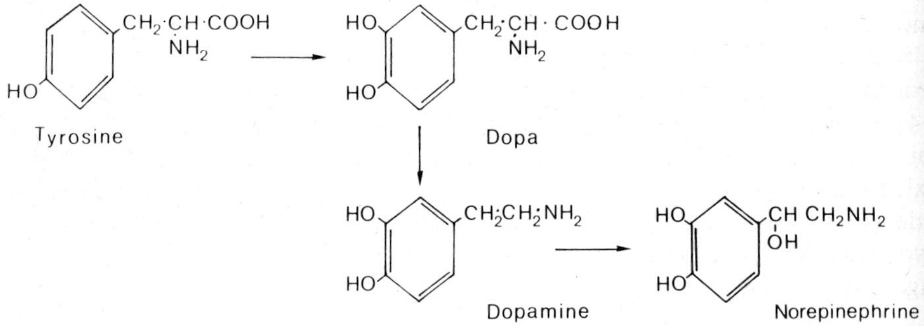

Fig. 8.5. The synthesis of dopamine and norepinephrine (noradrenaline).

8.5.4 Serotonin (5-Hydroxytryptamine; 5-HT)

Decarboxylation of the amino acid tryptophane by the appropriate enzyme produces another neuroactive amine—serotonin (*Fig.* 8.6). Present at a level of 0·2–0·23 µg/g in the human hind brain, 5-HT falls by a small but significant extent during senescence (Ordy). Timiras et al. (1980), however, studying various areas of the brain in rats, observed appreciable increases in the 5-HT levels between 4 and 24 months in the cerebral hemispheres, the mesodiencephalon and the pons medulla. The 5-HT levels in the corpus striatum and the hypothalamus, however, fell by 11% and 5% respectively over the same period. Of possibly greater significance were Timiras's observations that the ratios of 5-HT to norepinephrine and 5-HT to dopamine rose on average by 36·5% and 69% respectively, thus demonstrating that although the 5-HT level itself may fall with age, there was still a significant replacement of catecholaminergic neuronal transmission by seratonergic transmission as age progresses, due to a more rapid reduction in the dopamine and norepinephrine levels. Although they were able to demonstrate

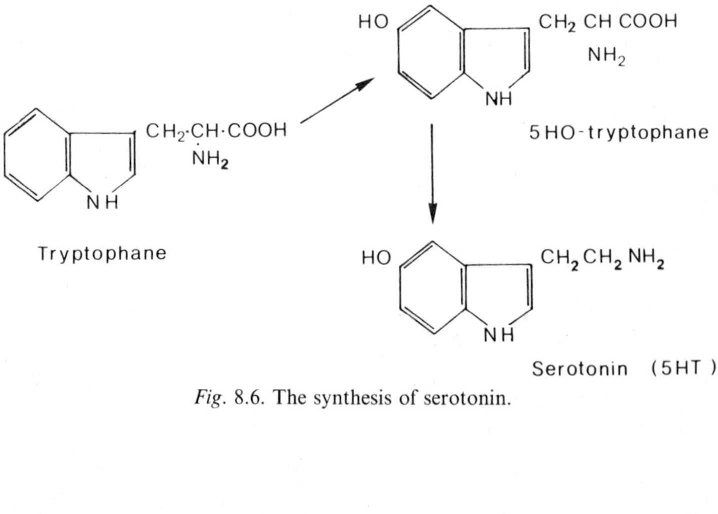

Fig. 8.6. The synthesis of serotonin.

arked physiological changes associated with a reduction in serotonin levels duced by dietary tryptophane restriction, they could not ascribe this specifically) neural changes since 5-HT also controls the hypothalamic induction of many ndocrine functions, and hence a reduction in 5-HT levels could have more than ne effect on the metabolism of the animal.

Serotonin is removed from tissues by the action of the enzyme monoamine xidase (MAO). In the adult human hypothalamus the activity of the enzyme is ·4 μmol/g/h, but this may double between 30 and 90 years of age. This accounts)r the fall in the 5-HT level in the hypothalamus mentioned above. Monoamine xidase inhibitors have been prescribed for the treatment of depression in the derly, but the protein level of the diet has to be reduced considerably since severe ypotension may occur as a side effect in those individuals who are simultaneously gesting appreciable amounts of cheese, meat or vegetable proteins.

.5.5 γ-Aminobutyric Acid (GABA)

lutamine, glutamic acid and GABA are related to one another (*Fig. 8.7*). GABA ppears to be the effective transmitter of this group. The other metabolites pparently induce the synthesis of GABA by activating the neurones to synthesize creasing amounts of glutamate decarboxylase. Levels of this enzyme, and hence vels of GABA are minimal in tissues other than the brain. Kraus demonstrated at 2 hours after the intraperitoneal injection of glutamate into mice, the utamate level in the brain reached a peak value 50% above the resting level. One our later, the glutamate decarboxylase content of the brain peaked at a level two mes higher than the resting value. There is little evidence that glutamate can ccumulate in the brain. It may be that the transport of this amino acid across the lood–brain barrier requires neutralization of the terminal carboxyl group. This is, 1 fact, the rationale of enzyme replacement therapy employing glutamine ynthetase (Hall P. et al., 1969). It has been reported (Hall P., 1971) that the

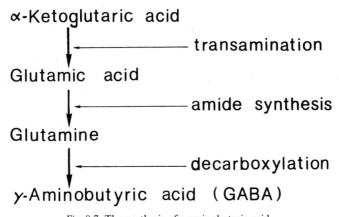

Fig. 8.7. The synthesis of γ-aminobutyric acid.

intramuscular injection of this enzyme can restore the active functioning of th
brain which is impaired in senile dementia. In mice, the synthesis of GAB.
glutamine and glutamate is reduced by 31–46% between 3 and 39 months (Timir
et al., 1973).

8.5.6 Synaptic Receptors and Ageing

The effective transmission of an impulse from neurone to neurone across th
synaptic cleft, depends as much on the integrity of the receptor sites located on th
dendrites of the second neurone as on the adequate synthesis of the transmitt
molecule itself by the synaptic terminal of the first axon. Samuel et al. (1982) ha
shown, using tritiated serotonin, that at the point of maximum absorption, whic
occurs when the microviscosity of the neuronal membrane is maintained at a lev
of 7·5 poises by incubation with lecithin, the amount of serotonin bound to th
receptors is halved in elderly mice.

Studies of the effects of various alkaloids on synaptic transmission ha
demonstrated the similarity of certain of the cholinergic receptors to muscarir
and nicotine. Tritiated quinuclidinyl benzilate, tubocurarine and α-bungarotoxi
combine preferentially with muscarine and nicotine-like receptors respectively (th
second and third compounds both react with nicotine-like receptors). Nordberg
al. (1982) using these compounds have shown that, following a very sharp fa
during the first 2 years, there is a slower but significant reduction in muscarir
receptors in the anterior portion of the human hippocampus (25% in nine decades
Nicotine-like receptors fall more rapidly, losing 40% of their number in the yea
between 60 and 90.

8.6 The Assessment of Neurological Change

8.6.1 Introduction

Variations in cerebral function can be assessed functionally by a variety c
methods, depending on the type of activity under consideration, and the region c
the overall nervous system which is involved.

The response to a stimulus identified by any organ or sensory unit, whethe
experienced by tactile, pain sensory, auditory or visual terminals, necessitates th
involvement of afferent, central and efferent nervous activity before the appro
priate action, be it muscular or mental, can be taken. The overall length of axo
and the number of synapses for instance which intervene between the activation c
the pain sensor in a finger tip immersed in boiling water and the neuromuscula
junction which stimulates the removal of this digit to a less hostile environmen
may be considerably greater than the network between the retina and the eyeli
when a bright flash stimulates the closure of the eye. Birren and Botwinick (1955)
however, have demonstrated that there is little difference between reaction time
for responses involving different lengths of efferent pathway. Where the majo

rtion of the network lies within the central nervous system, as when some ellectual function forms the main burden of the task, for instance the solution of complex mathematical problem in one's head, followed by an indication of mpletion of pressing a switch, the total processing time can be divided into a mber of separate stages:

a. peripheral identification of the task;

b. central identification of the task;

c. stimulation of short-term memory;

d. comparison of observation with information stored in long-term memory;

e. completion of task;

f. indication of task completion.

ge-related differences in the rate at which each of these stages is completed has en identified by Birren (1974).

In the elderly subject, in addition to speed reduction, which may be classified as a antitative change in mental capacity, there is also evidence of marked failure of a alitative nature in short-term memory and a failure to control the interneuronal ansmissions which permit ordered thought processes to occur.

6.2 *Psychological Changes in the Elderly*

he biochemical changes in the brain which occur with increasing age result in a riety of psychological defects which can be divided into three major categories:

a. memory changes;

b. intellectual defects;

c. behavioural disturbances.

Together, these result in the syndrome of senile dementia, an irreversible and rogressive reduction in effective brain function with increasing age. Ten per cent r more of the total population aged 65 years and over are affected by one or all of ie conditions listed above. The prevalence of dementia reaches its peak in persons ged 80 and above and since this portion of the population is predicted to increase Great Britain by some 1·7 millions before the middle of the last decade of the resent century, it is likely that the number of elderly individuals who can be lassified as being demented will increase proportionally.

Irreversible dementia of the elderly may be due to either atherosclerosis or to the egeneration of parenchymatous tissue of the brain. In the first category tissue egeneration does also occur, but only as a secondary factor to localized chaemia. The lesions may be focal or distributed through the cerebral body. In ome instances these lesions may be of a temporary nature resulting in transient chaemic attacks (TIAs) (Yates, 1976), which may result in mental or functional npairment lasting for a period of less than 24 hours. A single TIA may be ollowed by clinical improvement or even full recovery, but subsequent episodes, if hey do occur (Whisnant, 1976), will be followed by decreased capacity for ecovery until profound dementia may develop by a process of stepwise eterioration.

True senile dementia—degradation of the parenchymatous tissue is usual
progressive without intermediate recovery and is associated with the appearance
cellular abnormalities (*see* p. 192).

Loss of memory for recent events is the most conspicuous early manifestation
senile dementia whereas long-term memory is not impaired to anything like th
same extent. In later stages, all aspects of memory are affected, recollections of th
immediate past being completely lost, whereas earlier events may only be recalle
in a very patchy fashion. Short-term memory can be quantified by well-designe
questionnaires aimed at the assessment of the recall of information presented a fe
minutes to a few hours previously. Long-term memory can be measured b
questions aimed at probing the individual's recollections of his or her early life an
times. The questionnaires must, however, be devised in relationship to the elder
person's intellectual capabilities and personal history. It is impossible for anyon
to remember an event or the name of an individual which was of insufficier
importance to him in his youth to warrant its impression on his short-terr
memory, before its subsequent transfer to his long-term memory. Criteria of thi
type also determine the most appropriate methods for the assessment of in
tellectual and functional deterioration. Many methods have been designed for th
measurement of intelligence quotient, but if these are not related to the norma
capabilities of the individual, the results obtained will not provide a tru
assessment of any deficiency. Assessment of functional capacity in simple day-to
day acts such as dressing, washing, or filling and boiling a kettle of water fo
instance, is therefore probably more effective than approved psychological test
such as matching of shapes, etc. since the latter may be of little significance to th
elderly subject, whereas the former are more meaningful representing as they d
actions which are commonplace. Where such measurements are employed for th
assessment of therapy, it may on occasion be observed that some everyda
functions are not affected to the same extent as others. Cox et al. (1981) fo
instance, observed that the ability to feed themselves, was not improved in a grou
of patients treated with a preparation aimed at an improvement of cerebra
circulation, whereas they recovered to a significant degree in respect to their abilit
to move freely, dress and wash themselves unaided and also showed a marke
improvement in the powers of communication with nursing staff and a reduction ir
their overall level of confusion (*Figs.* 8.8 and 8.9).

Studies by Roth and his colleagues have demonstrated that some of these clinica
changes can be correlated directly with pathological lesions (Roth et al., 1967)
These changes, however, can be correlated more closely with more specifi
syndromes such as Alzheimer's disease, etc. than with less closely definec
conditions such as senile organic brain disease.

8.7 Conclusions

Although an appreciable amount of evidence has been forthcoming over the pas
two decades on the basis of which it may ultimately prove possible to relate the

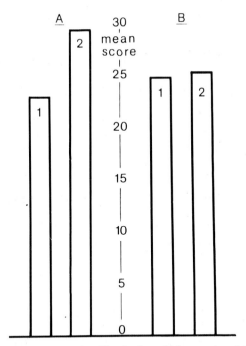

g. 8.8. The effect of an enzyme preparation, Vasolastive, which acts synergistically with lipoprotein
ase and also affects functional changes in elderly human subjects to whom it is administered
tramuscularly. Eight functional characteristics of the elderly were assessed on a four point scale
fore (1) and after (2) treatment with Vasolastine (A) or a comparable placebo (B). The scores
present the sum of individual ratings for 60 individuals in each group and indicate that the enzyme
eparation improves the overall assessment by about 10%, whereas the placebo is virtually without
ect. (However, see Fig. 8.9.)

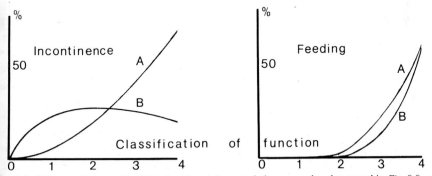

ig. 8.9. Although the majority of the functional characteristics assessed and summed in Fig. 8.8. were
ositively affected by the enzyme preparation Vasolastine, some were not altered appreciably, and
ence the overall score is lower than might have been recorded if those with a positive effect were
onsidered by themselves. The difference between the effects of Vasolastine on two typical functions,
continence and feeding, are recorded in this figure. The two curves in each case represent the numbers
f individuals classified in grades 1, 2, 3 or 4 for (A) Vasolastine and (B) placebo-treated groups. A far
rger proportion of individuals in the enzyme-treated group than in the placebo group showed
nproved control of urinary flow at the end of treatment. The enzyme did not, however, improve the
bility of elderly individuals to feed themselves to any greater extent than the placebo.

clinical symptoms of senile dementia unequivocally with various cellular a~
biochemical lesions, the whole story has not yet emerged. The major difficulti~
associated with any explanation of the ageing nervous system lie in t
morphological complexity of its structure and the ramifications of its biochemistr~
Because of the differences between the extracerebellar nervous system and t
various individual functional loci in the brain itself, it is difficult to ascribe t~
various types of senile defect to pathological alterations in any one section of t~
nervous system. Most elderly subjects would appear to demonstrate some degr~
of mosaic effect with separate areas of the brain affected to a greater or less~
extent. It is this phenomenon which results in the clinical symptoms of o~
individual often being both qualitatively and quantitatively different from those
another, and also makes it difficult to define dementia at the biochemical level

Recommended Reading

Seven of the most recent eight volumes in the series *Ageing* (Vols. 13–15 and 17–20) Raven Press, N~
York, are devoted to the various aspects of the ageing of the nervous system. Of these, Vol. 20 'T
Aging Brain: Cellular and Molecular Mechanisms of Aging in the Nervous System' Edited by
Giacobini, G. Filogamo, G. Giacobini and A. Vernadakis (1982), is the most general, presenting
series of most useful contributions to our knowledge of the cellular and biochemical changes associat
with the ageing neurone.
Brain Function in Old Age. Edited by F. Hoffmeister and C. Müller (1979), Springer, Berlin, also prese~
a useful study of cerebral ageing, including appreciable sections on the psychological assessment
senile dementia.

References

Airey C. M. (1983). The effect of the natural anti-oxidant vitamin-E on ageing mice. *Ph.D Thesis, Lee
    University*.
Airey C. M. and Hall D. A. (1983) Unpublished results.
Andrew W. (1952) *Cellular Changes with Age*. Springfield, Ill., Thomas.
Berlet H. H. and Volk B. (1980) Age-related microheterogeneity of myelin basic protein isolated fro~
    human brain. In: Amaducci I. (ed.) *Ageing of the Brain and Dementia*. New York, Raven Press, p. 8~
Birren J. E. (1974) Translations in gerontology—from lab to life. Psychophysiology and speed
    response. *Am. Psychol.* **29**, 808.
Birren J. E. and Botwinick J. (1955) Age difference in finger, jaw and foot reaction time to audito
    stimuli. *J. Gerontol.* **10**, 429.
Birren J. E. and Schaie K. W. (ed.) (1976) *Handbook of the Psychology of Aging*. Vol. 12. New Yor
    Van Nostrand, Reinhold.
Blackett A. D. and Hall D. A. (1980) The action of vitamin E on the ageing of connective tissue. *Mec
    Ageing Dev.* **14**, 305.
Blackett A. D. and Hall D. A. (1981a) Tissue vitamin E levels and lipofuchsin accumulation with age
    the mouse. *J. Gerontol.* **36**, 529.
Blackett A. D. and Hall D. A. (1981b) Vitamin E its significance in mouse ageing. *Age Ageing* **10**, 19~
Brody H. (1955) Organization of the cerebral cortex. *J. Comp. Neurol.* **102**, 511.
Brody H. (1970) Structural changes in the aging nervous system. *Interdiscip. Topics Gerontol.* **7**, 9.
Buell S. J. and Coleman P. D. (1979) Dendritic growth in the aged human brain and failure to grow
    senile dementia. *Science* **206**, 854.
Bugiani O., Salvarini S., Perdelli F. et al. (1978) Nerve cell loss with aging in the putamen. *Eur. Neur~
    17**, 286.
Cox R., Spanswick J. and Hall D. A. (1981) Enzyme therapy for vascular disease in the elderly. *J. Cl~
    Exp. Gerontol.* **3**, 77.
Dastor D. K., Lane M. M., Hansen D. B. et al. (1963) Effects of aging on cerebral circulation a~
    metabolism in man. *Human Aging: A Biological and Behavioural Study*. US Printing Office, 986, p. 5

eldman M. L. (1976) Aging changes in the morphology of cortical dendrites. In: Ordy J. M. and Brizee K. R. (ed.) *Neurobiology of Aging*. New York, Raven Press, p. 211.

eldman M. L. and Dowd C. (1974) Aging in rat visual cortex: light microscopic observations on layer V. Pyrimidal apical dendrites. *Anat. Rec.* **178**, 355.

all D. A., Middleton R. S. W., Elridi S. S. et al. (1980a) Serum elastase levels following stroke in elderly subjects. *Gerontology* **26**, 167.

all D. A., Middleton R. S. W. and Zajac A. R. (1980b) Related age changes in the elastase and lipid contents of normal and hemiplegic subjects of various ages. *Mech. Ageing Dev.* **14**, 293.

all D. A. and Wilkinson J. E. (1962) Elastase and thrombus formation. *Nature* **197**, 454.

all P. (1971) Enzymes in psychiatric illness. *Psychiat. Neurol.* **2**, 1.

all P., Hartridge G. and van Leeuwen G. H. (1969) Effect of catechol B-methyl transferase in schizophrenia. *Arch. Gen. Psychiat.* **20**, 573.

all T. C., Miller A. K. H. and Corsellis J. A. N. (1975) Variations in the human Purkinje cell population according to age and sex. *Neuropathol. Appl. Neurobiol.* **1**, 267.

anley T. (1974) Neuronal fall out in the ageing brain: a critical review of the quantitative data. *Age Ageing* **3**, 133.

eipetz R., Pilz H. and Scholz W. (1977) Fatty acid composition of sphingomyelin from adult human cerebral white matter and changes in childhood, senium and unspecific damage. *J. Neurol.* **216**, 57.

enderson G., Tomlinson B. E. and Gibson P. H. (1980) Cell counts in human cerebral cortex in normal adults throughout life using an image analyzing computer. *J. Neurol. Sci.* **46**, 113.

endley D. D., Mildvan A. S., Reporter M. C. et al. (1963) The properties of isolated human cardiac age pigment I and II. *J. Gerontol.* **18**, 144, 250.

önigsmark B. W. (1969) Neuronal population of the ventral cochlear nucleus in man. *Anat. Rec.* **163**, 212.

önigsmark B. W. and Murphy E. Q. (1970) Neuronal populations in the human brain. *Nature* **228**, 1335.

önigsmark B. W. and Murphy E. A. (1972) Volume of the ventral cochlear nucleus in man: its relationship to neuronal population and age. *J. Neuropathol. Exp. Neurol.* **31**, 304.

ow P. A., Okazaki H. and Dyck P. J. (1977) Splanchnic preganglionic neurons in man. *Acta Neuropathol. (Berl.)* **40**, 55.

onagle R. D. and Brody H. (1974) The effects of age upon the main nucleus of the inferior olive in the human. *J. Comp. Neurol.* **155**, 61.

ordberg A., Adolfson R., Marcusson J. et al. (1982) Cholinergic receptors in the hippocampus in normal aging and dementia of Alzheimer type. In: Giacobini E., Filogamo G., Giocobini G. et al. (ed.) *The Aging Brain: Cellular and Molecular Mechanisms of Aging in the Nervous System. Aging.* Vol. 20. New York, Raven Press, p. 231.

'Brien M. D. and Mallett B. L. (1970) Cerebral cortex perfusion rates in dementia. *J. Neurol. Neurosurg. Psychiatry* **33**, 497.

rdy J. M. (1982) Geriatric psychopharmacology: drug modification of memory and emotionality in relation to aging human and non-human primate brain. In: Hoffmeister F. and Müller C. (ed.) *Brain Function in Old Age*. Berlin, Springer-Verlag, p. 435.

rdy J. M. and Brizee K. (ed.) (1975) *Neurology of Aging*. New York, Plenum Press.

oth M. (1971) Classification and aetiology in mental disorders of old age. Some recent developments. In: Kay D. W. K. and Walk A. (ed.) *Recent Developments in Psychologeriatrics*. Ashford, U.K. Headley Brothers, p. 1.

oth M., Tomlinson B. E. and Blessed G. (1967) The relationship between quantitative measures of dementia and of degenerative changes in the cerebral grey matter of elderly subjects. *Proc. R. Soc. Med.* **60**, 14.

ouser G. and Yamamato A. (1969) Lipids. In: Lajtha A. (ed.) *Handbook of Neurochemistry*, Vol. 1. New York, Plenum Press, p. 121.

amorajski T. and Rolsten C. (1973) Age and regional differences in the chemical composition of brains of mice, monkeys and humans. In: Ford D. H. (ed.) *Neurobiological Aspects of Maturation and Aging*. Vol. 40. Amsterdam, Elsevier, p. 253.

amuel D., Heron D. S., Hershkowitz M. et al. (1982) Aging, receptor binding and membrane microviscosity. In: Giacobini E., Filogamo G., Giacobini G. et al. (ed.) *The Aging Brain: Cellular and Molecular Mechanisms of Aging in the Nervous System. Aging.* Vol. 20. New York, Raven Press, p. 93.

chiebel A. B. (1978) Structural aspects of the aging brain. Spine systems and the dendritic arbor. In: Katzman R., Terry R. D. and Bick K. L. (ed.) *Alzheimer's Disease. Senile Dementia and Related Disorders*. New York, Raven Press, p. 11.

Schiebel M. E. and Schiebel A. B. (1976) Structural changes in the ageing brain. In: Brody H., Harm D. and Ordy J. M. (ed.) *Aging*. Vol. 1. New York, Raven Press, p. 11.

Shefer V. G. (1972) Absolute number of neurons and thickness of the cerebral cortex during agir senile and vascular dementia and Pick's and Alzheimer's disease. *Zh. Nevropatol. Psikhiatr.* 7 1024.

Shock N. W. (1974). In: Rockstein M. (ed.) *Theoretical Aspects of Aging*. New York, Academic Pre p. 119.

Siakotis A. N. and Koppang N. (1973) Procedures for the isolation of lipopigments from brain, hea and liver and their properties. *Mech. Ageing Dev.* **2**, 177.

Strehler B. L. (1964) On the histochemistry and ultrastructure of age pigment. *Adv. Geriatr. Res.* **1**, 34

Strehler B. L. (1977) *Time, Cells and Ageing*. New York, Academic Press.

Strehler B. L., Mark D. D., Mildvan A. S. et al. (1959) Rate and magnitude of age pigme accumulation in the human myocardium. *J. Gerontol.* **14**, 430.

Stübel H. (1911) Du Fluorezenz tierische Gewebe in ultravioletten licht. (Fluoresence of animal tissu in ultraviolet light.) *Pflügers Arch. Gesamte Physiol.* **142**, 1.

Sun A. Y. and Sun G. Y. (1979) Neurochemical aspects of the membrane hypothesis of agir *Interdiscip. Topics Gerontol.* **15**, 34.

Timiras P. S., Hudson D. B. and Jones S. L. (1980) Pharmacologically induced changes in seroton and aging. In: Brombilla F., Racagni G. and de Wied D. (ed.) *Progress in Psychoneuroendocrinolog* Amsterdam, Elsevier/North Holland. Biomedical Press, p. 571.

Timiras P. S., Hudson D. B. and Oklund S. (1973) Changes in central nervous system free amino aci with development and aging. In: Ford D. H. (ed.) *Neurobiological Aspects of Maturation and Agir* Vol. 40. Amsterdam, Elsevier, p. 267.

Tomlinson B. E. (1980) The structural and quantitative aspects of the dementias. In: Roberts J. P. (e Biochemistry of Dementia. New York, Wiley, p. 25.

Tomlinson R. E., Blessed G. and Roth M. (1970) Observation of the brains of demented old people. *Neurol. Sci.* **11**, 205.

Tomlinson B. E. and Henderson G. (1976) Some quantitative cerebral findings in normal and dement old people. In: Terry R. D. and Gershon S. (ed.) *Neurobiology of Aging*. New York, Raven Pre p. 183.

Tomlinson B. E. and Irving D. (1977) The number of limb motor neurones in the human lumbrosacr cord throughout life. *J. Neurol. Sci.* **34**, 213.

Treff W. M. (1974) Die Involutionsmuster des Nucleus dentatus cerebelli. (The involution of t cerebellar nucleus dentatus.) In: Platt D. (ed.) *Altern*. Stuttgart, Schaltauer, p. 37.

Vijayashankar N. and Brody H. (1977) Aging in the human brainstem: a study of the nucleus of t trochlear nerve. *Acta Anat.* **99**, 169.

Vijayashankar N. and Brody H. (1979) A quantitative study of the pigmented neurons in the nucle locus coeruleus and subcoeruleus in man as related to aging. *J. Neuropathol. Exp. Neurol.* **38**, 49

Wang H. S., Obrist W. D. and Busse E. W. (1970) Neurophysiological correlates of the intellectu function of elderly persons living in the community. *Am. J. Psychiatry* **126**, 1205.

Whishant J. P. (1976) A population study of stroke and transient ischaemic attacks. In: *Stroke*. Pro 9th Pfizer Symp. Edinburgh, Churchill Livingstone.

Wilkinson A. and Davis I. (1978) The influence of age and dementia on the neurone population of t mammillary bodies. *Age Ageing* **7**, 151.

Yates P. O. (1976) Vascular disease of the central nervous system. In: Blackwood W. and Corsell J. A. N. (ed.) *Greenfield's Neuropathology*. 3rd ed. London, Arnold, p. 86.

The Immune System and Ageing

1 Introduction

ttempts have been made over the years to differentiate between so-called
athological and *physiological* ageing (Craciun, 1974) on the assumption that
any of the diseases to which the elderly are prey may be eliminated, leaving
ehind a degree of fundamental ageing which is in no way related to these
uperimposed pathological conditions. All animals, however, become more sus-
eptible to disease as they progress from adulthood to senility. Since the
immunological system is responsible for the various lines of defence thrown up by
he organism against invasion by bacteria, viruses, fungi, foreign proteins, etc., one
hould look towards changes in this system before assuming that pathologies due
o invasive action by external agencies are in no way age-related. The immuno-
ogical response of all vertebrates suffers a marked reduction with age, and hence
heir body's protective reaction to any form of foreign substance, be it living or
on-living, is less effective. As will be seen later in this chapter, the immune system
 not simple and hence its age changes are themselves complex, involving various
ssues and their component cells, various types of wandering cells and their target
ssues, and various circulating macromolecules. Once the individual component of
he immune system has reacted with the invader, the complex so formed is ingested
nd digested by phagocytic cells, thus introducing yet one further layer of systemic
nvolvement at which age changes in the body's defence mechanisms can manifest
hemselves.

9.2 The Constituent Elements of the Immune System

9.2.1 *The Cellular Composition of the Immune System*

In man and other mammals the immune system consists of the bone marro*
thymus, spleen and lymph nodes, together with humoral immunoglobulins in t*
circulation and in certain secretions such as saliva and tears (*Fig.* 9.1). In birds, t*
bursa of Fabricius performs the function of the bone marrow. The bone marro*
the thymus and the bursa of Fabricius represent the primary sites of B-lymphocy*
synthesis, whereas the spleen and lymph nodes act as secondary immune organ*
accumulating lymphocytes during the course of life and initiating the speci*
immune functions of the body. The significant cells for the immune system prese*
in these peripheral organs are lymphocytes, plasma cells and macrophages. The*
particular lymphocytes are responsible in the body for the humoral antiboc*
response, anaphylactic reactions, allergies and resistance to invasion by mo*
bacteria and against toxins originating within or without the body.

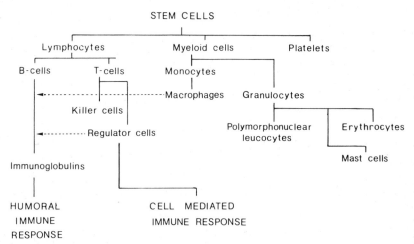

Fig. 9.1. The relationship of various components of the immune system with other cellular componen*
of the plasma.

The thymus, on the other hand, acts as the site for the maturation of another typ
of lymphocyte, namely the T-cell which is responsible for cell-mediated immur
responses such as delayed hypersensitivity, the host–graft reaction leading to th
rejection of foreign tissues, immunity against tumour cells which it recognizes a
'foreign' and resistance to viral and fungal invasion. B-cells may be distinguishe
from T-cells by their appearance in the electron microscope (*Fig.* 9.2) and by the
response to various stimuli. Both types of lymphocyte are roughly spherical b*
their surfaces are dotted with protruding villi. The surface of the resting B-cell h*
fewer villi than the T-cell, but after activation it develops a layer of long villi. A
intermediate stages they tend to be indistinguishable on purely morphologic*
grounds; B-cells are, however, readily distinguished from T-cells by their reactivi*

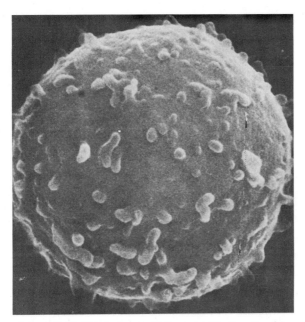

ﬁg. 9.2. Electron micrograph of a B-lymphocyte. Following activation, the villi on the surface of the ㅣl lengthen and the overall appearance of B- and T-cells is virtually identical since the latter have ﬁger villi than an unactivated B-cell. (Reproduced with the permission of Academic Press and the ﬁthors, Kay and Makinodan, from *Lectures on Gerontology* Vol. 1A. Viidik A. Ed. (1982).)

ﬁd response to stimulants such as antigens, mitogens, drugs and radiation (Stites, ﬁ80). The macrophages are much larger than the lymphocytes and have highly astic membranes which appear to 'flow' on surfaces permitting them to migrate ﬁd engulf antigen–antibody complexes and cells which have past their prime and ﬁst their viability (Kay, 1978). They do, however, have other functions in the ﬁmmune system (*see* pp. 215, 221) presenting antigens to the B-cells (Marchalonis, ﬁ980).

Antigens trigger B-cells to transform into plasma cells which are then capable of ﬁnthesizing the appropriate antibody, whereas T-cells are transformed into killer-ﬁmphocytes which can kill target cells without the aid of extraneous protein ﬁctors such as complement (Kay, 1976) and into lymphocytes which secrete ﬁgulating factors known as lymphokines (Gorczynski et al., 1972). These ﬁbstances control the differentiation of B- and T-cells into their appropriate ﬁfector cells: plasma cells of killer-lymphocytes. Certain T-cells activated by ﬁntigens are capable of modulating the immune response by intervening in immune ﬁsponse as helpers or suppressors.

.2.2 *The Thymus*

ﬁarly studies (Boyd, 1932; Andrew, 1952) demonstrated that the thymus, consist-ﬁg during the later period of fetal life of 20% medulla, 40–60% cortex and 40–20%

connective tissue and lipid, begins to lose cortical mass slowly during childho
and more extensively after sexual maturity is reached. By 40 years of age, t
cortex represents only 6–7% of the total mass of the thymus and the medulla is a
reduced to a similar proportion of the total, the remainder of the organ consisti
of connective tissue. The organ as a whole becomes atrophic (Kay, 197
Hirokawa (1977) observed that the epithelial tissue of the thymus which represer
that portion of the organ which produces the factors responsible for transformi
the T-cell precursors into the various forms of T-cell also atrophies during thyn
involution. Thymectomy carried out on young adult experimental anim
produces the same reduction in those aspects of the immune system which
mediated by the T-cells as does the ageing process, thus confirming that t
involution of the thymus results in T-cell loss.

9.2.3 *The Spleen*

The spleen weight remains constant in experimental animals (mice) until about 1
weeks of age. Thereafter there is an increasing likelihood of splenomega
(Makinodan and Peterson, 1964). Albright et al. (1969) observed that the transf
of spleen cells from old mice into the middle-aged syngenic animals reduced the
life expectancy, whereas the implantation of cells from neonatal animals did nc
Splenectomy of middle-aged mice resulted in an appreciable increase in li
expectancy (57 weeks instead of 34 for 97-week-old animals). It appears, therefor
that ageing animals develop a defective immune system, the main lesion beir
located in the spleen. This may explain why the ablation of this organ in hum
subjects following splenic injury does not result in any major long-term loss
immune response, because only part of the age-mediated reduction in the effectiv
ness of the immune system is located in the spleen.

9.2.4 *Stem Cell Mutation*

The cellular complement of the lymphoid tissues originates in undifferentiate
stem cells in the bone marrow. Burch (1965) has calculated that the number of suc
cells in the adult marrow is about 10^{10}. A proportion of these cells migrate to th
thymus where they are altered and pass into the circulation in the form of thymu
derived or thymus-processed lymphocytes (T-cells). It has been suggested that th
function of such cells is two-fold. Not only do they function as carriers of certai
elements of the immune system and are thus capable of reacting with those foreig
substances which they are able to reach (i.e. those which are not situated behind
blood–tissue barrier which lymphocytes are unable to penetrate), but they ma
also control the growth of specific target tissues by the release of antimitotic facto
following their fusion with the target cell. Burwell (1963) suggested that the growt
of all peripheral tissues might be controlled centrally (*Fig.* 9.3) and Burch (196
developing Burnett's (1959) forbidden clone theory, has suggested that the change

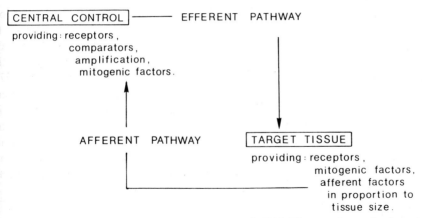

9.3. The central control of tissue size (Burch and Burwell, 1964). The central control unit receives afferent factors from the target tissue, compares this concentration (and hence the size of the target tissue) with a built-in standard, amplifies this signal where necessary and if it is low (indicating a abnormal target tissues size), elaborates efferent mitogenic factors which travel to the target tissue. These are received by the target and stimulate its mitogenic activity thus returning the size of the tissue mass to 'normal' levels.

tissue size and function observed in ageing and in cancer may be due to alterations occurring in the stem cells themselves prior to their differentiation into tissue-specific lymphocytes.

As an organism ages or as some of its tissues develop in an unchecked malignant fashion, the control exerted by the circulating lymphocytes is modified. In the ageing system (Burch and Burwell, 1964) the reaction between lymphocyte and target cell is not restricted to the control of mitosis—in fact, in adulthood a sizeable proportion of the cells of the body have reached the postmitotic state. The lymphocyte fails to recognize the target cell as 'self' and combines with it as it would with any foreign cell. This results in the formation of a complex which is removed from the tissue by macrophages. There are two possible ways in which this change in the relationship between lymphocyte and target cell can be accomplished. Either the target cell must have suffered some change—a somatic mutation, or the lymphocyte must have altered. Hall (1973) has pointed out that the likelihood of massive somatic mutation bringing about such changes in the target tissue as would result in the simultaneous recognition of these tissues in various regions of the body as 'non-self' is very slight. It is far more rational to believe with Burnett (1974) that such mutations as may occur take place at the opposite end of the lymphocyte–target cell pathway, namely in the stem cells themselves. Burnett suggested that individual stem cells which were destined to be precursors of certain strains of lymphocytes could suffer mutation. Such a mutated cell would then experience mitosis and from it would develop a clone of altered cells. Some of these clones would prove to be so altered as to cease to be viable, but some would multiply and provide the basis for a 'forbidden clone' of lymphocytes whose surface properties would be so altered as to render them incapable of identifying as 'self' the target cell for which their unmutated progenitor was specific and thus would precipitate the cellular interactions which the irreversible fusion of altered lymphocyte and target cell could induce. Burch (1965, 1968) and Burch and Jackson (1966) have developed mathematical relationships which related the age-specific rate of initiation of various age-related conditions to the age at initiation of the symptoms of the condition. For instance, Burch and Jackson have shown that the equation:

$$P_{nt} = (1 - e^{-kt})^n$$

describes the age-specific prevalences of the loss of teeth (P) against the age which this first occurs (t). The power (n) represents the number of individual incidents (most probably mutants in the stem cells) which must occur to initiate the phenomena which result in tooth loss. For the first permanent molars n = 1, for maxillary premolars n = 2, and for the mandibular incisors n = 5. Thus, the reaction which results in the loss of the molar teeth is simpler than that which controls the loss of the incisors, one mutation being adequate to initiate the periodontal changes which result in the loss of these teeth, whereas five are required for the loss of an incisor. This means that the gingival tissue which retain the incisors are under the synthetic control of five different types of cell each of which must be recognized as 'non-self' by circulating lymphocytes before the tooth is shed. It is also possible to calculate the latent period which intervenes between the initiation of the chain of events culminating in tooth loss and the actual time when the tooth is lost. In the case of all three teeth types, this is 14·5 years. When similar mathematical procedures are applied to figures for the age-specific mortality from coronary heart disease, it can be shown (Burch, 1968) that the latent period for males is 10 years, whereas that for females amounts to 20. This an interesting observation which does much to confirm the mathematical approach devised by Burch since there is a fully documented 10-year difference between the mean ages of onset of coronary heart disease in male and female subjects (see Fig. 3.14).

The 'insults' which the stem cells must suffer before the aggressive process can start may affect a series of different cells or may on the other hand be confined to one cell. Either of these possibilities can be dealt with by only slight alterations in Burch's fundamental equation. Burch (1968) suggested that this type of reaction between a forbidden clone of lymphocytes and the target tissues of their un mutated progenitor should be termed 'autoaggressive' rather than 'autoimmune' since he was of the opinion that the immunoglobulins which are responsible for humoral immune reactions have little effect in this form of reaction.

Since some of these autoaggressive reactions with target tissues may take place behind a blood–tissue barrier, impervious to lymphocytes, some of the control factors must be humoral in nature rather than consisting of active groups on the surface of the lymphocyte. Two such humoral agents are required for a complete feedback pathway, with efferent and afferent function. In the ageing situation, will be the efferent factor which, emanating from the mutated lymphocyte clone will lower the mitotic activity of those cells still capable of dividing and destroying those which are postmitotic. Under normal circumstances a reduction in cell mass

ɔuld lower the level of the afferent factor thus removing the inhibition of central
ll mitosis and hence re-established peripheral growth. The complex of aberrant
ferent factor and target cell, however, does not provide the feedback mechanism
hich ensures the homeostatic balance. Hence autoaggressive reactions of this type
sult in peripheral cell death and tissue atrophy.

2.3 B-cells and Immunoglobulins

the presence of an appropriate antigen, a specific form of T-cell and
acrophages, B-cells can be a stimulated to produce an antibody which is specific
ɔr the antigen. If the promotor activity of the T-cells is lacking, the B-cell fails to
roduce any antibody. The macrophage appears to 'combine' with the B-cell
assing cytoplasmic bridges into the lymphocyte body (Shoenberg et al., 1963) and
ossibly transferring RNA (Fishman and Adler, 1963) although doubts have been
ıst on the importance of such an interaction (Gottlieb et al., 1967; Roelants and
ɡoodman, 1969). It may be that the macrophage merely carries the antigen to the
ɪmphocyte to enable it to stimulate antibody synthesis (Claman et al., 1969). The
ɪmmunoglobulins consist of monomers or polymers of Y-shaped structures,
ɔntaining two heavy and two light protein chains (Fig. 9.4). The light chains
ɔnsist of c. 216 amino acids, the heavy chains consist of c. 430. The total
ɪolecular weight of the Ig monomer is thus of the order of 150 000 daltons. The
ɔur subunits are joined together by 4 disulphide linkages forming part of cystine
ɛsidues located by peptide linkage in the polypeptide structures of the subunits.
he amino-acid composition of the two thirds of the structure which is located

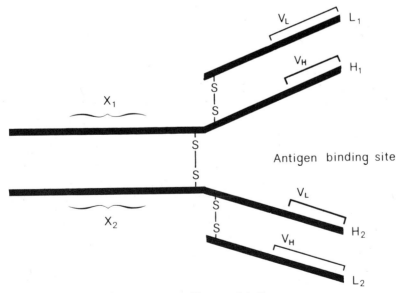

Fig. 9.4. The structure of immunoglobulin monomers.

towards the COOH terminal portion of all four chains (*Fig.* 9.4) is relative
constant, but two types of light chains (κ and λ) and five type of heavy chai.
(α, δ, γ, ε and μ) exist in which these 'constant' regions differ in amino-ac
composition. The 108 amino acids at the NH_2-terminal ends of all four chains a
of variable amino-acid composition. Of these variable regions, three short
sequences in each are hyper-variable, being the areas in which most variatic
between immunoglobulins occurs.

Five major forms of Ig have been identified by the type of heavy chain in th
molecule. IgG, IgA, IgD and IgE exist in the form of monomers. There are tw
forms of each depending on the nature of the light chain, which may be eith
κ or λ. The form of the heavy chain, may exist in any one of four subclass
($\gamma_1 - \gamma_4$). Thus there are eight forms of IgG. IgM and also IgA exist as polyme.
linked by an additional joining chain (J). IgA can exist in 16 different forms due
the two subclasses of the light chains, the two subclasses of the heavy chains and th
monomeric and three polymeric forms in which it can occur (*Box* 9.1). For eac
form of subclass the dimer can exist in two types depending on whether it occurs i
the circulation or is present in secretions such as saliva or tears. In the latter case
also contains a further polypeptide, the secretory component. Because of thes
variations in the so-called 'constant' regions of the molecules, there are, therefor
30 different basic Ig molecules on which the B-cells are able to superimpose th
specific structures of individual antibodies by manipulating the composition of th
hyper-variable portions of the molecules. It is, therefore, not surprising tha
electrophoresis of plasma results in the separation of a broad band of γ-globulin i
which all the 30 species overlay one another, or that methods providing a greate
degree of resolution such as isoelectric focusing result in the separation of a ver
large number of individual Ig species.

The various clones of B-cells synthesize specific types of Ig. Rabbits (1978) an
Valbuena et al. (1978) have demonstrated that the variable and constant regions c

---

BOX 9.1 Immunoglobulins

Name	Light Chain	Heavy Chain	Additional Proteins
IgM	κ	μ	J
	λ		
IgG	κ		
	λ	γ_1	
		γ_2	
		γ_3	
		γ_4	
IgA	κ		
	λ	α_1	
		α_2	
IgD	κ		
	λ	δ	J.Sc.
IgE	κ	ε	
	λ		

There are 2 forms of IgM; 8 forms of IgG; 4 forms of IgA; 16 forms of IgA which can assist i
monomeric, dimeric or trimeric forms and the dimer can also occur in a secretory form incorporatin
the Sc peptide in tears and salivary secretions. IgE can occur in 3 forms. There are, therefore, 32 basi
structures on which the full heterogenicity of the variable antibody structure can be built.

oth light and heavy chains are synthesized under the control of separate genes.
'he production of a specific antibody requires the selection of appropriate groups
·f genes and the combination of various nascent polypeptides. Similar losses to
hose in man have been observed in dogs (Jaroslav et al., 1974), hamsters (Mathies
t al., 1973), rats (Bilder, 1975), mice (Makinoden and Peterson, 1966), rabbits
Namagushi et al., 1976), guinea pigs (Baer and Bowser, 1963) and invertebrates
Hildermann, 1978). Although each of these individually lowered responses will
ave been due to the failure to produce a specific Ig, there is little evidence as yet as
o whether the synthesis of one species of Ig is more labile than another. It would
·e expected that the losses of the more complex polymeric forms of Ig—IgM and
gA—would be be greater than the losses of the monomers simply because the
·rganism would have to retain into old age the added ability to synthesize the
·olymers from nascent monomers and would moreover, have to be able to provide
·t the correct place and time and in the correct amounts the joining and/or
·ecretory components. Surprisingly enough, evidence has been provided which
ndicates that IgE, the species which is present in plasma in the lowest concen-
·rations does decrease in amount with increasing age (Hamburger, 1979).

The response of an organism to the administration of an antigen takes between
·5 and 7 days to occur. This primary response can be increased by booster doses
·f antigen at 7–10-day intervals. After a month no further increase in response
·ccurs, and if administration is then stopped, the level decreases to zero over the
·next 3 months. A secondary response can then be induced by further adminis-
·tration of the same antigen, when antibody can be identified in the plasma within
3–4 days. The rate at which B-cells produce Igs in response to an antigen shows a
·marked decrease with age immediately after the involution or ablation of the
·thymus. For instance, Rowley et al. (1968) have reported an 87% decrease in the
·production of the antibody to *Salmonella* flagellin in man between the ages of 20
·and 70, and Makinoden and Peterson (1964) recorded an almost complete loss of
·response to A iso-agglutinin in the nine decades from age 10 to 100.

9.2.4 *Histocompatibility and Ageing*

Walford (1970, 1974), Yunis et al. (1973) and Smith and Walford (1977) have
suggested that the main histocompatibility complex (MHC) is involved in the
ageing process. MHC is a super-gene complex containing several hundred
separate gene loci which together control a variety of immune functions, especially
those related to the thymus (Svejgaard et al., 1975; Shreffler, 1977; Walford, 1977,
1981) (*Box* 9.2).

In human subjects the complex which is located on chromosome 6 is called the
HLA system, whereas in mice it is the H-2 system and is part of chromosome 17.
Nearly all the functions listed in *Table* 9.2 are affected by ageing. Different
subregions (alleles) of the H-2 system confer differing survival capabilities (50%
survival and 100% survival) on strains of mice which are congenic in so far as the
whole H-2 system is concerned (Smith and Walford). Moreover, the longest-lived

---

BOX 9.2

The main histocompatibility complex (MHC) regulates the following functions in the immune system
1. Recognition phase of cellular immunity
2. Cell-mediated lymphocytotoxicity
3. Development of suppressor cells
4. Viral susceptibility
5. Susceptibilities to spontaneous malignant growth
6. Susceptibility to autoimmune conditions
7. Immune response to specific antigens
8. Age-specific rates of tissue maturation
9. The synthesis of the complement system
10. Production of cells which permit the collaboration of B and T cells
11. Recognition of 'self'
12. Involvement in the ageing of the immune system

MHC, therefore, represents a multifunctional factor in the immune system itself under the control of a
supergenic region of the nuclear substance.

---

strain maintains the highest response to the mitogen phytohaemogglutinin (PHA
throughout life.

Since the MHC is responsible for the T-cell response to PHA, it appears
probable that control of the immune response is located on the same genes as the
control of life-span. Meredith and Walford (1977) have also shown that mitogens
which are specific for B-cells and those T-cells which differ from the mainstream by
being resistant to cortisone, provide either no correlation of immune response to
longevity, or provide a relationship which is restricted to a limited number of
strains.

The autoimmune response bears many similarities to graft-versus-host reaction,
which foreign cells are lysed and disintegrated. In the mouse, this reaction is
controlled by K and D loci in the H-2 region; in human subjects by the A and B loci
of the HLA region.

9.3 Ageing and the Autoimmune Diseases

9.3.1 Rheumatoid Arthritis

Rheumatoid arthritis (RA) may commence at any age, but because of the low
mortality rate associated with the condition many elderly subjects carry the
symptoms of the disease with them into old age, and many subjects do not manifest
signs of skeletal involvement until late in life (Grahame, 1978). Adler (1966), Ebert
(1967) and Ehrlich et al. (1970) suggested that the development of RA followed a
different path in those who showed the first signs of the disease in old age. Ehrlich
et al. reported that the ratio of sexes differs; there being only 2·5 females to each
male in elderly groups as apposed to twice that number of females in groups
developing the disease in earlier life; other workers, however, reported a sex ratio
in the elderly only slightly above 1:1 (Exton-Smith, 1978). Splenic enlargement
and involvement of the lymph nodes was shown to be less in elderly onset RA.

The titre of the so-called rheumatoid factor often shows a high level in elderly subjects. This factor measured by the agglutination of activated latex particles is not a primary response of the body to a circulating antigen, but the response of the body to the antibody raised against the original antigen. Czekalowski and Hall (1977) have suggested that the development of rheumatoid factor and the inflammation associated with the immune response to the condition is in fact a cyclical reaction which may initially be instigated by the degradation of joint tissue (Fig. 9.5). The degradation of the joint results in the provision of relatively low molecular weight antigens which initiate an antigenic response. The antibodies raised against this and the rheumatoid factor raised against the antibody can both promote the release of prostaglandins with their accompanying inflammatory response and also initiate the release of proteolytic enzymes of the cathepsin type from lysosomes within the infiltrating cells in the joint. Thus a second cycle of degradation, immune response and inflammation can be started. The degradation of the articular tissues may be due to enzyme systems evolved by invasive organisms such as *mycoplasma* species (Czekalowski et al., 1973) which produce enzymes having a role to play in the degradation of the collagen fibres of the joint, or may be due to collagenases evolved within the tissues themselves (Woolley and

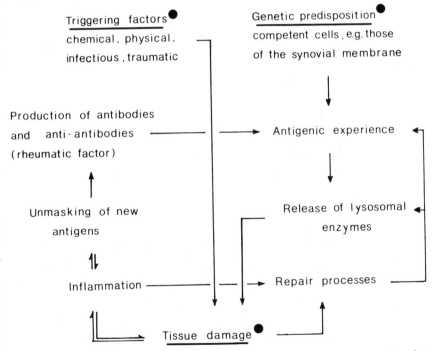

Fig. 9.5. Czekalowski and Hall (1977) suggest that the development of inflammatory processes in cases of rheumatoid arthritis may well be cyclical. The cycle can be stimulated by external or internal factors operative at various points in the cycle (indicated by the black dots). If, for instance, massive tissue damage occurs due to some triggering effect, antigens are produced which become involved at other points in the cycle. Such effects can, however, be amplified by genetic predispositon.

Evanson, 1980). Partial degradation or the initiation of the degradation cycle may occur early in life due to infection, only to be enhanced in old age by the further action of endogenous enzymes.

9.3.2 *Amyloid Disease*

In old age many tissues and organs become infiltrated by a metachromatic protein-containing fibrous mass which stains green with Congo Red when viewed between crossed Nicol prisms or polaroid screens (*Fig.* 9.6). It was originally suggested (Letterer, 1926, 1934) that amyloid consists of an immunoprecipitate, but the same author later (1968) demonstrated that the fibres are, in fact, a mixture of proteins only part of which might be immunoglobulin in nature. Schultz and Milgrom (1973) have suggested that the tissue toxicity of immune complexes may play a significant role in the synthesis. Stiller and Katenkamp (1971) have proposed that the formation of cardiac amyloid in elderly subjects consists of the progressive replacement of collagen fibres by amyloid fibres. Finally, after the deposition of large amounts of glycosaminoglycan, collagen fibres can no longer be demonstrated. They suggested that collagen synthesis and amyloid formation are controlled by the same fibroblasts. However, although some of the short chain mono-amino mono-carboxylic amino acids are present in high concentration as in

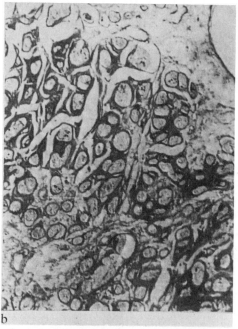

Fig. 9.6. Amyloid in ageing human cardiac tissue.

collagen and cystine is absent, numerous workers (Pirani et al., 1964; Harada et al., 1971) have reported the complete absence of hydroxyproline. More easily acceptable is Stiller and Katenkamp's (1975) suggestion that the macrophage has an important role to play in amyloid production. Their postulated sequence of reactions is as follows: circulating immunoglobulins or free light chains are phagocytosed by macrophages and partially digested by lysosomal enzymes (Glenner and Terry, 1973). These degradation products are transformed into material which on extrusion from the macrophage aggregates in fibrillar form as amyloid. Levin et al. (1973) have suggested that in addition to immunoglobulins, the macrophages may also ingest hyperimmunized cells. This would explain the fact that the amino acid composition of amyloid cannot be related directly to that of any single protein.

Amyloid is a complex tissue component, the composition of which will vary from organ to organ much in the same way that pdc (partially degraded collagen; Chapter 4) can be shown to be tissue specific. Moreover, again in close similarity to the diversity of pdc in various situations, there may well be superficial similarities between senile amyloid and amyloid evolved as the result of some specific pathological condition, whereas the primary or secondary protein structure may differ markedly.

9.4 Conclusions

Age changes in the immune system are apparently two-fold. There is an overall reduction in cellular activity resulting in a deficiency in both the cell-bound and the humoral immune response. In this, the immune system is in no way different from other cellular elements in the body. The aspect of age-modification to the immune system which does differ from cellular function elsewhere in the body is the alteration which induces an autoimmune reaction. Burnett's (1959) concept of stem-cell mutation and Burch's (1968) suggestion that this, rather than mutation of target cells, is the important factor in the development of autoaggressive disease, puts the immune system in a category which is markedly different from all other forms of cellular ageing. In fact, of course, these two facets of the ageing immune system act in opposition to one another. If the immune response is lowered as a result of ageing, this will apply to those aspects of this response which induce the progeny of the mutated stem cells to fail to recognize the appropriate target tissue cells as self. Hence the autoimmune—or autoaggressive—reaction in old age is not as pronounced as it might have been if the immune response in general were maintained at its youthfully optimum level.

Recommended Reading

There have been a number of contributions to multi-author productions over the past few years, which provide surveys of the various aspects of the effect of ageing on the immune system. For instance:

222 THE BIOMEDICAL BASIS OF GERONTOLOGY

Walford R. L. (1981) Immunoregulatory systems and aging. In: Danon D., Shock N. W. and Marois M. (ed.) *Aging: A Challenge to Science and Society. Vol. 1, Biology*. pp. 302–318. L'Institute de la vie and WHO. He presents a clear picture of the role of the main histocompatibility complex on ageing
Kay M. M. B. and Makinoden T. (1982) The ageing immune system. In: Viidik A. (ed.) *Lectures on Gerontology Vol. 1*. pp. 143–172. New York, Academic Press.
These authors provide a balanced story of the immune system in age.
Burch P. R. J. (1968) *An Inquiry Concerning Growth, Disease and Ageing*. Edinburgh, Oliver & Boyd, provides the background (with a lot of mathematics) to his unified theory,
and
Burnett F. M. (1974) *Intrinsic Mutagenesis*. Medical and Technical Publishing Co., deals in detail with the whole question of stem cell mutation and the concept of the forbidden clone.

References

Adler E. (1966) Rheumatoid arthritis in old age. *Isr. J. Med. Sci.* **2**, 607.
Albright J. W., Makinodan T. and Peterson W. J. (1969) Presence of life-shortening factors in spleens of aged mice of long life span and extension of life expectancy by splenectomy. *Exp. Gerontol.* **4**, 267.
Andrew W. (1952) *Cellular Changes with Age*. Springfield, Ill., Thomas
Baer H. and Bowser R. T. (1963) Antibody production and development of contact skin sensitivity in guinea pigs of various ages. *Science* **140**, 1211.
Bilder G. E. (1975) Studies on immune competence in the rat: changes with age, sex and strain. *J. Gerontol.* **30**, 641.
Boyd E. (1932) The weight of the thymus gland in health and disease. *J. Dis. Child.* **43**, 1162.
Burch P. R. J. (1965) Natural and radiation carcinogenesis in man. *Proc. R. Soc. (Series B)* **162**, 223.
Burch P. R. J. (1968) *An Inquiry Concerning Growth: Disease and Ageing*. Edinburgh, Oliver & Boyd.
Burch P. R. J. and Burwell R. G. (1964) Autoimmunity and chromosomal aberrations. *Lancet* **2**, 720.
Burch P. R. J. and Jackson D. (1966) The growth of hair and the loss of permanent teeth considered in relation to autoimmune theory of aging. *J. Gerontol.* **21**, 522.
Burnett F. M. (1959) *Clonal Selection Theory of Acquired Immunity*. Cambridge, Cambridge University Press.
Burnett F. M. (1974) *Intrinsic Mutagenesis: A Genetics Approach to Ageing*. New York, Wiley.
Burwell R. G. (1963) The role of lymphoid tissue in morphostasis. *Lancet* **2**, 69.
Claman H. N., Chaperon E. A. and Hayes L. I. (1969) Thymus-marrow immunocompetence IV. *Transplant* **7**, 87.
Craciun E. C. (1974) Fibroblast activity related to human pure senescence versus human common sensescence. *Proc. 4th Eur. Symp. Basic Gerontol*, Varberg, Sweden, p. 41.
Czekalowski J. W. and Hall D. A. (1977) Connective tissue degradation, a factor in rheumatoid arthritis. *VIth Congress of European Soc. Pathol*. p. 100.
Czekalowski J. W., Hall D. A. and Woolcock P. (1973) Studies on proteolytic activity of mycoplasmas. 1. Gelatinolytic properties. *J. Gen. Microbiol*. **75**, 125.
Ebert H. (1967) Der Verlauf der im alter auftrenden chronische Polyarthritis. (The course of age-related chronic polyarthritis.) *Z. Alternsforsch*. **20**, 259.
Ehrlich G. E., Katz W. A. and Cohen S. H. (1970) Rheumatoid arthritis in the elderly. *Geriatrics* **2**, 103.
Exton-Smith A. N. (1978) Bone aging and metabolic bone disease. In: Brocklehurst J. C. (ed.) *Textbook of Geriatric Medicine and Gerontology*. Edinburgh, Churchill Livingstone, p. 510.
Fishman M. and Adler F. L. (1963) Antibody formation initiated *in vitro* II. *J. Exp. Med.* **117**, 595.
Glenner G. G. and Terry W. D. (1973) The immunoglobulin origin of amyloid fibril proteins. In: Peeters H. (ed.) *Protides of the Biological Fluids*, **20**, Oxford, Pergamon, p. 55.
Gorczynski R. M., Miller R. G. and Phillips R. A. (1972) Initiation of antibody production to sheep erythrocytes *in vitro*. *J. Immunol* **108**, 547.
Gottlieb A. A., Glisin V. R. and Doty P. (1967) Studies on macrophage RNA involved in antibody production. *Proc. Natl Acad. Sci. USA* **57**, 1849.
Grahame R. (1978) Diseases of the joints. In: Brocklehurst J. C. (ed.) *Textbook of Geriatric Medicine and Gerontology*. Edinburgh, Churchill Livingstone, p. 528.
Hall D. A. (1973) Conclusions on the phenomenon of autoimmunity as applied to the ageing process. In: Steinman B. (ed.) *Gerontology*. Stuttgart, Hüber, p. 87.
Hamburger R. N. (1979) Heredity, IgE and the development of atopic allergy. In: *Allergy Unmasked*. Piscataway, New Jersey, Pharmacia Inc., p. 10.
Harada M., Isersky C., Cuatrecasas P. et al. (1971) Human amyloid protein, chemical variability and homogeneity. *J. Histochem.* **19**, 1.

Hilderman W. H. (1978) Phylogenetic and immunogenetic aspects of aging. In: Bergsma D. and Harrison D. E. (ed.) *Genetic Effects of Aging.* White Plains, NY, National Foundation-March of Dimes.

Hirokawa K. (1977) The thymus and aging. In: Makinodan T. and Yunis E. (ed.) *Immunology and Aging.* New York, Plenum, p. 51.

Jaroslav B. N., Suhrbier K. M. and Fritz T. E. (1974) Decline and restoration of antibody forming capacity in aging beagle dogs. *J. Immunol.* **112,** 1467.

Kay M. M. B. (1976) In: Meathe I., Florentin I. and Simmler M. C. (ed.) *Lymphocytes and Macrophages in Cancer Patients: Recent Results in Cancer Research.* Vol. 1. New York, Springer-Verlag, p. 111.

Kay M. M. B. (1978) The effect of age on T-cell differentiation. *Fed. Proc.* **37,** 1241.

Letterer E. (1926) Studien über die Entstchung des Amyloids (Studies on the composition of amyloids). *Zentralbl. Allg. Pathol.* **75,** 487.

Letterer E. (1943) Nene Untersuchungen über die Entstehung des Amyloid (New studies on the composition of amyloid). *Virchows Arch. Pathol. Anat.* **293,** 34.

Letterer E. (1968) History and development of amyloid research. In: Mandema E., Ruinen L. Scholten J. H. et al (ed.) *Proc. Symp. on Amyloid.* Amsterdam, Excerpta Medica, p. 3.

Levin M. E., Pras M. and Franklin E. C. (1973) Immunologic studies of the major nonimmunoglobulin protein of amyloid. I. Identification and partial characterization of a related serum component. *J. Exp. Med.* **138,** 373.

Makinodan T. and Peterson W. J. (1964) Growth and senescence of the primary antibody forming potential of the spleen. *J. Immunol.* **93.** 886.

Makinodan T. and Peterson W. J. (1966) Further studies of the secondary antibody forming potential of juvenile, young adult, adult and ageing man. *Dev. Biol.* **14,** 112.

Marchalonis J. J. (1980) In: Fudenberg H. H., Stites D. P., Caldwell J. L. et al (ed.) *Basic and Clinical Immunology.* Los Altos, Cal., Lange Medical Publications, p. 115.

Mathies M., Lipps L., Smith G. S. et al (1973) Age-related decline in response to phytohaemagglutinin and pokeweed mitogen by spleen cells from hamsters and a long lived mouse strain. *J. Gerontol.* **28,** 425.

Meredith P. J. and Walford R. L. (1977) Effect of age response on T and B cell mitogens in mice congenic at the H-2 region. *Immunogenetics* **5,** 109.

Nomagushi T. A., Okuma-Sakurai Y. and Kimura I. (1976) Changes in immunological potential between juvenile and presenile rabbits. *Mech. Ageing Dev.* **5,** 409.

Pirani C. L., Bestetti A., Catchpole H. R. et al. (1964) Isolation and characterization of amyloid. *Arthr. Rheum.* **7,** 338.

Rabbits T. H. (1978) Evidence for splicing of interrupted immunoglobulin variable and constant region sequences in nuclear RNA. *Nature* **275,** 291.

Roelants G. E. and Goodman J. W. (1969) The chemical nature of macrophage RNA-antigen complexes and their relevance to immune induction. *J. Exp. Med.* **130,** 557.

Rowley M. J., Buchanan H. and Mackay I. R. (1968) Reciprocal change with age in antibody to extrinsic and intrinsic antigens. *Lancet* **2,** 24.

Schoenberg M. D., Mumaw V. R., Moore R. D. et al. (1963) Cytoplasmic interaction between macrophages and lymphocytic cells in antibody synthesis. *Science* **143,** 964.

Schulz R. T. and Milgrom F. (1973) Role of casein in casein-induced amyloidosis of mice. *Int. Arch. Allergy Appl. Immunol.* **44,** 21.

Shreffler D. C. (1977) The H-2 model: genetic control of immune functions. In: Dausset J. and Srejgaard A. (ed.) *HLA and Disease.* Copenhagen, Munksgaard, p. 33.

Smith G. S. and Walford R. L. (1977) Influence of the main histocompatibility complex on aging in aging in mice. *Nature* **270,** 727.

Stiller D. and Katenkamp D. (1971) Die senile Amyloidose des Herzeus. (The senile amyloidosis of the heart.) *Dtsch. Ges. Wes.* **26,** 2179.

Stiller D. and Katenkamp D. (1975) Histochemistry of amyloid. *Exp. Pathol.* Suppl. **1,** 9.

Stites D. P. (1980) In: Fudenberg H. H., Stites D. P., Caldwell J. I. et al. (ed.) *Basic and Clinical Immunology.* Los Altos, Cal., Lange Medical Publications, p. 382.

Svejgaard A., Platz P., Ryder L. P. et al. (1975) H-LA and disease associations—a survey. *Transpl. Rev.* **22,** 3.

Valbuena O., Marcu K. B., Weigert M. et al. (1978) Multiplicity of germline genes specifying a group of related mouse K-chains with implications for the generation of immunoglobulin diversity. *Nature* **276,** 780.

Walford R. L. (1970) Antibody diversity, histocompatibility systems, disease states and aging. *Lancet* **2,** 1126.

Walford R. L. (1974) The immulogic theory of aging: current status. *Fed. Proc.* **33**, 2020.

Walford R. L. (1977) Human C-cell alloantigens, their medical and biological significance. In: *Proc Internat. Congr. of the HLA system—New Aspects, Bergamo, Italy*. Amsterdam, Elsevier, North Holland, p. 105.

Walford R. L. (1981) Immunoregulatory systems and aging. In: Danon D., Shock N. W. and Marois M. (ed.) *Aging: A Challenge to Science and Society. Vol. 1*. Geneva, L'Institute de la Vie and WHO p. 302.

Woolley D. E. and Evanson J. M. (1980) *Collagenase in Normal and Pathological Connective Tissues* Chichester, Wiley.

Yunis E. J., Fernandes F. and Greenberg W. J. (1973) Immune deficiency, autoimmunity and aging In: *Immunodeficiency Workshop: Birth Defects. Orig. Art. Ser. 11*.

10 *Prospects*

If it is accepted, on the evidence presented in Chapter 2, that at least part of the ageing process is under genetic control, it can be assumed that before long mankind will be tempted to extend the typical human life-span, whether it be taken nowadays as three score years and ten or four score years and ten, by indulging in genetic engineering. At present it is possible to induce the synthesis of substances such as interferon and insulin in commercial amounts, by incorporating appropriate genes into the nuclei of cells which were previously incapable of such syntheses.

The major difficulty which will be encountered when attempts are made to graft genes for longevity onto human cells is the complexity of the ageing process. The maintenance of total bodily function—physical, mental and metabolic— necessitates the adequate production of a vast array of functional and structural components (*Fig.* 10.1). The synthesis of each of these is under separate genetic control and as yet no single locus has been identified which controls the many-sided manifestations of the ageing process. Even relatively simple and common-place ageing phenomena such as the loss of teeth (Burch and Jackson, 1966) can be shown to be under multi-genic control. Although there is some evidence that the control of the immune response and longevity may be sited on related groups of genes (Meredith and Walford, 1977) effects such as autoxidation which might be assumed to be universal in its effects on cellular activity throughout the body do not effect ageing phenomena and survival equally at all points of the life-span (Blackett and Hall, 1981). Mice fed vitamin E are protected against death during the early months of their life (*Fig.* 10.2) but the total life-span is either unchanged

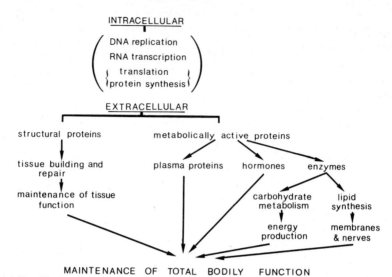

Fig. 10.1 Simplified schematic representation of the pathways which result in the maintenance of total bodily function and which originate in intracellular protein synthesis.

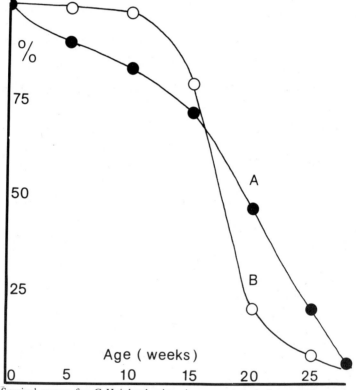

Fig. 10.2 Survival curves for C₃H inbred mice; A, on a control diet and B, on the same diet supplemented with 0·25% vitamin E, showing that the 'vitalizing' effect of the anti-oxidant is restricted to the first half of the life-span.

or possibly even shortened and other parameters of ageing are equally only modified favourably during the period which precedes the point of 50% survival.

It appears that it will be necessary to consider the possibility of recombining a number of separate genes with the host nuclei before even a semblance of life extension can be hoped for. Although this would entail some complicated manipulations, they should not prove to be beyond the wit of man. It will, however, be necessary to consider the effects of such modifications of life-span on the higher levels of the organizational ladder (see Fig. 1.5). How will society be able to feed the vastly increased number of individuals which will be present in the world, if the mean life-span is extended by 20, 30 or 40 years?

In fact, this may not be as difficult a problem to deal with as it appears at first sight. If the world's governments were suddenly saddled, in addition to the increment due to the progressively increasing birth-rate of developing countries, with a sudden 20% increase in population, no doubt the strain on supplies of food, water, energy and living space would be insurmountable. Enhanced longevity would not by itself, however, affect the population in such a dramatic fashion. The population explosion would not be cataclysmic, but progressive and despite those doomwatchers who claim that the present increase in population is too great for the world's resources to meet, no doubt man would continue to demonstrate the innate biological flexibility by which he has been characterized over the 30 million years since he developed into a separately identifiable representative of the primate order. He should be able to overcome problems of overcrowding, undernourishment, etc. even if (to be very cynical) he could only accomplish this by engaging in a more than usually disastrous war! Such a holocaust should not, however, be necessary since, if man were to prove capable of employing the degree of genetic engineering which would permit him to add x years to his own life-span, he should also be capable of modifying the yields of crops, utilizing non-destructive forms of energy production and undertaking such recycling programmes as might be necessary to conserve those elements which he is at present using up too rapidly. It will be abundantly obvious that I am an incurable optimist. The most cogent aspect of prophecy is that the seer is seldom around to appreciate the failure of his own predictions, but I do feel that if mankind were ultimately to resort to the use of recombinant DNA to extend his life, he would ipso facto have in his hands the necessary tools to meet the sociological challenge which would accompany his actions.

In fact, it might be thought that unless mankind is pushed along this pathway by the acceptance of the necessity for genetic manipulation, he will not have the incentive to control his present lemming-like stampede to self-destruction by over-utilization of food, energy and resources. Energy of a different type will have to be expended to bring our ageing world society out of its state of increasing entropy or run-down-ness, and one possible source of this social energy might lie in the revision of man's genetic constitution. It may prove necessary to consider the possibility of 'adding years to life' in order that man can be stimulated to 'add life to years' in its true sense of providing the necessities for a healthy and fruitful life-style for all of mankind.

References

Blackett A. D. and Hall D. A. (1981) Vitamin E, its significance in mouse ageing. *Age Ageing* **10**, 191.
Burch P. R. J. and Jackson D. (1966) The growth of hair and the loss of permanent teeth considered in relation to autoimmune theory of ageing. *J. Gerontol.* **21**, 522.
Meredith P. J. and Walford R. L. (1977) Effect of age response on T and B cell mitogens in mice congenic at the H-2 region. *Immunogenetics* **5**, 109.

Index